VOICE STUDIES

Voice Studies brings together leading international scholars and practitioners, to re-examine what voice is, what voice does, and what we mean by "voice studies" in the process and experience of performance. This dynamic and interdisciplinary publication draws on a broad range of approaches, from composing and voice teaching through to psychoanalysis and philosophy, including:

- voice training from the Alexander Technique to practice-as-research
- operatic and extended voices in early baroque and contemporary underwater singing
- voices across cultures, from site-specific choral performance in Kentish mines and Australian sound art, to the laments of Krahô Indians, Korean *p'ansori* and Javanese *wayang*
- voice, embodiment and gender in Robertson's 1798 production of *Phantasmagoria*, Cathy Berberian's radio show and Romeo Castellucci's theatre
- perceiving voice as a composer, listener, or as eavesdropper
- voice, technology and mobile apps.

With contributions spanning six continents, the volume considers the processes of teaching or writing for voice, the performance of voice in theatre, live art, music and on recordings, and the experience of voice in acoustic perception and research. It concludes with a multifaceted series of short provocations that simply revisit the core question of the whole volume: What *is* voice studies?

Konstantinos Thomaidis is Lecturer in Drama and Theatre at the University of Portsmouth. He is joint founder of the Centre for Interdisciplinary Voice Studies, co-convenes the Performer Training working group at the Theatre & Performance Research Association and is a founding co-editor of the *Journal of Interdisciplinary Voice Studies*.

Ben Macpherson is Senior Lecturer and Course Leader for Musical Theatre at the University of Portsmouth. He is joint founder of the Centre for Interdisciplinary Voice Studies, a founding co-editor of the *Jou   sical theatre.

D1145575

VOICE STUDIES

Critical approaches to process, performance and experience

Edited by
Konstantinos Thomaidis and Ben Macpherson

Routledge
Taylor & Francis Group

LONDON AND NEW YORK

First published 2015
by Routledge
2 Park Square, Milton Park, Abingdon, Oxon OX14 4RN

and by Routledge
711 Third Avenue, New York, NY 10017

Routledge is an imprint of the Taylor & Francis Group, an informa business

British Library Cataloguing-in-Publication Data
A catalogue record for this book is available from the British Library

Library of Congress Cataloging in Publication Data
Voice studies : critical approaches to process, performance and experience / edited by Konstantinos Thomaidis and Ben Macpherson.
pages cm
Includes index.
1. Singing--Instruction and study. 2. Voice. I. Thomaidis, Konstantinos.
II. Macpherson, Ben.
MT820.V6253 2015
783--dc23
2014044507

ISBN: 978-1-138-80934-5 (hbk)
ISBN: 978-1-138-80935-2 (pbk)
ISBN: 978-1-315-75006-4 (ebk)

Typeset in Bembo
by Taylor & Francis Books

Printed and bound by Ashford Colour Press Ltd.

MIX
Paper from
responsible sources
FSC
www.fsc.org   FSC® C011748

CONTENTS

FIGURES

CONTRIBUTORS

'**Femi Adedeji** is the Head of Music and Professor of Music and African Musicology at Obafemi Awolowo University, Ile Ife. He is President of the Association of Nigerian Musicologists, a gospel singer, vocal coach and choral director. He has researched extensively on African music theory, composition and Ifa/Christian religious music. He is responsible for propounding Sacred (Bibliological) Musicology and Transformative Musicology as new subfields in African musicological studies.

Paul Barker trained as a composer and pianist at the Guildhall School of Music and Drama, winning several prizes including the Royal Philharmonic Society award. His compositions have been performed at major festivals internationally, including works in opera, music theatre, vocal and choral music, orchestral and concert music. He works particularly with musicians to refine performance through an experience of theatre in relation to music. Three CDs of his music are available and his book, *Composing for Voice*, was published by Routledge in 2004. He is Professor of Music Theatre at the Royal Central School of Speech and Drama.

Yvon Bonenfant is Professor of Artistic Process, Voice and Extended Practices at the University of Winchester. He likes voices that do what voices don't usually do. He likes unruly bodies. He makes artworks starting from these voices and bodies. He currently holds a Large Arts Award from the Wellcome Trust and funding from Arts Council England, collaborating with speech scientists on the development of a series of participatory, extra-normal voice artworks for children and families. His publications range from traditional academic formats to creative and online alternatives. He has presented, taught and exhibited work in fourteen countries in the last ten years. www.yvonbonenfant.com.

George Burrows is Senior Lecturer and Course Leader on the BA(Hons) Drama and Performance degree at the University of Portsmouth, having previously worked for the Open University, Newcastle University and the Royal Opera House. His scholarship is interdisciplinary and aims to bring new critical approaches to the study of music, while also using music as a critical tool to explore other disciplines. His published work thus articulates psychoanalytical, sociological and philosophical understandings with musical theatre and jazz of the interwar period. He is founding co-editor of the journal *Studies in Musical Theatre* (Intellect) and the international Song, Stage and Screen conference series. George has a background in musical performance, having trained as a trombonist, singer and conductor. He currently directs the Portsmouth University choirs.

Marios Chatziprokopiou works in the intersections between performance practices and ethnography, focusing on voice and its relationship with language and politics. He holds an MA in Anthropology (School for Advanced Studies in the Social Sciences, Paris) and is currently a doctoral candidate and part-time tutor in Performance Studies at Aberystwyth University. His thesis is entitled *Displaced Laments: Voicing Mourning and Exile in Contemporary Athens.*

Lyn Darnley has teaching qualifications from the University of South Africa and Trinity College London, an MPhil from the University of Birmingham's Shakespeare Institute and a PhD from Royal Holloway, University of London. She was Head of Voice for the BA in Community Theatre and the BA (Hons) in Theatre Arts at Rose Bruford College (1981–92), after which she joined the RSC, becoming the Head of Voice, Text and Artist Development in 2003. She remained with the RSC until 2014, working with actors in the UK and abroad. Alongside articles for voice journals, her writing includes *The Voice Sourcebook* (Winslow Press, 1992), *The Teaching Voice* (Whurr, 1996) and *The Voice Box* (Speechmark, 2013), all co-authored with Stephanie Martin.

Piersandra Di Matteo is a performance theorist and independent curator, working as Romeo Castellucci's dramaturg since 2008. As a scholar of visual and performing arts media at the University of Bologna, her research interests range from contemporary theatre to experimental performance, from linguistics to continental contemporary philosophy, with a current focus on the linguistics, ethics and politics of voice. She has collaborated with a number of European artists as a theoretical consultant and editor on *performance writing* projects.

Nina Sun Eidsheim is a faculty member of the Department of Musicology, UCLA. Her current projects include monographs *Sensing Sound: Singing and Listening as Vibrational Practice* (Duke University Press, forthcoming), *Measuring Race: Listening to Vocal Timbre and Vocality in African-American Popular Music* and co-editing the *Oxford Handbook of Voice Studies* and a special issue on voice and materiality for the journal *Postmodern Culture*. In addition, she is the principal investigator for a transdisciplinary research project entitled *Keys to Voice Studies: Terminology, Methodology, and Questions across Disciplines.*

Ella Finer is a writer, artist and lecturer whose practice in theatre, performance and sound explores the relationship of the gendered body and voice. She holds a PhD from Roehampton University (2012) and is a member of London-based collective The International Western.

Jarosław Fret is the founder of Teatr ZAR, director of the Grotowski Institute and lecturer at the Ludwik Solski State Theatre School, Wrocław. With Teatr ZAR he has worked in places including Athos mountain Greece, Sardinia, Corsica, Armenia and Turkey. He has directed *Triptych: Gospels of Childhood*, parts of which have been seen in over ten countries internationally. Teatr ZAR was named Best New Music Theatre by the *LA Times* (2009) and won a 2010 Wrocław theatre prize.

Päivi Järviö is a mezzo-soprano, specializing in the singing, researching and teaching of Baroque and Renaissance music. She has performed and recorded with numerous Baroque ensembles and orchestras. Her doctoral thesis focused on embodied performing practice in Italian Early Baroque music, and recently she has studied the rhetorical *actio* in the embodied performing practice of the 17th and 18th century French repertoire. Järviö has worked as a research fellow at the Orpheus Institute (Belgium), and is currently a lecturer at the DocMus Doctoral School (Sibelius Academy, University of the Arts Helsinki).

Pamela Karantonis is Senior Lecturer in Voice in the Department of Performing Arts, Bath Spa University. Her performance experience has included opera, classical recital work and 20th century popular Greek music. Publications are largely in the areas of voice, drama and performance theory. From 2010 to 2014, she was co-convenor of the Music Theatre Working Group of The International Federation for Theatre Research. She is joint editor and contributing author for: *Cathy Berberian: Pioneer of Contemporary Vocality* (Ashgate, 2014), *The Legacy of Opera: Reading Music Theatre as Experience and Performance* (Rodopi, 2013), *Opera Indigene: Re/presenting First Nations and Indigenous Cultures* (Ashgate, 2011). Her recent research interests involve vocality, cultural alterity and the intersection between music and the theatrical avant-garde.

Mikhail Karikis is a London-based Greek artist who works internationally, with projects exhibited at the 19th Biennale of Sydney, Australia (2014); Mediacity/Seoul Museum of Art Biennale, South Korea (2014); Assembly, Tate Britain, UK (2014); the Aichi Triennale, Japan (2013); Videonale, Germany (2012); Manifesta 9, Belgium (2012); the 54th Venice Biennale, Italy (2011). Karikis's three solo albums have been released by Sub Rosa records and he has contributed to records by Bjork and DJ Spooky. His texts have been published by Tate Publishing and ArteEast. Karikis is also a researcher at the University of Brighton.

Tim Kjeldsen trained in theatre at Dartington College of Arts, and subsequently as a teacher of the Alexander Technique. Since 1984, he has worked in private practice in Cardiff, and as a lecturer in the Royal Welsh College of Music and Drama. He represented Alexander Technique teachers at the Federal Working Group that established the government-supported regulator for the complementary and natural healthcare profession (CNHC). His research interests are mainly in the philosophy of action, phenomenology and Wittgenstein, and he is currently undertaking postgraduate studies in philosophy at the University of Southampton.

Johanna Linsley is a researcher and London-based artist. She is currently a post-doctoral research projects officer in Drama, Theatre and Performance at the University of Roehampton. Between 2011 and 2013 she worked on the research project Performing Documents at the University of Bristol, and she is currently co-editing a book arising from the project. Her research has been published in *Performance Research* and *Contemporary Theatre Review*. She is part of the London-based performance collective I'm With You, and she is co-founder of UnionDocs, a centre for experimental documentary in Brooklyn, New York.

Ben Macpherson is Senior Lecturer and Course Leader for the BA (Hons) Musical Theatre at the University of Portsmouth. He gained his PhD from the University of Winchester in 2011, and his research interests include the intersection of voice and body in musical theatre performance, and the role of British musical theatre in cultural identity formation. Publications include articles in *Studies in Musical Theatre*, *International Journal of Performance Arts and Digital Media* and several chapters in edited collections. He is joint founder of the Centre for Interdisciplinary Voice Studies and a founding co-editor of the *Journal of Interdisciplinary Voice Studies* (Intellect).

Tara McAllister-Viel is Head of Voice at East 15 Acting School, University of Essex, and Associate Editor-in-Chief of the *Voice and Speech Review* (Routledge). Previously, she led the voice programmes for Music Theatre and Collaborative and Devised Theatre specialties at The Royal Central School of Speech and Drama, and was Visiting Professor (Voice) at the Korean National University of Arts, Seoul. In Seoul, she studied Korean *p'ansori* under Human Cultural Treasures Han Nong Son and Song UHyang, and Chan Park in Ohio. She has worked internationally as an actor, director and voice director for twenty years.

Jan Mrázek is Associate Professor in the Department of Southeast Asian Studies at the National University of Singapore. He has studied, performed and taught Javanese performance for many years. He wrote *Phenomenology of a Puppet Theatre: Contemplations on the Art of the Javanese Wayang Kulit* (Kitlv Press, 2006), edited *Puppet Theatre in Contemporary Indonesia: New Approaches to Performance Events* (University of Michigan, 2002), and co-edited *What's the Use of Art? Asian Material and Visual Culture in Context* (University of Hawai'i Press, 2008). His current research concerns poetry, fiction and travelogues written by Czechs who journeyed to Southeast Asia in the colonial period.

Norie Neumark is Professor and Chair in Media Studies, La Trobe University, Melbourne, and a sound/media artist and theorist. Her research is currently focused on voice and the new materialist turn. Publications include *Voice: Vocal Aesthetics in Digital Arts and Media* (MIT Press, 2010; lead editor and contributor) and *Voicetracks: Voice, Media, and Media Arts in the Posthumanist Turn* (MIT Press, forthcoming, 2016). Her collaborative art practice with Maria Miranda (www.out-of-sync.com) has been seen nationally and internationally. She is Director of the Centre for Creative Arts, Melbourne (www.centreforcreativearts.org.au).

Diana Van Lancker Sidtis is Professor of Communicative Sciences and Disorders at New York University (NYU), where she served as Chair from 1999 to 2002. Her graduate work includes an MA in Anglistics from the University of Chicago, graduate studies at the UCLA Phonetics Laboratory, and a PhD in Linguistics from Brown University. Her clinical studies in Communication Sciences were enhanced by an NIH Postdoctoral Fellowship at Northwestern University. She currently teaches, mentors students and performs research in speech science, voice studies and neurolinguistics at NYU and the Nathan Kline Institute for Psychiatric Research.

Amanda Smallbone is Programme Leader and Senior Lecturer on the BA Vocal and Choral Studies at the University of Winchester. She trained as a singer and pianist at the Guildhall School of Music and has enjoyed a varied career as a singer, performer, teacher and lecturer in the UK and abroad. On completing an MA in Performing Arts in 2006, she began lecturing and researching in the area of voice studies at the University of Winchester, where she established the BA Vocal and Choral Studies programme in 2010.

Konstantinos Thomaidis is Lecturer in Drama and Theatre at the University of Portsmouth. His PhD explored the materiality of voice in intercultural pedagogies. Konstantinos works as an opera director and movement director. He was a visiting lecturer at the University of London, the University of Winchester, and the Aristotle University, Thessaloniki. He has published in *Theatre, Dance and Performance Training*, *Studies in Musical Theatre* and edited collections. He co-convenes the Performer Training working group at the Theatre & Performance Research Association and is joint founder of the Centre for Interdisciplinary Voice Studies and a founding co-editor of the *Journal of Interdisciplinary Voice Studies* (Intellect).

ACKNOWLEDGEMENTS

This book resulted from the research activities of the Centre for Interdisciplinary Voice Studies. We wish to thank all involved in these events, particularly Amanda Smallbone, with whom we co-founded the Centre and who helped shape and drive our thinking about voice studies.

Special thanks go to all contributors along with their illustrators and photographers for their hard work and enthusiasm in making this volume happen. We could not have produced this collection without the support of our colleagues in the School of Media and Performing Arts, and the Faculty of Creative and Cultural Industries at the University of Portsmouth. Thanks must also go to our peer-reviewers and editing team at Routledge, particularly Harriet Affleck, Andrew Watts, Andy Baxter, and our commissioning editor Ben Piggott.

Konstantinos wishes to thank David Williams, Alison Hodge, Katie Normington, David Wiles, Experience Bryon, Andrei Biziorek, his collaborators at Gardzienice (Poland) and the Gugak Center (Korea), alongside the A. Onassis and Leventis Foundations. Ben wishes to thank Millie Taylor, Malcolm Floyd and June Boyce-Tillman along with Dominic Symonds, George Burrows and Philip Drew. We both thank our wives, Natalia and Lauren, for their constancy, support and encouragement.

FOREWORD

With one voice: Disambiguating sung and spoken voices through a composer's experience

Paul Barker

> My voice is, literally, my way of taking leave of my senses.
>
> (Connor 2000: 7)

Imagine a curious child wants to understand more about fish. The child goes and looks at a fish in a lake. Getting closer, the child places a hand into the water and is dismayed to watch the fish swim away. In a flash of understanding the child goes to find a net. The child now picks the fish easily out of the water and places it carefully on the grass bank. Fascinated by the fish's dancing movements, unknowingly the child watches the fish, slowly and painfully, die.

My voice in my body might be usefully compared to the fish in the water. I imagine that from the perspective of a fish, there is only water. Whatever a fish sees, whether the object of its vision is really inside or outside of the water, the difference is not discernible through a fish's eyes, as the water *is* the element through which a fish sees and has all contact with the world. Indeed, the fish breathes water. For the boy in the story, the fish was the object of fascination and the water was irrelevant, perhaps as irrelevant as the air that intervened between his eye and the water he saw through. I should like to suggest that for most human beings, our voice shares a relationship to ourselves as the water does to the fish: both are the medium with which we communicate with our worlds. If perception as we understand it were possible for a fish, I doubt that *wateriness* would be conceptually available. From a similar perspective, our perception of *voiceness* is limited, if possible at all. So, if we want to understand what a voice is, perhaps we might best learn from those who have no voice. Let us hope it is not as tragic as the fish without water.

Losing your voice

When someone loses their voice through illness or accident, if they are lucky, they will eventually encounter the world of vocal synthesis and prosthetics and be offered a voice, in a box, typically operated from a keyboard. A researcher or technician will somehow ask them what sort of voice they would like to have, what it should sound like. At that moment most individuals encounter the limits of linguistic knowledge in their perception of *voiceness*. Even if they could speak, few words could accurately describe the individual and unique qualities of our voice, or any voice, in any way meaningful or recognizable. Paradoxically, the very instrument which we use to communicate and with which we both identify ourselves and are identified by others, has remained largely impervious to any useful vocabulary. Steven Connor clearly articulates the uniqueness of our voice:

> Nothing else about me defines me so intimately as my voice, precisely because there is no other feature of myself whose nature it is thus to move from me to the world, and to move me into the world. If my voice is mine because it comes from me, it can only be known as mine because it goes from me.
>
> *(2000: 7)*

Often, the unfortunate recipient of the voice-in-a-box is not merely vocally, but also physically, incapacitated. When we communicate with our voice, our body is crucially involved. The loss of a voice is not only a loss of communication, but also of identity; perhaps the body itself. Unfortunately for the recipient of the prosthetic voice, voice is far more than a sounding box: "The voice does not merely possess phonetic measure and pattern; it works to confer a dynamic shape on my whole body" (Connor 2000: 10).

Technology helped Stephen Hawking find a voice. He still uses a slightly modified version of the voice-in-a-box given to him in the 1980s. He controls the text it speaks for him by minute eye movements, all of which are left in the control of his body by his mind. Hawking's is perhaps the most recognizable artificial voice in the world, which may account for why he has refused to update or change it: it is part of his identity. It is also eerily inhuman – perhaps superhuman – and sounds at best bearable or monotonous.

Recently, I was asked to write a short theatre work, a melodrama that Hawking's synthetic voice would perform. The writer, Chris Newell, devised a plot around a fictitious opera singer who lost his voice in a production of Leoncavallo's *Pagliacci* in the 1980s, thus encountering the same voice-in-a-box as Hawking. The ex-singer is ostensibly on a tour, promoting his biography, called *My Voice and Me*. He tells the story of how he lost his voice whilst rehearsing the opera, which he recounts through the synthesizer while playing the piano. The challenge of the music was to give feeling and life to the voice, the text being well-written but delivered, in effect, by the poorest voice actor imaginable. *My Voice and Me* (2013) attempts to endow a human feeling and form to a voice-in-a-box, through music articulated by a piano; a different but more traditional species of voice-in-a-box.[1]

Sensual imbalance

The epigraph to this chapter is from Connor: "My voice is, literally, my way of taking leave of my senses" (2000: 7). Taking leave of my senses perhaps sums up one major discourse explored in this volume. The concept that through our senses we have contact with the world exemplifies the idea that our senses rarely (if ever) work independently of each other and their apparent collaboration can easily fool us. The McGurk effect demonstrates how sight tends to take precedence over our hearing in terms of perception, demonstrating how our eyes may dominate our ears.[2] This imbalance has been demonstrated to pervade into perceptions of musical performance by Behne and Wöllner (2011).

I experienced Clemens Wöllner's research at the Royal Northern College of Music in 2006. He invited a group of us to compare two pianists on video playing the same piece of music. He asked us to discuss and decide on our preference, which we were all able to justify from different perspectives. But we had heard the same performance twice, with some clever video editing over the second recording with a different pianist. As a pianist myself, the experience was both humbling and enlightening. Far from independent, our senses work together but trick us because their relationship is hierarchical. Despite this, we continue to pursue our evidence for the world through a concept of the five senses: by dividing something into constituent parts we create the illusion we are getting closer to it. If we do not allow ourselves to step back and see the whole, the fish *and* the water, the end result may be tragic.

Tyrannies of understanding

Mary Midgley asks us to stand back; she considers unity a core human concept and rails against universal over-specialization. She describes a relentless atomization of education mimicking 20th century scientists' pursuit of the smallest recognizable and indivisible particle, perpetuated long after the scientists themselves have moved on to other pursuits:

> What is new in this century […] is the contribution of academic specialization to the splitting process. […] Each is supposed to be discussed in its own appropriate terms, and any area so far neglected is suspect; since there is no proper way of discussing it, it tends to look like unsuitable ground for academic consideration altogether. Within each discipline, there is a further tendency […] to be suspicious of outlying areas and concentrate only on things which can be made to look perfectly clear and complete […]. The only remedy for this fragmentation is to stand back and take a wider view of the key concepts as parts of a whole.
>
> *(1981: 10)*

Midgley goes on to consider the processes and perspectives by which we comprehend our life. For her, the arts and the sciences share more in common with each other than they contest. She transgresses traditional scientific and artistic barriers through the commonality of *feeling* as an integral, rather than adjunct or even insignificant, constituent of thinking and being:

> We are in fact so constituted that we cannot act at all if feeling really fails. When it does fail, as in cases of extreme apathy and depression, people stop acting [...]. We do not live essentially by calculation, interrupted occasionally by an alien force called feeling. Our thought (including calculation) is the more or less coherent form into which our perceptions and feelings constantly organize themselves.
>
> *(Midgley 1981: 4)*

In this, she elaborates Hume's famous phrase, "reason is, and ought only to be, the slave of the passions." We need then to stand back from our specialisms and explore the connections between things, their synthesis, symbiosis and interdependence. The danger of perpetuating a fractured worldview is all too obvious to some, such as Henry Maudsley:

> [We have] a sufficiently strong propensity not only to make divisions in knowledge where there are none in nature, and then to impose the divisions in nature, making the reality thus comfortable to the idea, but to go further, and to convert the generalisations made from observation into positive entities, permitting for the future these artificial creations to tyrannise over the understanding.
>
> *(in McGilchrist 2009: 62)*

I had an insight into such a "tyranny of understanding" when I met the singer Keel Watson some years ago. I auditioned him as a baritone and took him on for an opera of mine. One day, I heard a high dramatic tenor phrase coming from the men's dressing room and I found him singing it there. He also introduced me to his bass range, topped of course by an impressive falsetto. He had learned early on that no-one would believe he could do everything and had CVs for each voice-type. We think we see a pattern and suddenly we impose it on our understanding, which is tyrannized by a false perception of reality. The more sophisticated development of the *fach* system in Germany took this concept to an industrial level at a time when opera was more dominant. It reflects a similarly over-enthusiastic will to order over a more complex reality: many voices simply cannot fit the box and some break. Mozart rewrote arias to suit different singers. The same objective is shared by the technician who asks the voiceless patient what kind of voice is preferred.

Voice and meaning

It is only experience that can challenge received information. The effect of over-specialization on our understanding of the voice has led to its being broken in so many ways. As I write this, a government minister in the UK is advocating less play and more written assessments for four-year-olds, even against educationalists who advocate the pre-eminence of speaking before writing, and play as a primary learning tool.[3] The voices of children are being silenced in favour of the concept of the pre-eminence of the written word over the spoken, twenty years after this warning by Patsy Rodenburg:

> If a teacher denies the importance of voice in the classroom, sees the sound of the voice as a distracting nuisance and refuses to make it part of the classroom environment, I fear that our oral skills will continue to decline even further. A vital part of education dies with the dying voice.
>
> *(1993: 22–23)*

The spoken word would still seem to be in retreat from the onslaught of the written word. On this subject, Connor helps us take leave of our senses again:

> In a culture in which the oral and the aural have been more generally subjected to the ordering powers of the eye, this process [of the subordination of our senses to sight] is presumably likely to occur earlier and more systematically than in a culture in which orality is more dominant. The result of this cooperation of the biological with the cultural relations between the senses is the simultaneous demotion and exaggeration of the powers associated with sound and with hearing.
>
> *(2000: 23)*

Spoken words may be richer, with more layers, than written words. The voice is multi-modal, working on many different levels and parameters simultaneously. According to McGilchrist, "[i]t is estimated that even now 90 per cent of communication between humans is by non-verbal means, through body-language and perhaps especially through intonation" (2009: 106). Although the percentage may be contested, the wealth of evidence accrued indicates non-verbal importance.

The voice itself is often segregated in pedagogy into the spoken and the sung, approached as if they were separate entities, with separate theories and practices. This act of dislocation or segregation often affirms limitations and prejudices assumed by the owner of the voice. Singing and speaking are often treated as vehicles or instruments designed to deliver text. This represents the compartmentalized thinking that excludes experience as a primary tool for understanding. Let us stand back and take Midgley's wider view: there are many who consider that singing predated speaking in terms of the development of our species, that singing is a more basic, fundamental and primal way of communicating. Many philosophers have supported this argument, such as Rousseau in the 18th century, von Humboldt in the 19th and Jespersen in the 20th. Stephen Mithen (2005) suggests there is some fossil evidence to that effect. Whereas the phylogenetic proof may be questionable, the ontogenetic evidence is witnessed by almost every family. When we are born, we cry, and our crying becomes refined over the first couple of years through the development of language which gradually takes precedence over sound itself. Singing may be described as refined screaming, through the practice of Maria Huesca.[4] The adult path to singing often requires a re-patterning, an unlearning of the bad habits we develop which obstruct the open voice with which we are born. If we are to divide voice into two, the spoken and the sung, let us acknowledge a third division which separates sound and language. Those who speak and sing professionally are acutely aware of the primary importance of the sound of their voice as a harbinger of meaning, before and beyond the word itself.

There is an instance where the printed word, the sounded word and the embodied word all potentially synthesize to form a single, unified voice. James Joyce was by no means the first writer to synthesize sound and meaning on the page, but *Ulysses* (1922) remains unusual in that it demands the reader collaborate to that end. It might be seen – or heard – as an unusual attempt to synthesize what I call *voiceness* through the printed page and its effect on a reader. In Chapter 11, "The Sirens," written language dissolves into a melange of sound, finally becoming the sound of the sea itself.

> A sail! A veil awave upon the waves.
> Lost. Throstle fluted. All is lost now.
> […] Listen!
> The spiked and winding cold seahorn. Have you the? Each and for other, plush and silent roar.
> Pearls: when she. Liszt's rhapsodies. Hissss.
> […] Fro. To, fro.
> […] Fff! Oo!
>
> *(Joyce 1986: 210–11)*

In my setting of these extracts, recorded by Cantamus Girls Choir, the singers are divided into *The Sirens and The Sea*, which is the name of the work. The Sea perform Joyce's text out of which comes "The Sirens' Song," my setting of the original Greek song that Ulysses heard in Homer's *Odyssey*. It is my conviction that sound and language exist together in a precarious balance in our voice. The orthodox view of language being more precise in meaning, and music being more general, was neatly addressed two centuries ago by the composer Mendelssohn:

> People often complain that music is so ambiguous, that what they are to think about it always seems so doubtful, whereas everyone understands words; with me it is exactly the reverse; not merely with regard to entire sentences, but also to individual words; these, too, seem to me so ambiguous, so vague, so unintelligible when compared to genuine music, which fills the soul with a thousand things better than words. What any music I love expresses to me, is not thought too indefinite to be put into words, but on the contrary, too definite.
>
> *(Mendelssohn Bartholdy and Mendelssohn Bartholdy 2001: 276)*

Mendelssohn clarifies the negative sense of disambiguation to which the title of this chapter refers: when spoken and sung voice, text and music are differentiated or disambiguated, something may be lost.

Language, music and meaning

Another orthodox perspective distinguishes between the way the voice is approached in the practices of musical theatre and opera. It reflects an argument that has its roots in the *prima prattica* and *seconda prattica* of Monteverdi, distinguishing between the ancient style of polyphony which he felt obscured textual meaning and his monophonic settings which served the text. Contemporary performance practice transposes this argument to an operatic predilection for favouring voice as the primary expressive tool, whereas musical theatre serves the text first. I was never happy with these generalizations, and I began to write a series of forty-eight songs without texts, which I called *Songs Between Words* (2004).[5] They were taken up by several singers and I was subsequently approached by the Teatro de Ciertos Habitantes theatre company in Mexico to create an opera without text for actors. They wanted a work they might perform to any audience without translations, surtitles or programme notes. The result was *El Gallo*, a wordless opera for six actors and two string quartets. I replaced language with phonemes composed for the singers in the same way I composed the music, adapted to the individual idiosyncrasies of each performer. *El Gallo* demonstrates how an absence of language never prevents us from detailed, vocal communication, even in a full-length opera. Perhaps it reflects something of the spirit of Mendelssohn's quotation.[6] The plot concerns the relationship between a composer and five singers over rehearsals and the premiere of a new work. The composer has his favourites and demonstrates his impatience with one singer who is increasingly traumatized by him. Shaptes is the name of that character in *El Gallo*, who we might see as vocally damaged: an affliction both common and under-resourced today.

Vocal damage

Some of us sing, most of us speak, few enjoy speaking in public. These reactions might be seen as the result of vocal damage. Our vocal damage is often administered by the voice of someone else: for instance, at some stage we might have been told that we cannot sing in tune or in time, or that we speak badly and cannot be understood. It often happens at a time before we are able to consciously question the authority of those who judge. The result may be one person being confident at singing but not speaking, or vice-versa. Yet if the voice was perceived as a synthesizer of these actions, such a situation might seem irrational and more avoidable. Their separation justifies another example of Maudsley's tyranny of understanding. Sometimes the damage physically manifests itself as a stutter or some other vocal challenge. A deeper understanding of our own voice might lead us to doubt the apparent authority we endow to others and help defend against damage at many levels.

Mediatized singing

This division between spoken and sung voices is eclipsed by the fragmentation of the singing voice itself. I once had the pleasure of working with the soprano Shauna Beesley, who understood how to explore and play with her voice. My opera, *La Malinche* (1989), is set in pre-Hispanic Mexico and the opening uses a setting of the language of Nahuátl, the classical language of the Aztecs.[7] In the opening scene Shauna was evidently able to produce a full, rich operatic sound, even in Nahuátl, but in a concert tour with her I played for her singing like Nina Simone, Louis Armstrong and Joni Mitchell, alongside Berio and scat-singing. The pop voice, the jazz voice, the opera voice and many variations were all accessible to her through play and imagination because she understood these as colours of her voice, not as *voices*. It made writing music for her an exciting, multi-dimensional challenge.

One of the contributing factors is the increasing ubiquity of the mediatized voice; microphones and recordings have opened a new and beguiling vocal universe of expression, as Connor describes:

> The microphone makes audible and expressive a whole range of organic vocal sounds which are edited out in ordinary listening; the liquidity of the saliva, the hissings and tiny shudders of the breath, the clicking of the tongue and the teeth, and the popping of the lips. Such a voice promises the odours, textures and warmth of another body.
>
> *(2000: 38)*

This intimate, private world epitomizes much popular music and has come to provide an almost constant sound-track to many people's lives. Arguably, the singing voice has never been heard more, but paradoxically there is little evidence to suggest that the flood of recorded voice encourages people to sing. The singing voice may be more available, but the fear of not being perfect may cause untold damage. How many people regularly hear any live voice singing without a microphone? Voices confront us and challenge us emotionally. A big operatic sound provided one extreme for many centuries before universal mediatization; vocal concepts of large and small, grand or intimate, intense or relaxed have become inextricably confused as a result. The sheer volume – statistically and dynamically – of sung mediatized voices in our lives paradoxically demonstrates how little we know our own voice; we will never hear it as others do.

Empathic listening

My concern with the fully developed, athletic, efficient voice for which opera is designed, is not merely its failing competition with the mediatized voice, but that few young musicians and composers ever work with it. My earliest musical experiences were singing as a boy soprano, but I was in my late twenties working with some extraordinary singing teachers as a pianist before I started to listen *inside* a voice, rather than perceive it as a selection of pitches joined by a certain tonal colour. The concept of listening inside a voice is discussed in terms of empathic listening by McGilchrist: "empathy is associated with a greater intuitive desire to imitate [...]. By inhabiting the body of the other: is this how language ('musilanguage') began?" (2009: 122). McGilchrist describes how Rudolf Laban discovered how sub-Saharan drumming communicated: "the reception of these drum or tom-tom rhythms is accompanied by a vision of the drummer's movement, and it is this movement, a kind of dance, which is visualised and understood" (Laban in McGilchrist 2009: 122). These observations encourage my understanding of a phenomenon shared by many who teach voices: as we listen to a voice, our physiology unconsciously mimics the physiology of our subject. Although this may be illuminating in identifying what is going on, it also becomes physically painful for many of us when listening to a poorly produced voice. As we listen to a voice, our bodies may reflect the physiology of the singer, and we are able to feel how the singer creates the sound; how they feel.

For much of my formal education, composition was discussed formally as structure divided into harmony, rhythm and melody. How I listened, how I heard and perceived sound often remained outside the curriculum – another example of Maudsley's observation about the tyrannies of understanding. I was fortunate that my fascination with the singing voice led me to work with great teachers and great voices, but the segregation of singers into opera and non-opera, the segregation of singers from instrumentalists, and the isolation of composers in some institutions only serves to perpetuate these same prejudices and the tyrannies of understanding.

Vocal engagement

When a composer does not understand how the voice works, the composition implies the singer must comply with the misunderstanding, to fit the box. I will illustrate this by referring to one detail: dynamics in music. Dynamics came to be used by composers regularly in their scores by the time of Beethoven, but even his songs rarely place dynamics in the vocal part, following Mozart's lead. Dynamics evolved over several centuries partly to give insight into instrumental music when there was no text. Singers delivering a vocal line had for centuries allowed text to inform how the music was performed. The rapid increase in popularity of instrumental music went hand-in-hand with this developing sophistication of written dynamics, codes suggesting degrees of volume. Over a period of time after Beethoven, singers became increasingly confronted with complex dynamics, often applied without an understanding of the essentially complex, emotional nature that dynamics implied. It was not until Berio – and perhaps in particular his "Sequenza III for Female Voice" (1965) – that composers started to understand again how an emotional quality suggested by adjectives could fire the imagination of an actor–singer in a way that rendered *pianissimo* and *fortissimo* as merely abstract or disembodied ideas.

Manén, in fact, goes further and discusses the schism between vocal tone and emotion, perpetuated by a singer's misunderstanding: "Loud and soft tones replace changes of mood, and frequently singers today use only one of the potentialities of their vocal organ, one timbre, according to their own psychological make-up" (1974: 11). Manén also refers to the subjugation or repression of emotion mentioned by Midgley, describing how it affects a singer. She points out how the absence of any audience in a recording studio may lead a singer to believe that the sound of the voice is the only value, who then stops acting or performing, with dire consequences:

> The internal make-up of the singer has changed also. Man has been taught and has learned to hide external signs of emotion. A schism has developed between vocal tone and emotion. This situation has been further aggravated by performing without an audience in radio or recording studios, where tones can be produced without the simultaneous facial and emotional expression. Singers have moved further and further away from the unique power of the voice to produce vocal colouring based on the exclamatory vowels as a means of interpretation.
>
> *(1974: 11)*

Through global mediatization, the voice has become truly disembodied in a way that our ancestors, with their mythical and religious concepts of *hearing voices*, could not have imagined. What was once mysterious and supernatural has become normal. Whilst there may be much to learn from the disembodied voice and the way it speaks to us, I only hope that its ubiquity will not reduce our expectations and experience of the live voice. The philosopher Heidegger is associated with the idea that language houses the truth of Being, that *it* speaks, rather than ourselves. I should like to suggest a corollary: it is our voice which speaks, not we who speak with it. If that is so – whether we have no voice or many voices – who or what is speaking?

Notes

1 *My Voice and Me,* for actor–pianist, 1983 Dec Talk DTC 01 Speech Synthesizer and soprano, written and directed by Chris Newell, commissioned by University of Hull. Premiered on CreST Roadshow as installation and performed live at Woodend House, Scarborough, UK, 26 January 2013. See www.youtube.com/watch?v=CXHHouy 9KiM.

2 McGurk and MacDonald (1976) discovered through video editing that in seeing a speech pattern spoken while listening to a related but different one, the visual information in our brain takes precedence over the aural. See http://youtu.be/G-lN8vWm3m0.

3 "Specialists call for children to be allowed to learn through play, but Gove spokesman dismisses 'badly misguided lobby'" (Malik 2013).

4 Maria Huesca is a singing teacher of rich international experience with whom the author maintains a long professional practice with a research trajectory.

5 Some *Songs Between Words* may be heard on the CD *Entre Palabras*, Quindecim QD134 (2005).

6 To see excerpts from *El Gallo*, visit http://youtu.be/76TPYQzCCX4 and www.paula lanbarker.net/id36.html. Also available on CD, *El Gallo*, Quindecim QD11207 (2011).

7 *La Malinche* (1989), libretto by composer after historical sources, in four languages. Performed by the Modern Music Theatre Troupe, London International Opera Festival: http://youtu.be/i1A77hvjwnk or www.paulalanbarker.net/id45.html.

References

Behne, K-E. and Wöllner, C. (2011) "Seeing or hearing the pianists? A synopsis of an early audiovisual perception experiment and a replication," *Musicae Scientiae*, 15(3): 324–42.

Connor, S. (2000) *Dumbstruck: A Cultural History of Ventriloquism*, Oxford and New York: Oxford University Press.

Joyce, J. (1986) *Ulysses*, London: Penguin Books.

Malik, S. (2013, 12 September) "Early schooling damaging children's wellbeing, say experts," *The Guardian*, www.theguardian.com/education/2013/sep/12/early-years-schooling-damaging-wellbeing.

Manén, L. (1974) *The Art of Singing*, London: Faber Music Ltd.

McGilchrist, I. (2009) *The Master and his Emissary*, New Haven and London: Yale University Press.

McGurk, H. and MacDonald, J. (1976) "Hearing lips and seeing voices," *Nature*, 264: 746–48.

Mendelssohn Bartholdy, P. and Mendelssohn Bartholdy, C. (eds) (2001) *Letters of Felix Mendelssohn Bartholdy from 1833 to 1847*, Elibron Classics: Adamant Media Corporation.

Midgley, M. (1981) *Heart and Mind*, New York and Oxford: Routledge.

Mithen, S. (2005) *The Singing Neanderthals: The Origins of Music, Language, Mind and Body*, London: Weidenfeld and Nicolson.

Rodenburg, P. (1993) *The Need for Words*, London: Methuen Drama.

Part I
Introducing voice studies

INTRODUCTION

Voice(s) as a method and an in-between

Konstantinos Thomaidis and Ben Macpherson

Oskar is a young boy who cannot let go. He has hidden an answering machine with the final six messages from his father still on the tape; he plays them repeatedly just to hear his father's voice, although he is no longer there, and is not coming back. In an effort to understand the loss he suffered on 9/11, Oskar scours New York, on a journey to reconnect with his dad. His grandfather often accompanies him on trips around the city, yet the grandfather is silent, communicating only through the written word, gesture and facial expression. This focus on voice is central to the film adaptation of Jonathan Safran Foer's 2005 novel *Extremely Loud and Incredibly Close*, directed by Stephen Daldry (2011). Its importance to the way in which Oskar mourns his father's passing, and bonds with his grandfather, suggests something about voice as a powerful entity of connection, emotion and support – whether material, mediated or mute.

In any of these forms, voice has the power to create what Erika Fischer-Lichte terms a "liminal space of permanent transitions, passages, and transformations" (2008: 128). It is voice that allows Oskar to stay connected with his father. Considering the centrality of recorded and silent voices to Foer's narrative, Fischer-Lichte's observation that voice is in a state of *permanent* impermanence – an aural space, defined only by its evanescence – is telling. This sense of voice as the "in-between" – as the space that allows Oskar to hold on to his past while dealing with his present – in many ways represents the starting point of this collection, through which the transitions, passages and transformations made possible through voice are brought together and explored. Before introducing this volume as a whole, further perspectives on voice as an "in-between" will provide a context for this collection, and establish certain positions assumed at the outset.

Conceptualizing the "in-between"

This sense of "in-betweenness" pervades discourses about voice. Mladen Dolar has previously explored this "in-betweenness" of voice in vividly Lacanian terms.

Conceptualizing voice as the nexus of body and language, Dolar suggests it represents "the place where what cannot be said can nevertheless be conveyed" (2006: 31). Ben Macpherson (2012) reconsidered Dolar's paradoxical hierarchy of voice, body and language with reference to sung voice, but in this case, the place that "conveys" rather than "says" – the embodied in-between of vocality – implicitly relies on Fischer-Lichte's suggestion of transformation and transition. Roland Barthes famously defined the "grain of the voice" as "the materiality of the body speaking its mother tongue," while asserting it is not linguistic, timbral or tonal (1977: 182). The "grain," then, might be permanent, whilst the aural space it activates is rendered transitional.

In each case, whether through song, speech or silence, voice becomes complex and ineffable, with scholarship of the past two decades challenging the fetishized voice-as-object (Abbate 1991; Cavarero 2005). The voice of Oskar's grandfather is certainly ineffable in its absence, yet in contrast to the mediatized recordings of his father, can silence be understood as a vocal act? What kind of aural space does it inhabit? Conversely, Oskar's treasured answering machine messages are technologically reproduced, "fixed" by a date stamp, and representative of a moment in time. With the panicked reassurances of his father's messages now historical utterances, does the voice of his father "convey" something, rather than "say" something, facilitating Oskar's passage from the past to the present? Might Oskar's grandfather and father occupy the same aural space, the same "in-between," in their silence and their mediated utterance?

One possible way to begin answering these questions is to consider the point at which voice becomes "in-between." With further reference to sung performance, musicologist Simon Frith has observed that listeners hear voice all at once as a musical instrument, a body, a person and a character in performance (2008: 68). Voice, then, is a plurality – and the aural "in-between" is the junction point for multiple encodings of experience to be negotiated and understood. This is the first position of the book.

Despite their ontological or sonic disparities, the voices on Oskar's answering machine and his mute grandfather may occupy the same space, enabling the young boy's journey. In short, the "in-between" of voice offers an interdisciplinary space for such plurality, wherein multiple renderings work together in a process of transition, passage and transformation. In this important sense, then, when seeking to ask what voice *is* and what voice studies *might be*, there is no definitive answer and no definite article: *the* voice does not exist. This is the second position that led us to develop this volume.

This collection responds to a growing academic interest in voice, encapsulated in a proliferation of recent publications (Neumark, Gibson and van Leeuwen 2010; Karpf 2007; Kreiman and Sidtis 2013; Utz and Lau 2013; Bernhart and Kramer 2014; Connor 2014), and the establishment of related degree programmes in the UK, the US and Australasia. However, until now, there has been little concerted attempt to bring together the disparate disciplinary scholarship that effectively addresses voice, not merely as a theme, but as a discrete area or critical methodology. Taking our cue from Paul Barker's Foreword, we wish to ask what it means to reflect on "voiceness" in its own right, and what efforts are needed to disentangle ourselves from the "tyrannies of understanding" voice in strict musicological or linguistic terms. In concluding Part I, Konstantinos Thomaidis deconstructs the epistemologies of voice in training and research programmes, seeking "to find a voice for voice" within the academy. If the voices of Oskar, his father and his grandfather occupy the same space in a state of "in-betweenness," is there a way to reorganize this space to make its analysis less hierarchical?

This volume is a decisive step towards such a reordering, arguing for voice studies as an inter-discipline with distinctive approaches and concerns. It proposes such a turn by questioning and exploring the concepts and practices of "voice" in the following three parts: Process (Part II), Performance (Part III) and Experience (Part IV), which we understand as interrelated and interconnected.

"Process" might allude to such creative practices as composition, dramaturgy and devising. Part II interrogates "the *makings* of this making" (Thomaidis 2013: 61; original emphasis); the vocational training of voice and cultural assumptions associated with mundane and extra-daily voice(s). In Chapter 2, Päivi Järviö focuses on the vocal studio for Baroque music. She uses Michel Henry's non-intentional phenomenology to bring the singular experience of the singer – in their contingent dialogue with the teacher's bodied self – to the forefront of learning as experiencing. Tim Kjeldsen, in Chapter 3, revisits Sartre's concept of internal negation through Merleau-Ponty's critique, to examine the singer's facticity through application of the Alexander Technique. Tara McAllister-Viel's contribution then critically interrogates her experiences of drawing on Linklater's techniques to teach voice in a South Korean university. Her intercultural/interdisciplinary methodology derives from her students' and her own training in traditional *p'ansori*. Jan Mrázek unpacks the complexities of another form of in-betweenness. His writing attends to the space occupied by spoken voice in Javanese *wayang,* as it resonates between music and text, the puppet, the puppeteer and the audience, or tradition and in-performance innovation.

"Performance" (Part III) might therefore refer to musico-theatrical practices where voice is the primary means of expressivity, or it may be seen *as* a performative agent in-and-of-itself within its own socio-political context. Mikhail Karikis foregrounds – from a practitioner's perspective – two concerns around generating material for devising: the acoustics of a lived space in site-specific performance and the unsettling potential of nonsense, as proposed by Cage or Connor. In Chapter 7, Piersandra Di Matteo traces voice as a consistent preoccupation in Romeo Castellucci's theatrical work. Her analysis of physical, textual and sonic dramaturgies unfolds against a palimpsest of theoretical discourses that debate voice as present *and* disembodied. Chapter 8 sees Nina Sun Eidsheim revisit an earlier article in which she uses Juliana Snapper's underwater singing performances as a nodal point towards an expansive web of critical associations on the sensuality and materiality of voice. Marios Chatziprokopiou roots his live art practice in his study of the Krahô Indians' ritual lamentation, alongside his personal experiences of mourning and protest in the urban Greek context. In the final chapter of Part III, Norie Neumark frames the voices of seminal Australian sound artists within questions of enchantment. In weaving together their compositional strategies and conceptual preoccupations, Neumark simultaneously lends an attentive ear to the performative and affective qualities of voice.

In Part IV, "experience" is understood as multi-modal engagement with voice in process, in practice and in performance. Yet it is also understood as listening, receiving and documenting. Ben Macpherson conceptualizes an intricate dialogue between "body musicality" and neumatic, cheironomic, orthochronic, graphic and mediatized notation. His analysis centres around Alexander Truslit's notion of the inner motion of music as a key to unlocking the interface between the visual, the virtual and the visceral (in) voice. Pamela Karantonis, in Chapter 12, traverses a broad historical and geographical landscape, focusing on the cultural politics of classical singing as exemplified in key pedagogic manuals, international initiatives and opportunities afforded by technology – including Berberian's radio show. Ella Finer asserts that voice "carries a body and no body simultaneously: existing as vibrations through space and simultaneously as the aural promise of some*body*," interrogating cases whereby voice as an acoustic property emanated from a female voicer. Concluding Part IV, Johanna Linsley advocates the methodological benefits of eavesdropping as a research strategy. Listening-in and overhearing are critically approached as fertile tools in analysing differing performance settings, in which the spectator is first and foremost invited to occupy the in-between place of the (intentional or inadvertent) auditor.

Vocal multiplicities

Let us, however, return to Oskar. Stephen Daldry's screen adaptation of Foer's novel (2011) does not merely address voice as paradoxical; it celebrates its in-betweenness. What could be termed the ontological ineffability of voice is presented, not as something to be marvelled at – presupposing an essential topos of voiceness – but as an "in-between," a unique point of departure; remarkable, omnipresent, but a given nonetheless.

In many ways, Daldry fashions a self-conscious meditation on the cinematic voice – expanding or even challenging the thinking of Doane (1980) and Chion (1999) on audiovisual body-voices. It is not just that Oskar's dad has become a series of secret voice messages, or that his mute grandfather scores and communicates his utterances through copious amounts of notes. The key for characterization throughout the scripted plot is vocality. Oskar and his mother do not talk frequently; a whispered "I love you" behind a closed door – without any certainty of reciprocity – is the closest they come to vocal exchange. Oskar, resorting to legal terminology, accuses her of being "*in absentia*"; the un-heard voice, the absent mother. His grandmother responds to his late-night walkie-talkie calls from across the street but when they find themselves in the same flat, what fills the acoustic sequence is the disparity in their accents. They share the same lineage but inhabit different cultural milieus and moments. Daldry's sublimation of the (historical, psychological, biological, mediated) voice denies the existence of a single subject as its bearer. There can be no undeniable protagonist in this unfolding of vocal fragmentation and excess.

This evidences a further concern of this volume: methodology. The dramaturgy of the film is itself metonymic of methodology, revolving around a (lost-and-found) key and Oskar's development of strategies that could help turn the enigma of his father's loss into something manageable. It is not merely the plot that abounds with vocal references; voice is also deployed as a core filmic device. The all-familiar tactics of the acousmatic narrator and the dialogic exchange persist in this case too. However, as a child on the autistic spectrum, Oskar is oftentimes overwhelmed in his perception of the world, particularly when wracked with guilt and grief, conveyed as a tide of acoustic waves – alluding to Oskar's internality – or as bouts of extra-linguistic cries, sobs and gasps – framing his inter-relationality. Oskar's voice is a problem and Daldry's approach is to resort to a *variety* of techniques and representational tools.

Acknowledging the in-betweenness of voice is a provocation to methodological multiplicity. Approaching voice as an emerging field of creative and scholarly practice, this collection therefore refocuses a wide array of lenses drawn from cultural studies, musicology, performance studies, ethnography, visual studies, somatics, sound studies, and training and pedagogy, to establish voice as an area of study and a methodological tool. Voice is taken here to be at once between existing disciplines and an emerging enquiry. All authors' writing embodies a relation to the praxical, that which is in-between the practical and the exegetic. Järviö, for example, interlinks philosophy with first-person accounts of teaching. Eidsheim reads Snapper's performances as an observer and delves into the practice through experimentation. Chatziprokopiou journeys from anthropology to artistic practice through an auto-ethnography of loss. At the same time, voice is used as a method and a tool. Barker and Thomaidis use voice – either voiceness or revocalization – to question epistemic categories. Neumark and Fret remind us that voices engender *doing* but what they do is not easily accounted for, or tangible. Linsley proposes a type of listening to voices – eavesdropping – as a research methodology and a tool for documentation.

The content responds to this multifaceted engagement with voice, foregrounding a move away from understanding voice as a singular or unquestioned category. A stimulating mixture of leading voices in the field combined with cutting-edge work from emergent academics balances scholarly enquiry and empirical contributions by practitioner–scholars. Moreover, in bringing together contributors from Finland, Italy, Greece, Poland, Nigeria, Canada, Singapore, Australia, the UK and the US, and presenting case studies from the above geopolitical contexts along with those from South Korea, Indonesia, Brazil, Germany, France and the Czech Republic, this edited collection is avowedly international in its scope. We aim to reflect on the globalized contexts within which voice is produced and circulated.

This multiplicity of content translates into the format of the volume. Several contributions (Kjeldsen, Karikis, Neumark, Macpherson) tightly weave analysis with the use of scores, diagrams, rehearsal photos and illustrations, allowing for multimodal engagement with the authors' concerns. In a similar vein, we developed the final section (Part V) as an invitation to new modes of enquiry. Presenting the volume as a platform of interrogation and not a final statement, we asked researchers and practitioners to share their personal experiences prompted by the question "What is voice studies?" In lieu of more traditional concluding remarks, their responses, alongside our own reflections, form what we have called the "polyphonic conclusion" to this collection.

In the chapters that follow, twenty-two voices from six continents offer divergent, disparate and interdisciplinary perspectives on voice, enlivening each section with a multiplicity of experiences, arguments, concepts and opinions. The richness, praxicality and in-betweenness of the material invites a plurality of thematic journeys. Readers interested in intercultural voice will source relevant information in the extensive discussions by McAllister-Viel and Mrázek, and in the texts by Fret, Karikis, Chatziprokopiou or Adedeji. Alongside Part II, pedagogy is a concern of Eidsheim, Karantonis, Smallbone, Thomaidis and Darnley. Psychoanalytic perspectives thread through Di Matteo or Burrows; a multidisciplinary interest in the biomedical and expressive characteristics of voice is forged in Sidtis or Kjeldsen; and Barker, Macpherson, Bonenfant, Neumark and Linsley reflect on technology and voice. Therefore, this sense of interdisciplinarity is not only to be found within each chapter, but "in-between" them, and we invite you to find your own connections as you engage with the range of topics and ideas that follow.

References

Abbate, C. (1991) *Unsung Voices: Opera and Musical Narrative in the Nineteenth Century*, Princeton: Princeton University Press.

Barthes, R. (1977) *Image Music Text*, trans. S. Heath, London: Fontana Press.

Bernhart, W. and Kramer, L. (eds) (2013) *On Voice*, Amsterdam: Rodopi.

Cavarero, A. (2005) *For More than One Voice: Toward a Philosophy of Vocal Expression*, trans. P.A. Kottman, Stanford: Stanford University Press.

Chion, M. (1999) *The Voice in Cinema*, trans. C. Gorbman, New York: Columbia University Press.

Connor, S. (2014) *Beyond Words: Sobs, Hums, Stutters and Other Vocalizations*, London: Reaktion.

Doane, M.A. (1980) "The voice in cinema: the articulation of body and space," *Yale French Studies*, 60: 33–50.

Dolar, M. (2006) *A Voice and Nothing More*, Cambridge, MA: MIT Press.

Fischer-Lichte, E. (2008) *The Transformative Power of Performance*, trans. S.I. Jain, New York and Abingdon: Routledge.

Frith, S. (2008) "The voice as a musical instrument," in Clayton, M. (ed.) *Music, Words and Voice: A Reader*, Manchester and New York: The Open University.

Karpf, A. (2007) *The Human Voice: The Story of a Remarkable Talent*, London: Bloomsbury.

Kreiman, J. and Sidtis, D. (2013) *Foundations of Voice Studies: Interdisciplinary Approaches to Voice Production and Perception*, Boston: Wiley-Blackwell.

Macpherson, B. (2012) "A voice and so much more (or, when bodies say things that words cannot)," *Studies in Musical Theatre*, 6(1): 43–57.

Neumark, N., Gibson, R., and van Leeuwen, T. (eds) (2010) *Voice: Vocal Aesthetics in Digital Arts and Media*, Cambridge, MA: MIT Press.

Thomaidis, K. (2013) *The Grain of a Vocal Genre: A Comparative Approach to the Singing Pedagogies of EVDC Integrative Performance Practice, Korean* Pansori, *and the Polish Centre for Theatre Practices "Gardzienice,"* Ph.D. thesis, London: University of London.

Utz, C. and Lau, F. (eds) (2013) *Vocal Music and Contemporary Identities: Unlimited Voice in East Asia and the West*, New York and Abingdon: Routledge.

1

THE RE-VOCALIZATION OF LOGOS?

Thinking, doing and disseminating voice

Konstantinos Thomaidis

Prologue/pre-logos: the "Cavarerian project"

In her seminal *For More than One Voice: Toward a Philosophy of Vocal Expression* (2005), Italian cultural theorist Adriana Cavarero traced the historical processes whereby Western philosophy has developed its core strategies and principles of logos at the expense of the lived materiality of the voice. A series of "close read-ings" of a diverse array of thinkers and artists, ranging from Aristotle and Levinas to Monteverdi and Borges, problematized "the devocalization of logos" (Cavarero 2005: 40), the systematic exclusion, marginalization or silencing of the experienced, contingent and intersubjective voice, of *phone*, in the realm of philosophical enquiry.

I employ Cavarero as a productive point of departure in order to probe the role of voice in contemporary practice as research (PaR) in the performing arts. In unpacking recent trends and prevailing idioms in the UK academe, my interests lie mainly in what I term the "Cavarerian project," what I see as Cavarero's invitation to unveil, critique and deconstruct devocalization. For this research at least, the "Cavarerian project" revolves around two major axes: the positioning of voice against (traditional, patriarchal and Eurocentric) understandings of logos *as reason* and of logos *as language*. Cavarero's line of enquiry seems to necessitate further probing of the pedagogy and creative praxis of voice: how do we conceptualize voicing? How does voice emerge from and reflect back on its discursive domains? How can we bridge the chasm between ontology and epistemology in the study of voice? Ulti-mately, how do we think and do voice, particularly within graduate and postgraduate programmes and, by extension, in our explorations as voice practitioner–scholars? This chapter questions the underlying principles that fertilize core concerns around, and approaches to, voice, but recognizes that answers can only be explored fully in practice. Therefore, in examining how institutionalized scholarly activity engages with voice, this chapter investigates the interface between theory and practice in the emerging field of voice studies.[1]

This analysis extends a post-structuralist interrogation of the knowledge structures embedded in the study of voice in the current landscape of UK higher education, particularly the dissemination of research into/for/through voice. As such, the analysis – whilst informed by Cavarero's philosophical argument and primarily concerned with a meta-narrative or metaphysics of knowledge – will be grounded in "case studies" of doctoral projects and their respective publication (and/or assessment) formats. This discussion follows closely both axes of the "Cavarerian project," mainly concentrating on logos-as-language/dissemination. The overarching aim is of wider relevance, however: I argue for non-hierarchical, less-predictable models of engaging with voice that allow for its phonic element to reclaim its space in epistemological approaches to voice-related research.

Devocalizing research: voice versus logos-as-reason/knowledge

Unpacking Platonic metaphysics, Cavarero denounced the privileging of thought as the internal, unexpressed and therefore uncontaminated by experience dialogue of the mind with the self. Cavarero is not alone in postulating logos as coinciding with "the mute, visible order of the ideas contemplated by pure thought" (2005: 57). From art and education philosopher John Dewey's condemnation of a "spectator theory of knowledge" (Quinton 1977: 3) to the recent rise of embodied cognition and somatics, arts practitioners and scholars have contested "[t]he primacy given to the sense of sight," which "combined with the discovery of perspective as a Western aesthetic, has created distance between the position of the subject and the object" (Reeve 2011: 7). The construction of logos-as-reason on the metaphor of sight is evident in the etymology of a litany of related terms, such as idea (from the Greek *idein*, meaning to see and to know), theory (from the Greek *theorein*, meaning to see carefully and to contemplate) or science (from the Latin *scientia*, meaning to perceive through looking and to comprehend). Metaphors premised on sight, perspective and distance establish theory as a means of spatializing knowledge in a way that hierarchizes the knower over the known (Salmond 1982: 68–70). The constitutive presumption here is that reasoning, and by extension scientific research, involves observing from a distance, clarifying through examination or relating to the sphere of ideas.

This is an endeavour often assigned to quantitative approaches to research, which make claims at a "possible degree of separation between the researcher and the researched" (Smith and Dean 2009: 4). Is it possible, however, to research voice – which we thought of as an in-between in the Introduction to this book – only as a measurable, distanced or objectified phenomenon? According to Smith and Dean, "[a]t the basis of the relationship between creative practice and research is the problematic nature of conventional definitions of 'research,' which are underpinned by the fundamental philosophical quandary as to what constitutes 'knowledge'" (2009: 2). Cavarero's disputation of the mute order of consciousness from the perspective of voice could be deployed to challenge any notion of "knowledge as being an understood given" (Smith and Dean 2009: 3).

In considering these comments, and in interrogating knowledge-production processes in the study of voice, I see traditional conservatoire training as fostering a training focused on *phone*, the embodied knowledge of vocal practice. Logos-as-reason in this instance is tacit (see Polanyi 2009), muted, as it were, but implicit in the bodily disciplining of the vocal apparatus. However, in interrogating paradigms of vocal knowing from a Cavarerian perspective, even established training pedagogies, with their devotion to transmitting a set of canonical works (especially in the realms of opera and musical theatre), can be unpacked as complex, logocentric strategies of disciplining *phone* into voicing the logos/texts of the repertoire. In undergraduate university programmes, the other prevailing model of vocal education, logos appears to take precedence within units on historical and contextual knowledge of voice (opera studies, musical theatre milestones or poetics and linguistics, to name but a few). Practical units are on offer but, although more frequently than not delivered by practitioner specialists, they can be subject to criticism. Freeman, surveying actor training, warned against the dangers of merely imitating the conservatoire sector: "the links and overlaps between drama schools and non-vocational programmes provide little more than opportunities for boutique borrowing, with each group singing from the same sheet until such time as our innate differences of intent and possibility emerge" (2013: 86). Institutional pressures on timetabling and resources mean that the number of hours devoted to practical voice sessions in degree courses may be significantly less than in conservatories. But should it be different?

The problem is one of underlying paradigms; undergraduate programmes, when not explicitly vocational, need neither aspire only to tacit knowledge – nor do they have to aim at purely logocentric analysis. Universities *are* changing and Nelson's call for new categories in which "knowing–doing is inherent in the practice and practice is at the heart of the inquiry" (2013: 10) can have a decisive effect on the framings of voice across undergraduate higher education. To revocalize the logos/reason of vocal knowledge, foundational paradigms can be set up and developed in order to embed methodologies constituent to the PaR enterprise more commonly applied at postgraduate/doctoral levels. Crucially, what is at stake is not a mere silencing of logos but a project of re-imagining voicing as praxical and intimately connected to practice *and* knowledge production.[2]

Devocalizing dissemination: voice versus logos-as-language/symbol

The second component of Cavarero's criticism relates to logos as a system of signification, to the "side" of logos that "coincides with language" (2005: 57). In the logocentric world, which is premised on a model of communication seen as the exchange of signs, voice – bound to the sonorous component of signifiers – ought to serve the expression of signifieds. Linguist Ferdinand de Saussure conceptualized voice as such: "In any case, it is impossible for sound alone, a material element, to belong to language. It is only a secondary thing, substance to be put to use" (1959: 118). Voice in the process of signification is just a remainder, a leftover, not worthy of much elaboration outside its role as bearer of utterances. In the immaterial universe of signs, language can exist with no connection to corporeality, and signs have no need for voice to exist. In Cavarero's words,

> [t]he voice thus becomes the limit of speech – its imperfection, its dead weight. The voice becomes not only the reason for truth's ineffability, but also the acoustic filter that impedes the realm of signifieds from presenting itself to the noetic gaze.
>
> *(2005: 42)*

Nonetheless, what is it that voice expresses, and how? Is any study of voice destined to investigate language? In an attempt to challenge logos as signification, I will now focus on the dissemination of voice-related research.

The previous section mapped some of the challenges with which the Cavarerian critique of logos-as-reason presents existing modes of knowledge-production in undergraduate or conservatoire-type environments. What happens, though, when researchers share their knowledge on a doctoral level? Which systems of signification do they employ, activate or object to? In other words, which is the place of voice, and vocal praxis, in relation to the logos-as-language of scholarly dissemination? For Smith and Dean, the answer seems straightforward when "knowledge is normally verbal or numerical"; however, "[s]ince it is clear that a sonic [...] artwork can sometimes transmit knowledge in non-verbal and non-numerical terms, we believe that any definition of knowledge needs to acknowledge these non-verbal forms of transmission" (2009: 3).

This section questions the presuppositions and underlying assumptions of existing modes of dissemination. I also discuss the potentialities that a PaR approach can trigger and foster in the field of voice studies (or in related disciplines, when a voice studies approach is employed). Dissemination is taken here as an umbrella term, encompassing not only the various types of public sharing, presentation and publication in the professional arena, but also the broad range of disseminating practices during the educational process, normatively thought of as assessments.

A decisive "rite of passage" that links these two worlds is the final assessment of a researcher and, supposedly, the very first sharing of their research in a peer-reviewed context, the viva. Mladen Dolar's analysis of this moment can further illuminate the tensions between logos and voice/*phone*. Building on Giorgio Agamben's observations on the extimate connections between *bios* and *zoe* as the core organizational principle of politics,[3] Dolar argued that "the voice, in its function as the internal exterior of logos, the apparent pre-logos, the extra-logos, is called upon and necessary in certain well-defined and crucial situations" (2006: 107), such as the ritual readings of the Holy Scripture, the interrogation of witnesses in judiciary processes, and elections. Crucially, in an educational system whereby a university student is mainly expected to engage with various manifestations of logos, primarily through readings, written exams or essay-type assignments, the performative "limen" between being a student and adopting the vocational identity of the researcher is an act of voice; namely, the defense of a doctoral thesis *viva voce*. The viva is "indeed simply a question of vocal display; the supposed testing and questioning of the candidate's knowledge has very little to do with that knowledge itself, and has an entirely ritual and vocal character" (Dolar 2006: 110). This is not a mere case of acknowledging the importance of the voice; it is a regulatory process whereby the unruly, ephemeral, I–thou character of the voice (as the equivalent of Agamben's biological life, *zoe*) is allocated a strictly delineated space within the educational process. Voice is therefore subordinated to the main object of the examination, the thesis, the research results presented as logos-set-in-stone. To return to Cavarero, this is yet another strategy of devocalizing knowledge, even in its dissemination.

However, a PaR approach can open up fresh possibilities as it "offers a clear challenge to conventional thinking in its premise that the practice of performance can be at once a method of investigative research and the process through which that research is disseminated" (Freeman 2010: 7). This challenge extends to the significance afforded to the researcher's voice in the quasi-ritual tactic of the viva. The assessment – and dissemination – of the practical component of a PaR thesis project could reposition the voice to the forefront and establish new balancing acts between the traditionally accepted logos/thesis and the voice/practice.

Having said that, it would be naïve to consider the mere presence of a musical/vocal/sound performance piece as automatically presenting logos with a challenge (or as activating disciplinary resistance, to stretch this logic to its Foucauldian limits). The exigency of disseminating research "in a communicable and retrievable form" (Freeman 2010: 113) can reposition voice in relation to logos in various ways. This section will build on Freeman's refashioning of Frayling's (1993: 2) research *into, for* and *through* art, in order to map these differing positionings and tensions from the perspective of dissemination.

A research *into/of* practice (RiP) approach addresses the practice as the object of study, with the term "object" bearing all the philosophical complexity 20th-century critical analysis has bequeathed to us (see Böhme 1993). Research projects that offer semiotic analyses of musical theatre pieces, or historical and historiographic reflections on compositional processes in the format of a written dissertation, exemplify such an approach. In this instance, despite voice being the central object of study, *phone* as lived materiality remains a point of reference or material relegated to an appendix. RiP transposes the contingency and impermanence of the voice within systems of logocentric signification. Recent instances of such an approach are Experience Bryon's (1998) or Konstantinos Thomaidis's (2013) theses.[4] Bryon, for instance, developed a critique of performing strategies and pedagogical models available to the interdisciplinary (voicing) performer, drawing on historical examples and research on deconstructionist models of meaning-making in performance. It is indicative that throughout her doctoral research Bryon's emerging methodology was conceived as Integrative Performance *Theory*, whereas during later stages of her studio-based explorations it transformed into Integrative Performance *Practice and Theory* (2014).

In other words, although the doctoral project was informed by practical research and was completed by a professional singer, coach and opera director, vocal practice was used as a necessary point of reference but the mode of submission was the conventional written thesis and the research findings informed subsequent practice. Similarly, my thesis on intercultural voice pedagogies aimed to frame the discursive bodies they produce and documented training fieldworks in the appendix. This appendix also included transcriptions of a workshop session that capitalized on the research findings and proposed a new pedagogical methodology for voice. In both instances, the lived voice was secondary to its discussion and only came decisively to the foreground, structurally, as a side project and, chronologically, as the "afterlife" of the research; what was facilitated instead was logos, a study *in* voice, a critical analysis that found its most appropriate expression in a monograph-type final submission.

Research *for* practice (RfP) establishes a binary between logos and voice, and, in a way, reverses the paradigm of seeing/observing from a distance; what is being investigated/seen/observed is used as a springboard that informs the practice. Such an approach is geared towards application; a theoretical issue is studied and resolved in discursive terms and the practice exemplifies the proposed critical schemata. For example, an RfP project would encompass the theorization of the ideological nexuses embedded in a particular vocal mannerism or stylistic approach to a piece of repertoire, the deconstruction of latent ideologies through a meta- or extra-generic philosophy, and, finally, the materialization of a practical piece informed by this new knowledge. Zachary Dunbar, for example, devised a musical theatre adaptation of *Oedipus* inspired by his contextual research on classical theatre and methodological probing of interdisciplinary approaches (2007). In this and similar instances, dissemination is effected both through the text and the practice, but, crucially, the practice is not emerging but predicated on and determined by traditional analysis. Voice is an application of logos, it exemplifies and demonstrates the theoretical research. As Freeman put it, "[t]he practice *informs* the thesis without ever (despite the efforts of a fearless few) satisfactorily standing *as* the thesis" (2010: 64; original emphasis).

Another pertinent example is Chan E. Park's thesis (1995) on Korean *p'ansori* (particularly its extended and reworked form of 2003). Park first investigated this musico-theatrical practice from a joint historiographic and ethnomusicological perspective. In noticing the dangers of current codification, she developed new musical narratives that encompass the modes, rhythms and vocal tropisms of the *p'ansori* lineage but derive new inspiration from recent stories and use English recitatives alongside Korean sung parts. Significantly, these new performances and scores were presented as the culmination of the project and the conclusion of the argument (Park 2003: 245–76). Her suggested model of cross-cultural/transnational performance came as the direct application of her theoretical examination of the genealogy and aesthetics of the genre; consequently, and even though the comprehensive communication of the argument requires both thesis and practice, voice seems to depend on the needs of the theoretical research and to come as a response to its discoveries.

Research *through* practice (RtP), however, invites the practical component as a partner indispensable to the research process. The theoretical context is not predetermined, and the limits and boundaries between theory and practice are constantly negotiated. As a result, the mode of dissemination accommodates a relationship between the exegetical/written, the practical/creative and the documented in a manner that foregrounds the ineluctable uniqueness of both the project undertaken and its "publication" and embraces the fact that the "'outcomes' of artistic research are *necessarily* unpredictable" (Barrett and Bolt 2007: 3; original emphasis). A fluid, non-linear, studio-based, laboratory-inspired approach results in an idiosyncratic presentation/publication formula, in which the thesis cannot operate as distinct from the practical work or the plethora of supporting media that proliferate in tight connection to RtP projects (artists' websites, reflexive blogs, audio-visual DVDs, interactive appendices and the like).

A number of theses in the broader area of music theatre result in this idiosyncratic amalgamation of practice and research. Karikis's project (2005) is a particularly useful example. The introduction states that "the project embarks on a methodological experiment whose starting point is a 'multi-vocal' approach to writing and the simultaneous employment and equal consideration of artistic practice and theory" (Karikis 2005: 10). Building on the hypothesis that voice accords presence, the thesis argued that voice is not a representation of the self but a continuous strategy of identity-making, a listening out for the self (Karikis 2005: 126). Karikis situated voice at the very centre of his project through a series of strategies. The first half of the written submission, which corresponded to the expected literature review of a conventional thesis, was framed as the transcript of a "domestic lepidopterist" and deployed a pseudoscientific mode of speech; in the second part, the thinking voice was replaced by the empirical voice as Karikis embarked on a walk in the streets of London and charted his vocal reactions to sonic events, discovering this process as constant and never fully reaching a clear distinction between the perceiving self and the environmental acoustics. The writing was presented as a transcript and Karikis highlighted the performative and contingent character of voice by coopting voicing personae rather than seeking recourse to a single or impersonal logos. Logos was further challenged through shifting typefaces and neologisms, which negated the language of dissemination as a rigid system of signification and foregrounded its contingent and arbitrary qualities. Second, the phonic and aural took precedence over the written; the thesis was accompanied by CDs with compositions that exemplified and challenged the ruptures in the acoustic identity that the first half conceptualized. Further, they documented the sonic events without which it would not be possible for the second half to articulate its argument. Karikis also proposed a methodology according to which the text was produced by reading and voicing instead of the silent (muted, in Cavarero's understanding) act of writing (2005: 31). Most importantly, the CDs included a full reading of the text, voiced by speakers of diverse ethnic backgrounds; this was presented as the main submission, while the text was postulated as secondary. What is significant in this case is that the vocal was pervasive and predominant, the linguistic and textual assisted the practice instead of replicating it, studying it or applying its findings, and the mode of dissemination ("exploded" textuality, multi-vocal reading, recourse to vocal personae) was inextricably connected to the core argument on the fragmented and essentially ruptured sense of the acoustic self. This written account, among others, engaged with newly composed musical pieces, sonic materials or training exercises in mutually dependent, fluctuating and dynamic symbiosis.

One must not forget, however, that this seemingly ever-expanding field of possibilities operates within the fence lines of given assessment criteria (in the case of university examinations) or models of scholarly publication, which, albeit shifting and adapting, tend to prioritize logos over vocal praxis. Haseman and Mafe cautioned that "[a]round each creative work there is a wide field of possible interpretive contexts and it is in the exegesis that some of these can be delimited. This delimiting act, […] is seldom comfortably arrived at" (2009: 226). It is perhaps in the field of the "uncomfortable," of that which is not either *a priori* prescribed or *a posteriori* imposed, that the emergent, indeterminate and immediate character of the voice can find its place in the dissemination of research through voice (parallel and in addition to research into or for voice). If logos is to be revocalized – to follow Cavarero – or, if voice is to assume less of a ritual role – to employ Dolar – while also addressing the problematics of research significance in PaR projects, it is imperative to re-imagine dissemination too as a dialogic framework, a nexus of tensions between logos and voice. I will now return to, and further refine, this notion of tension between the practical and the exegetic.

Epilogue/epi-logos: PaR as revocalization

Yet another question needs to be asked: what is the relation between the two aspects of logos, between language and thought? Cavarero saw "the ideas" as "the origin of both verbal language and the empirical world" (2005: 41). "Thinking and speaking," "the two components of logos," are "arranged in hierarchical order" (Cavarero 2005: 57). This implies that "[a]s a specific object of interest for philosophy, the human voice is grasped within a system of signification that subordinates speech to the concept" (Cavarero 2005: 34). It is in the traditional dualism between the vocal/aural and the conceptual/seen that Cavarero located the devocalization of logos, the dichotomy between embodied phonation and critical enquiry – and this dichotomy prioritizes the sign over vocality and the idea over the sign.

In the words of Simon Jones,

> [o]ur greatest challenge is to find ways – and I stress here the plural, as there may well be as many ways as there are bodies or combinations of bodies active within the academy – of *housing the mix* of performative and textual practices alongside each other.
>
> *(2009: 29; original emphasis)*

In this spirit, and after applying and extending the critique of logos to the study and research of voice, it is timely to ask: which is the alternative that Cavarero proposed? Cavarero, in reading Calvino, called for "a vocal phenomenology of uniqueness" and explained: "This is an ontology that concerns the incarnate singularity of every existence insofar as she or he manifests her- or himself vocally" (2005: 7). It is here, then, that the overarching intentionality of her project is revealed: Cavarero criticized logos in order to reclaim some breathing space for the contingency, temporality, presence, vulnerability and relationality of the lived voice, which she understood as "not being but becoming" (2005: 37). In a similar vein, I would recognize that perhaps the ultimate aspiration of this chapter is to define a place for voice within the academy, to find a voice for voice.

At a first glance, this may sound like a valorization of practice *over* research; Bolt seems cautious, however, when diagnosing the risks ingrained in such a claim: "practice-only postgraduate research can disable practice-led research by confusing practice with praxical knowledge and severing the link between the artwork and the work of art" (2007: 33–34). Research and knowledge *can* be implied in the very act of voicing, but voicing *per se* is not necessarily the sole enabling *a priori* of any related research or knowledge. Cavarero too does not seem to advocate a simplistic overthrow of metaphysics in favour of phenomenology; her "project," as earlier defined, is a philosophical one after all. She rather claimed "a kind of reversal": "to understand speech from the perspective of voice instead of from the perspective of language" (Cavarero 2005: 14) and to (re)consider how for pre-Platonic thought it was "the *phone* that decide[d] the physiology of thought" (Cavarero 2005: 63).

For this author at least, as a voice studies practitioner–scholar, this shift in perspective is crucial in re-imagining the role of voice in research. However, Cavarero's propositions seem to imply a methodological scheme of wider interest or application. In the suggested reading of *For More than One Voice* (2005), voice is not only *expressive* of logos-as-reason, but it also constructs and generates it; equally, voice is not the *facilitator* of logos-as-language, of a supposedly set-in-stone system of signification, but it participates in its shaping and construction. I read Cavarero's dismantling of devocalization as a critique of a presupposed and essentialist hierarchy between thinking, speaking and voicing.

On this basis, and in agreement with Pitches's argument that "any claim to a singular and expert account of training [or research, I would add] methods or methodologies should be treated with considerable suspicion and skepticism" (2011: 140), I propose an approach to PaR that unfolds as a triangular continuum between logos-as-reason, logos-as-language and practice (which, in the instance of voice studies, is, or involves, voice). This scheme, as evident in Nelson's triangular, dynamic model for mixed-mode research, mixed-mode practices and "theoretical practices" (2006: 18), can facilitate a multimodal, "mixed" and emerging engagement with the voice. Extrapolating Nicolescu's triangle of the included middle (2002: 156), what I find particularly intriguing is that each point of the proposed triangular continuum can be seen as operating on a different plane where the other two points can be seen as non-contradictory; if seen as the two points of a line, for example, practice and research are either separated or draw from each other and result in each other (as in the examples of research *in* voice and *for* voice). In classical geometry, after all, each point signifies location and points in a line imply opposing directionalities. The third point can provide opportunities for inclusion, complex interaction and non-contradiction. The emerging format of Karikis's thesis, as shown, challenged the opposition of his vocal practice and (voiced) writing and offered a new plane in which the dissemination allowed for a dynamic, nascent, praxical understanding of voice.

Building on my reading of Nicolescu and Nelson, I see this type of triangulation as an ongoing *process*, as a shifting away from the spatial/visual metaphor of the static shape. This paradigm rejects linear trajectories from logos/thinking towards the conceptualization of practice or, reversely, from practice towards the generation of exegetical logos, and embraces the potential of the "uncomfortable" briefly sketched out in the previous section. In the specific context of "uniqueness" within which its PaR project operates, analysis, praxis and dissemination (including the languages and protocols of sharing at play) are equally generative "partners." In this case, the major challenge is to maintain each of the three synergetic parameters activated in the dynamic flow between them. If the mode of dissemination is always-already implemented, then logos-as-language is inescapably posited as immobile and hierarchically placed above thinking and practising. For example, if the dissemination is fixed as conservatoire-type exams, voice remains in the pre-determined realm of the know-how, whereas if the assessment is always-already in writing, voice is trapped within logocentric dissemination, what Symonds has called "the logocentric archiving of knowledge" (2013: 212). A flexible, contingent and unique thesis/assessment formula could maintain the inventive and unexpected dialogues between logos and practice. As a self-reflective aside, if this analysis of vocal PaR is predestined to be published as a chapter, can it achieve more than making a theoretical claim and proposing a schema, a desire for the praxical possibilities of a triangular continuum to be fulfilled *elsewhere*? More importantly, this scheme, which, I am aware, comes as a cadence to a rethinking of Cavarero's work and needs further expansion to gain currency in its own right, does not only encapsulate a call for a revocalization of logos. It also points to the reverse side of the coin, that the revocalization of knowledge cannot come at the expense of the de-logosization of practice.

Notes

1 This research first appeared in *Studies in Musical Theatre*. I thank the editors for granting me permission to publish this reworked version. My ongoing collaboration with Amanda Smallbone and Ben Macpherson at the Centre of Interdisciplinary Studies has been central to the development of this chapter.

2 In this volume, McAllister-Viel and Smallbone reflect further on voice training within undergraduate courses.

3 For Agamben, the Greek term *zoe* denotes life as a biological phenomenon and *bios* refers to socio-political coexistence. Their connection is extimate in that *bios*, the structured life of the *polis*, orders and marginalizes *zoe* but inevitably, the natural life of instincts and biological needs remains at the very centre of human activity. Dolar elaborated on the concept of extimacy in seeing logos as the structured system of signification, the organized language of the social order, and voice/*phone* as the suppressed, controlled but unavoidably present equivalent of *zoe* (2006: 119–24).

4 I do not intend to compare or evaluate the significant contributions to knowledge effected through the selected theses; the emphasis is on the *mode* of dissemination, understood within specific knowledge-making paradigms and therefore assessment criteria and corresponding institutional standards.

References

Barrett, E. and Bolt, B. (eds) (2007) *Practice as Research: Approaches to Creative Arts Enquiry*, London and New York: I.B. Tauris.

Böhme, G. (1993) "Atmosphere as the fundamental concept of a new aesthetics," *Thesis Eleven*, 36(1): 113–26.

Bolt, B. (2007) "The magic is in handling," in Barrett, E. and Bolt, B. (eds) *Practice as Research: Approaches to Creative Arts Enquiry*, London and New York: I.B. Tauris, 27–34.

Bryon, E. (1998) *The Integrative Performance Theory: An Anti-Hermeneutic Approach for Opera*, Ph.D. thesis, Victoria: Monash University.

——(2014) *Integrative Performance: Practice and Theory for the Interdisciplinary Performer*, New York: Routledge.

Cavarero, A. (2005) *For More than One Voice: Toward a Philosophy of Vocal Expression*, trans. P.A. Kottman, Stanford: Stanford University Press.

de Saussure, F. (1959) *Course in General Linguistics*, trans. W. Baskin, New York: Philosophical Library.

Dolar, M. (2006) *A Voice and Nothing More*, Cambridge, MA: MIT Press.

Dunbar, Z. (2007) *Science, Music and Theatre: An Interdisciplinary Approach to the Singing Tragic Chorus of Greek Tragedy*, Ph.D. thesis, London: University of London.

Frayling, C. (1993) "Research in art and design," *Royal College of Art Research Papers*, 1(1): 1–5, www.transart.org/wp-content/uploads/group-documents/79/1372332724-Frayling_Research-in-Art-and-Design.pdf.

Freeman, J. (2010) *Blood, Sweat and Theory: Research through Performance*, Faringdon: Libri Publishing.

——(2013) "Performance studies, actor training and boutique borrowing," *Studies in Theatre & Performance*, 33(1): 77–90.

Haseman, B. and Mafe, D. (2009) "Acquiring know-how: research training for practice-led researchers," in Smith, H. and Dean, R.T. (eds) *Practice-led Research, Research-led Practice in the Creative Arts*, Edinburgh: Edinburgh University Press, 211–28.

Jones, S. (2009) "The courage of complementarity: practice-as-research as a paradigm shift in performance studies," in Allengue, L., Jones, S., Kershaw, B. and Piccini, A. (eds) *Practice-as-Research in Performance and Screen*, Basingstoke and New York: Palgrave Macmillan, 19–32.

Karikis, M. (2005) *The Acoustics of the Self*, Ph.D. thesis, London: UCL.

Nelson, R. (2006) "Modes of PaR knowledge and their place in the academy," 1–23, www.westminster.ac.uk/__data/assets/pdf_file/0011/74594/RobinNelson.pdf.

——(2013) *Practice as Research in the Arts: Principles, Protocols, Pedagogies, Resistances*, Basingstoke and New York: Palgrave Macmillan.

Nicolescu, B. (2002) *Manifesto of Transdisciplinarity*, trans. K-C. Voss, Albany: State University of New York Press.

Park, C. (1995) *P'ansori Performed: From Strawmat to Proscenium and Back*, Ph.D. thesis, Hawai'i: University of Hawai'i.

——(2003) *Voices from the Straw Mat: Toward an Ethnography of Korean Story Singing*, Honolulu: University of Hawai'i Press.

Pitches, J. (2011) "Performer training: researching practice in the theatre laboratory," in Kershaw, B. and Nicholson, H. (eds) *Research Methods in Theatre and Performance*, Edinburgh: Edinburgh University Press, 137–61.

Polanyi, M. (2009) *The Tacit Dimension*, Chicago: University of Chicago Press.

Quinton, A. (1977) "Inquiry, thought and action: John Dewey's theory of knowledge," in Peters, R.S. (ed.) *John Dewey Reconsidered*, London: Routledge, 1–17.

Reeve, S. (2011) *Nine Ways of Seeing a Body*, Axminster: Triarchy Press.

Salmond, A. (1982) "Theoretical landscapes: on cross-cultural conceptions of knowledge," in Parkin, D. (ed.) *Semantic Anthropology*, London: Academic Press, 64–87.

Smith, H. and Dean, R.T. (2009) *Practice-led Research, Research-led Practice in the Creative Arts*, Edinburgh: Edinburgh University Press.

Symonds, D. (2013) "'Powerful spirit': notes on some practice as research," in Symonds, D. and Karantonis, P. (eds) *The Legacy of Opera: Reading Music Theatre as Experience and Performance*, Amsterdam and New York: Editions Rodopi, 209–28.

Thomaidis, K. (2013) *The Grain of a Vocal Genre: A Comparative Approach to the Singing Pedagogies of EVDC Integrative Performance Practice, Korean Pansori, and the Polish Centre for Theatre Practices "Gardzienice,"* Ph.D. thesis, London: University of London.

Part II
Voice in training and process

2

THE SINGULARITY OF EXPERIENCE IN THE VOICE STUDIO

A dialogue with Michel Henry[1]

Päivi Järviö

Philosophers of the 20th century, such as Sartre, Heidegger and Merleau-Ponty, have concentrated primarily on aspects of the visual, which offers a good starting point for discussions of intentionality. In the history of Western philosophy, the singular, live, embodied voice has given way to the study of seeing and reading – of the interior, silent voice, *logos*. The live human voice is simply absent from these discussions. As Adriana Cavarero argues, this ignoring of the uniqueness of the voice has been systematic (2005: 9). Cavarero tracks in detail how early philosophy closed its ears and ignored uniqueness in whatever mode it manifested itself, arguing that the live voice has only recently been given a place in the work of philosophers such as Cixous, Arendt, Nancy and Derrida.

The phenomenology of Michel Henry (1922–2002) and his views on the embodied singularity of the living human being helped to shape my thinking when I was writing my doctoral dissertation on the experience of the professional singer of Early Italian Baroque music (Järviö 2011). The aim of the dissertation was to study music making from the point-of-view/being of the present-day musician, a hitherto largely ignored position on which Cusick (1994) and Potter (2000: 158–62), among others, have called for more research.[2] My focus was on so-called Early Music Studies,[3] which tend to ignore the embodied experience of the present-day performer, even though many of the authors have been performing musicians.[4] I aim to demonstrate how the non-intentional phenomenology of Michel Henry can enhance understanding of the live, singular voice, of singing, and also of vocal pedagogy.[5] Considering the experience of singing music from the 17th and 18th centuries, my discussion focuses on the embodied "now" of the musician–singer–pedagogue who performs, for example, works by Monteverdi or Rameau.

The study of singing and human voice has tended to focus on phonetics, acoustics, anatomy and physiology, which – in Henry's phenomenology – represent an outside perspective; that of somebody observing, listening, measuring and defining the singer, the singing and the vocal instrument, or voice. Although these studies are invaluable for anyone attempting to understand the workings of the human voice, I have chosen another point of being: that of the musician–singer.[6] The experience discussed is mine, and links my research to the autoethnographical tradition (see Ellis and Bochner 2000 and 2002). Autoethnography – which tends not to be linked to an articulated philosophical background such as phenomenology – has only recently been applied more systematically to the study of music and performance (see Bartleet and Ellis 2009).

In this chapter, an overview of the main points of Henry's material phenomenology is interspersed with descriptions of the rehearsing and teaching situation in the vocal studio. The aim is to depict the body of the singer–teacher of Baroque vocal music as the singular, live point of intersection between her experience as a professional singer, a voice teacher, a teacher of chamber music, an expert on performance practices of the 17th and 18th centuries, and a human being whose whole life is present in the rehearsal or lesson, as embodied in her singer's body. The discussion is, therefore, not pedagogical in the sense that the reader might be given practical tools directly applicable to teaching. Rather, I propose a mode of understanding the human voice based on the material phenomenology of Henry, which might serve as a potential starting point for pedagogical thinking.[7]

Searching for a mode of thinking about singing

Gazing inside and listening to what is unfolding in one's body is characteristic of studying singing. Learning to do this is one of the challenges for inexperienced voice students: the interiority of the body does not seem to exist for us unless we concentrate on it, be it through breathing-centred modes of exercise such as yoga, Pilates or martial arts, or singing. When she is singing, a singer is powerfully aware of the experience of the interiority of her body, and, I would argue, not necessarily so much of her relationship with the exterior world. If the body and voice are in balance, or the singing is easy, there is nothing in the experience that would be "thrown forward," or would be an ob-ject.[8] Breathing that moves me, and makes me sound, forms a unity with the music I sing, with the score, with the space, and with all the knowing and experience that *is* me. My presence is filled with the music I sing. My presence *is* the music I sing:

> I close my eyes and inhale letting my lower torso and rib cage relax and spread out. Even though I inhale through my nose to fill my lungs, the experience is not about air flowing into a container through a tube. Rather, I inhale with my whole body.
>
> I start to hum. I sense the vibration on my lips, on my cheeks, on the top of my head, in my pharynx, around my rib cage, on my back, on my stomach, on my thighs, all the way down to my feet – in my whole body and around it. I do not pay much attention to the quality of the sound that I make. I do not listen to it with my ears. Rather, I attempt to let every part of my body

as well as my surroundings be overwhelmed with this buzzing feeling. I inhale and hum time and time again, each time inspiring new, yet unfound parts of my body to vibrate. I am this sound.[9]

Singing, therefore, is not exclusively about the concrete, physical movement of body parts such as the diaphragm, the sides, the back, the throat, the larynx and the mouth, studied in terms of vocal anatomy and physiology. Nor is it only about the definable, measurable qualities of the sound departing from the singer's body and entering the body of the listener – or a recording and/or measuring device. Above all, it is about the live movement in the singer's body. If she had not been shown an anatomical image of the diaphragm, for example – a two-dimensional image of a chanterelle-shaped, immobile, lifeless muscle – she probably would not know that she had one, and would have no idea what it was like. What is foregrounded in the experience of producing voice is a powerful presence, the quality of which seems to transcend perceptible reality in modes that make verbalization particularly challenging.

Distanced from methodological approaches such as anatomy, physiology, acoustics and phonetics, the construction of modes of thinking about singing becomes cumbersome. At first, phenomenology seems to provide a serviceable frame of reference. As I proceed to consider my own embodied experience of singing, the centrality of vision in phenomenological studies on human experience seems to miss the key experience of singing: this occurrence in my body that encompasses *all* of my body and all of its senses, of which vision would certainly not be the primary one. The idea of the human being as a subject "in the world" and intentionally directed *towards* the world, in a relationship with the world that is "there," outside me, simply does not seem to match my embodied experience of singing.[10]

One possible perspective on the living body and the interiority of singing that does not rely on vision is the phenomenology of Michel Henry. Whilst Henry did not write extensively about music or voice, art and culture have a special place in his thinking. He discusses music and singing only in passing, and specifically from the position of the listener – a position that, incidentally, has long dominated discussions on musical experience.[11] Henry's contribution to present-day thinking about music in his article (2004) on the musical drawings of the Hungarian-born artist August von Briesen is nevertheless inspiring. Further, his passion for the work of Wassily Kandinsky motivated his short discussion of music in *Seeing the Invisible* (2009).

Life, the world and the living body of the singer

For Henry, the world occurs in the body of a human being – of a singer as well as a listener – according to one principle. The foundation of this occurrence is life, which means that each person is "charged with self [forever] without having wanted it"; that life is given to the human being to be lived as a burden to be carried, to be suffered (Henry 2003: 199). Henry understands life as fundamentally different from the world, which means that he stands for ontological dualism and the acceptance of two aspects of reality: interiority–exteriority, invisible–visible, subjective–objective, life–world. However, this does not necessitate resorting to Cartesian dualities. Rather, as expressed by Zahavi, Henry's idea is about recognizing "the existence of an absolute dimension of subjective self-manifestation without which no subjective manifestation, without which no hetero-manifestation would be possible" (1999: 231). Life, then, is what differentiates living human beings from lifeless objects and enables them to touch objects outside of themselves and to be touched by them, to orientate themselves towards the world as sensing creatures. Life enables a singer to stand with a score in her hand, to read the score, to study the context of the piece she is working on, to produce a vocal sound, to pronounce the lyrics, to hear the musicians playing with her, and to see the audience. It is also the basis on which the vocal pedagogue can hear the singing of the student in a particular way, both as professional singer and pedagogue.

My subjective body is always present to me before my body is pro-jected (lat. *pro-iectō*) towards the world, before it perceives the world and represents it. This presence of the subjective body to itself is, according to Henry, life's only and real substance (Dufour-Kowalska 2003: 32). What Henry calls *auto-affection* is, for him, "an *immediate, non-objectifying* and *passive* occurrence" that does not stop occurring in us as long as we are alive (in Zahavi 2007: 137; added emphasis). Without life as auto-affection there is no being and no thinking. Henry maintains that it is possible for a human being to experience what comes from the world only in his or her own living body, without the distance and difference created by intentionality. All knowledge, including so-called objective knowledge, is based on auto-affection.[12]

When a person sings, the body's subjective, invisible life is strongly present, an experience that all singers probably share. Hemsley identifies in singing the power of life and energy that is essential for the expressing of emotion. This vital energy, or the "breath of life," has been called *l'élan vital* by Bergson, *prana* by the Hindus and *chi* by the Chinese. The Italian word *fiato* ("breath") also carries this meaning – the breath of life (Hemsley 1998: 22). Life is the foundation of everything, a source from which we all drink and that allows for a shared reality between people, a community – or *communauté* – in which each person has his or her own, unique, singular share of what can be shared – of life (Dufour-Kowalska 2003: 66–67). Life makes possible activities such as singing and studying historical performance practices, even though most of the time what allows us to manage all of this effortlessly is in oblivion. The idea of *communauté* is not identical to the notions of commonness, generality or universality, something that can exist only in theory and not in a reality based on singularity. Auto-affection is not some exceptional occurrence in the life of a human being, such as flow, even though sensing the presence of life can be an extremely moving experience.[13] Rather, it is something that occurs incessantly within us.

Life – what Henry calls the "subjective body" – occurs in what he terms the "organic body," referring to the boundaries that limit the movement of the subjective body. In the case of a singer, it is the resistance of the singing body that reveals these limits. Henry uses breathing as one of the instances of this resistance

(2000: 212–14). When a human being inhales, there is an interior opening that persists as long as possible. When the inhalation has reached its limits, the action stops and the human being returns to her original state by exhaling.

> I wake up in the morning feeling my body stretched out on the mattress, rested but slightly stiff from hours of virtual immobility. My singer's working day begins here. My first conscious inhalation is cautious and shallow. I can feel my ribs expand while inhaling and return to their resting position while exhaling. Breath by breath, I persuade my sleepy muscles to give in to my conscious breathing. There is always a limit, which it is not possible to surpass without forcing.

As noted earlier, it is possible to study the body from an objective point of view, from the outside, or, in Henry's terms, to study the objective body (2000: 145–46). The knowledge produced in branches of "the new science" (Henry 2000: 146) such as anatomy and physiology is nevertheless, according to Henry, lifeless and free of sensations, something that can be subjected to measuring and calculating. From this perspective, the singing voice is an object, an instrument that is used to produce sound. Like a dancer's body, the singer's body – and the vocal organs as a whole – can be worked on, trained and disciplined like a well-functioning machine (Parviainen 1998: 20–23).

The organic body reflects the affective and sensing relationship of the subjective body to everything that it is not: to others and to the world. Henry considers the world of a human being a "living cosmos," a world of life (Dufour-Kowalska 2003: 48). For me, this world exists in all the details embedded in my body. For somebody else, the living cosmos is different. A singer lives and works in her body or *as* her body, and senses the resistance offered by her body and by the world. When working on her singing, she aims to connect to the whole of her singing body that carries all her ever-changing experience and knowledge, both visible and invisible.

Following Henry's idea of passivity, I understand my body as compost that has become what it is in the course of time.[14] As an organic space open to the reining-in of the world, my body has received – and will continue to receive – every moment that enters me from the world: everything from historical knowledge to the understanding of rhetorical figures, from the process of building a vocal instrument to the peculiarities of the pronunciation of the French language, from certain experiences of making music to other experiences in life, without end. This compost is by no means an organized, articulated whole from which material that has been thrown into it can be picked out unchanged.

> I was born into a family where singing and playing jazz, sometimes in the late hours of the night, occurred without the need for sheet music. I then began to play by ear at around the same time as I started taking piano lessons. Later, I joined numerous choirs. During my studies, I was always more interested in chamber music than in solo singing. Sounds in themselves, such

as a beautiful singing voice, did not fascinate me. I was rather enchanted by the rhythm and swing in the music, and delighted in learning foreign languages. I chose none of these things, but they grew out of what I had been absorbing from the world since early childhood. In hindsight, it is of course possible to see all of this as something linear, to trace connections between things and to construe it as a story.

The composed material is always present in the singer, at the moment when she works on the music, for example. Part of this material is in her consciousness and can be verbalized while most of it has sunk into her living body, and she is no longer conscious of it. Practically everything that has come from the world into the body and has left its mark is potentially present at the moment of singing; things past and forgotten, and everything present in the moment; being tired or alert, lame or inspired, feeling ill or well, being depressed after having insulted a friend, being content after having found the right words at the right moment – endlessly. The living body is never the same from one moment to another, even though a human being inevitably needs to have some sense of continuity. Singing is the making audible of life in the now.

The world is manifested to us in a fundamentally neutral, indifferent way, or as Henry formulates it: "there are victims and executors, merciful deeds and genocide, rules and exceptions, wind, water, earth; and all of it appears before us in the same way" (2000: 60).[15] As long as what is in the world is not in us, we cannot make choices concerning it because it does not exist for us. Once it has entered us, it is too late to choose. According to Henry, the world and the objects in it that enter a human being from it are not capable of carrying any sensible qualities even though they might awaken an impression in us. A building is not grey or yellow any more than it could be hot or sad. A wall, subjected to the scorching sun, does not ask for water because of the heat. It is not hot because there are no such impressions in the manifestation of the world (Henry 2000: 74).

Similarly, sounds that comprise the material of music are not high or low, compositions are not more or less expressive, the voice is not more or less controlled, and dissonances in Baroque recitatives are not more or less harrowing. For me, they only have qualities when they occur in me. In the range of my own singing voice I can call certain sounds high, and others low. Some compositions might be expressive for me, my voice can be controlled or out of control, the dissonances I sing might be harrowing for me – or then again, maybe not. The experience of a human being is radically singular.

Sounds and words in the body of the singer and the listener–singer

As far as Henry is concerned, the sung words are a secondary factor in singing because the human voice is what actually "speaks" to the listener. The force of life present in the live voice is manifested in a particular way when the sung language is foreign to the listener (Henry 2004: 252–53). In this, Henry's thinking seems to connect with Roland Barthes's ideas of "the grain of the voice," and his use of Julie Kristeva's concepts of *phenosong* and *genosong* to separate two modes of singing: the first one concentrating on the nuances of the text, communication, expression and personal interpretation, and the second making present the singing, living body, the flesh of the singer.[16]

For somebody specializing in a repertoire in which the sung text is of crucial importance to every choice the performer makes, this is a challenging thought to digest. Is Henry implying that words as something referring to the reality of the world might distract the listener's attention from the living voice? Or that a listener who does not understand the words would be somehow safer from the connections to the world, simultaneously more sensitive to the fleeting moments of the presence of life in the singer's voice? This might be the case with regard to the experience of somebody listening. I argue, however, that for the singer or the speaker, the sung words exist in a different way from what might be characteristic for the listener. For the one producing the sound, meanings are always present in the voice in some way or another, whatever the sounds produced. A totally foreign language, even gibberish or seemingly senseless howling, is instantly connected to meanings, be they vague or explicit.

A singer working with a piece of music is expected to study both the meaning and the pronunciation of the text in detail, whether in her own mother tongue or in a foreign language. The text may become something more, however: a tool of embodiment, a space in which she might carve the "speaking in tones" into her living body.[17] With time, this will allow her to draw forth a voice that connects seamlessly to her living body and to her life. The sung words turn into the movement of live speaking and singing in her body, and – once embodied – they will remain in her flesh. Every new encounter with the music and the text will *re*-present the carving into the body of the text once performed.

This presence of the text in the body of the singer is not limited to her own singing. When she listens to others singing a piece she knows well, the moments of working on the text and the interior movements of her singing body will be re-presented in her own singer–listener's body as silent singing. The voice that she hears – that enters her from the world and becomes part of her body – occurs in her in a way that being a singer makes possible. As a vocal coach, she can "sing with her student," sense herself singing in and with another singer, sense the limits of the other singer's body in her own body. Her whole body, not just her ears, listens to this other live body and sings with her.

> For me, this was not always the case. When I was beginning my studies in vocal pedagogy, I was still struggling with my technique. My ears could tell me that my student's singing was somehow out of balance but I could not locate or verbalize, let alone solve the problem. Later, I learned to experience my own singing in a new, more conscious way, and began to feel a kind of embodied empathy in the teaching situation: my body could feel – or

"hear" – that the student's lower back was hollow, and my back would respond by imitating this movement. Finally, my body would begin to solve the problems of the student's singing. When the student's lower back was hollow my lower back would respond by widening outwards. When the student stretched her neck forward, my neck would open backwards and my pharynx would expand and relax. Only then was I able to help her find modes of working with the problem.

It is both possible and probable that teachers of Early Music will have students who choose not only well-known pieces of music that the teacher might have performed herself, but also pieces unknown to the teacher, as well as anything between these two extremes. In such situations, the music will be realized in the singer–teacher's body in different ways depending on the mode in which it is present in her body.

I am working with a chamber music group comprising a soprano, a cellist and a harpsichordist who are very experienced in working on the repertoire. I have neither heard nor sung this particular piece. They have sent me the music, the text and a rough translation of it in advance. The piece consists of several short sections, and one of the keys to performing it seems to be in understanding the character of these short recitatives and arias.

The messiness of the hand-written score tires me but I start playing and humming it, first without words. Accompanying myself on the harpsichord, I work to and fro between the hand-written scribble of a score and the typed text. When I enter the classroom, the piece is not finalized in my body, although I have some general idea about it as a whole.

When I hear the first run-through of the piece, I notice that my whole body is not yet involved in the listening. Quite pleased with what I hear, I start by discussing the different triple sections (in 3/4 and 3/2). Why would the composer use different time signatures if he wanted them to be played in the same tempo and character? Strict proportions do not seem to be in place, however. We experiment with a slow, tender 3/2 and a quicker, even whipping, 3/4.

In the course of the session, I feel my body beginning to live and move with the singing, sensing the moments of dramatic inhaling, expressive swellings, fleshy vowels and consonants. I transform from the motionless listening ear into a whole body in motion, no longer moving with the music but moving the music, silently, inside my singer–listener's body. As my body learns the piece, and as the speaking in tones is carved into my body, I begin to miss something in the singing that I am listening to. My singer's body has found spots to lean on in the piece, frictions in the embodied feel of the text, a flexible *legato* rooted in the body, all of which allow me to articulate the text more boldly and to connect the singing more closely into my living body. The music and the text are in my body. My body is the music and the text.

Sharedness and art in singing

According to Henry, connection between human beings is not possible in the world, which is a lifeless collection of objects. It is only possible in life, in the possibility of sharedness. A moment of sharedness, the becoming present of life, the foundation of all being – doing and thinking – is rare and often fleeting, and it touches us in a way that we recognize. Maybe it is just a passing look, a word, a nuance.

What is the role of art in sharedness? Henry's philosophy mainly concerns the visual arts, traditionally and intuitively understood as the painting or drawing of what the artist sees. Henry questions this seemingly obvious connection between painting, the eye and the visible, however, as well as the basis for thinking of a piece of art as something in the visibility of the world (2009: 7–8). In this line of thinking, the study of the worldly elements of music or singing – the minute analysis of the signs on the score or the sounds heard – can be questioned.

> I listen to her sing "Ahi!" on a two-line E note. Her onset is strong but controlled, leading on to a well-resonating but initially straight sound. The voice is beautiful. I would prefer a slightly less equalized, more Italian [a] to match the skilfully created impression of pain in her voice. She performs the Early Baroque *esclamazione* perfectly. Her singing is admittedly professional, and she controls her immaculate vocal technique admirably. Her vocal timbre reminds me of a well-known lyrical mezzosoprano.

For Henry, however, this is not the true being of art; art has the potential to make visible life that would otherwise be hidden or invisible. In his words: "To paint is to show, but this showing has the aim of letting us see what is not seen and cannot be seen" (Henry 2009: 10).

> I listen to her sing "Ahi!" on a high E note. She hits the note with a strong, even rough onset, crashing her voice into the sound. First, she quickly withdraws from the sound as if she were taken aback by the pain pressed out of her body. I sense myself shrinking with her. Then, I sense her gradually leaning on her body. The sound as measured might be getting louder but in my singer's body the quality is that of leaning down on my body. The question of the beauty of the sound seems irrelevant. I forget that my ears are perceiving sound.

Henry's description (2004) of August von Briesen's musical drawings illuminates this quality of art.[18] Sitting in an almost dark space, von Briesen listens to an orchestra play, and draws – without looking at it – dots and lines on a piece of white paper. The speed and force of the drawing occasionally pierces or even rips the paper. The edge brutally cuts the lines. At times, he turns a clean page and continues to draw.

Michel Henry argues that von Briesen's musical drawings represent traces of what never appears in the world and is not part of it, and not the reality of the world. He draws *no-thing*, the invisible being – something that exists before the world. He translates the life he senses in the music into signs on the paper, makes the invisible visible. He senses in the music the same overwhelming, drowning force of life that he has been given in life as a burden to be carried. This force throws itself forward as a cry or as traces of the movement of the hands holding the pencil. Here, von Briesen's lines are vibrating signs of the invisible, the immediate consequence of the bodily force of the one drawing. The line *is* a movement, a push originating from the human being drawing, from the pen, hard or soft, against the paper, gliding on it or ripping and piercing it, the length of the line being the same as the length of the movement of the living body (Henry 2004: 264).

The drawings might resemble compositions, the parts and the whole of which have a particular relationship with each other, but the only thing in them that connects these movements with a true and deep bond is the force that produces them. Henry's term for the drawings is "a-compositions," within which each singular line exists independently of the other lines appearing on the paper, in the same space, self-sufficient, indifferent to the other (2004: 277).

The human voice is some-thing that does not represent anything that is in the world: it represents the force of life dwelling in the body of an individual. One sound, one swiftly passing moment in the singing, can touch the listener in a special way that she may find impossible to verbalize. Then again, this might not be the case as the person next to her might not be moved at all. The explanation for this is that life is not a measurable quality of sound that works in the same way for any listener. Could this imply that any spontaneous scream is more expressive than a technically flawless performance of a piece of music? Where is the line between somebody screaming because she is scared for her life, and somebody singing a pain-filled "Ahi!" on a two-line E note? Inspired by Henry's thinking, I believe that there may well be no difference between these two. In any case, the difference cannot be determined in accordance with the measured quality of the sound or by defining the genre of music – by analysing aspects of music manifested in the world. Although creating art could be considered a conscious attempt to *re*-present the invisible, life can touch and move us in any situation.

Henry is not alone in his thinking of art as having an ability to make visible some-thing invisible: the potential of sharedness, of life. In Vladimir Jankélévitch's words, "the mystery transmitted to us by music is not death's sterilizing inexplicability but the fertile inexplicability of life, freedom, or love" (2003: 71). Life can become visible or audible anywhere, unexpectedly, without having been invited. To be able to experience the presence of life in singing, you need to be somebody who is alive, sharing in the singularity of lived experience. The sounds produced in the body of the singer are vibrating traces of the invisible force of life that is pressed out – or, ex-pressed – of her, and thrown forward. It is a cultivated cry that, for a moment, relieves the singer of the burden of the force of life. In this sense, singing becomes the art of life's suffering and joy, of the unexpected, and of occurring in the living moment.

Notes

1 The chapter is based on a paper given at the symposium "Interdisciplinary Studies in the Philosophy and Praxis of Voice" (London, 2013), as well as on my doctoral thesis (Järviö 2011). An early version of my thinking on singing with Michel Henry can be found in Järviö (2006).

2 On the point of being, see de Kerckhove (1995: 324).

3 Bruce Haynes (2007), for example, has questioned the term "Early Music," with good reason.

4 See Cook (2001). Le Guin's (2006) study on playing Boccherini's cello music is an exception.

5 For one of the rare discussions of Henry's philosophy and music, see Welten (2009) who, however, focuses on the experience of listening.

6 On the structure and function of the voice organ, see Sundberg (1987) or Boston and Cook (2009: 17–67).

7 In contrast, the contributors to Boston and Cook's collection (2009) articulate their understanding of breathing and voice as well as practical modes of working on them. Linklater (2006), for her part, focuses on presenting a progression of exercises for the voice.

8 Latin *ob-iectus* (pp. of *obicere*), "to throw, or put before or against."

9 The body of the text is written from the *point of being* of the musician–researcher. The second narrative voice in the indented paragraphs is that of the singer–pedagogue articulating her embodied experience of singing and listening to singing. The use of two voices makes visible the distance between the discussion and the embodied experience of singing and the singing voice, the distance being greater in the body of the text than in the indented paragraphs.

10 When I started my postgraduate studies, my rejection of the ideas of Heidegger and Merleau-Ponty, who served as frames of reference in numerous studies on the human experience, such as dance (see Sheets-Johnstone 2011; Rouhiainen 2003; Monni 2004; and Parviainen 1998), was undoubtedly due to my lack of experience in reading philosophical texts. I now find them more understandable and relevant to the study of singing than I did at the time.

11 See Poizat (1992), Barthes (1990) and Duncan (2004).

12 These are central ideas that are present on virtually every page of Henry's works. As de Sanctis (2009) notes, auto-affection could be considered a *leitmotiv* or a watchword in Henry's philosophy introduced in *L'Essence de la Manifestation* (1963) and retained until *Incarnation* (2000).

13 See Csíkszentmihályi (2008).

14 A novel by Diane Setterfield (2007: 53) inspired the idea of human experience as compost.

15 All the translations from the French are mine unless otherwise specified.

16 Duncan (2004) also discusses the voice as such as a resonant force with physical effects.

17 Numerous terms (*stile rappresentativo, in armonia favellare, recitar cantando, imitar col canto chi parla*, among others) were used at the beginning of the 17th century to describe the new dramatic style of vocal solo music (Sternfeld 1983–84). "To speak in tones" is an expression Hitchcock used in his translation of Giulio Caccini's foreword to *Le Nuove Musiche* (1982: 44).

18 August von Briesen (1935–2003) was a painter, lithographer and illustrator, born in Budapest. His father was German, his mother Hungarian. After the Second World War, he was deported to Siberia for three years because of his German roots. Returning from the prison camp in 1952, he began his studies at the Academy of Fine Arts, Budapest. He left Hungary after the Budapest insurrection of 1956, moving to England and, then, having travelled to the Netherlands, Germany and Italy, finally, settled in France in 1972. He lived his last years in solitude and, like many lonely people, died in Paris as a consequence of a heatwave in the summer of 2003. The city of Paris decided to commemorate the victims of the heatwave by placing one of von Briesen's works in the foyer of the National Museum of Modern Art.

References

Barthes, R. (1990) *Image Music Text*, trans. S. Heath, London: Fontana Press.

Bartleet, B-L. and Ellis, C. (2009) *Music Autoethnographies: Making Autoethnography Sing/ Making Music Personal*, Bowen Hills, Queensland: Australian Academic Press.

Boston, J. and Cook, R. (eds) (2009) *Breath in Action: The Art of Breath in Vocal and Holistic Practice*, London and Philadelphia: Jessica Kingsley Publishers.

Cavarero, A. (2005) *For More than One Voice: Towards a Philosophy of Vocal Expression*, trans. P.A. Kottman, Stanford: Stanford University Press.

Cook, Nicholas (2001) "Between process and product: music and/as performance," *Music Theory Online*, 7(2), www.mtosmt.org/issues/mto.01.7.2/mto.01.7.2.cook.html.

Csíkszentmihályi, M. (2008) *Flow: The Psychology of Optimal Experience*, New York: Harper Perennial.

Cusick, S. (1994) "Feminist theory, music theory, and the mind/body problem," *Perspectives of New Music*, 32(1): 8–27.

de Kerckhove, D. (1995) "Kybermedianäkökulmasta olokulmaan," in Huhtamo, E. (ed.) *Virtuaalisuuden arkeologia. Virtuaalimatkailijan uusi käsikirja*, Rovaniemi: Lapin Yliopisto, 315–25.

de Sanctis, F.P. (2009) "Le problem du temps chez Michel Henry: l'origine de l'espacement," *Bulletin d'Analyse Phénoménologique*, 5(1): 1–25, http://popups.ulg.ac.be/1782–2041/.

Dufour-Kowalska, G. (2003) *Michel Henry: Passion et Magnificence de la Vie*, Paris: Beauchesne Éditeur.

Duncan, M. (2004) "The operatic scandal of the singing body: voice, presence, performativity," *Cambridge Opera Journal*, 16(3): 283–306.

Ellis, C. and Bochner, A. (2000) "Autoethnography, personal narrative, reflexivity," in Denzin, N.K. and Lincoln, Y.S. (eds) *Handbook of Qualitative Research*, Thousand Oaks, CA: Sage, 733–68.

Ellis, C. and Bochner, A. (eds) (2002) *Ethnographically Speaking: Autoethnography, Literature, and Aesthetics*, Walnut Creek, CA: Alta Mira Press.

Haynes, B. (2007) *The End of Early Music: A Period Performer's History of Music for the Twenty-First Century*, New York: Oxford University Press.

Hemsley, T. (1998) *Singing and Imagination: A Human Approach to a Great Musical Tradition*, New York: Oxford University Press.

Henry, M. (1963) *L' Essence de la Manifestation*, Paris: Presses Universitaires de France.

——(2000) *Incarnation: Une Philosophie de la Chair*, Paris: Éditions du Seuil.

——(2003) *I Am the Truth: Toward a Philosophy of Christianity*, trans. S. Emanuel, Stanford: Stanford University Press.

——(2004) "Dessiner la musique: théorie pour l'art de Briesen," in *Phénoménologie de la Vie. Tome III. De l'Art et du Politique*, Paris: Presses Universitaires de France, 241–82.

——(2009) *Seeing the Invisible: On Kandinsky*, trans. S. Davidson, London and New York: Continuum.

Hitchock, H.W. (ed.) (1982) *Guilio Caccini: Le Nuove Musiche*, 2nd edition, Madison, WI: A-R Editions, Inc.

Jankélévitch, V. (2003) *Music and the Ineffable*, trans. C. Abbate, Oxford: Princeton University Press.

Järviö, P. (2006) "The life and world of a singer: finding my way," *Philosophy of Music Education Review*, 14(1): 65–77.

——(2011) *Laulajan sprezzatura. Fenomenologinen tutkimus italialaisen varhaisbarokin musiikin laulaen puhumisesta* [Acta musicologica fennica 29], Jyväskylä: Suomen musiikkitieteellinen seura.

Le Guin, E. (2006) *Boccherini's Body: An Essay in Carnal Musicology*, Berkeley and Los Angeles: University of California Press.

Linklater, K. (2006) *Freeing the Natural Voice: Imagery and Art in the Practice of Voice and Language*, London: Nick Hern Books.

Monni, K. (2004) *Olemisen poeettinen like. Tanssin uuden paradigman taidefilosofisia tulkintoja Martin Heideggerin ajattelun valossa sekä taiteellinen työ vuosilta 1996–1999*, Helsinki: Teatterikorkeakoulu.

Parviainen, J. (1998) *Bodies Moving and Moved: A Phenomenological Analysis of the Dancing Subject and the Cognitive and Ethical Values of Dance Art*, Tampere: Tampere University Press.

Poizat, M. (1992) *The Angel's Cry: Beyond the Pleasure Principle in Opera*, trans. A. Denner, Ithaca: Cornell University Press.

Potter, J. (2000) *Vocal Authority: Singing Style and Ideology*, Cambridge: Cambridge University Press.

Rouhiainen, L. (2003) *Living Transformative Lives: Finnish Freelance Dance Artists Brought into Dialogue with Merleau-Ponty's Phenomenology*, Helsinki: Theatre Academy.

Setterfield, D. (2007) *Kolmastoista kertomus*, trans. S. Moksunen, Helsinki: Tammi.

Sheets-Johnstone, M. (2011) *The Primacy of Movement*, 2nd edition, Amsterdam and Philadelphia: John Benjamins.

Sternfeld, F.W. (1983–84) "A Note on 'Stile Recitativo,'" *Proceedings of the Royal Musical Association*, 110: 41–44.

Sundberg, J. (1987) *The Science of the Singing Voice*, DeKalb, IL: Northern Illinois University Press.

Welten, R. (2009) "What do we hear when we hear music? A radical phenomenology of music," *Studia Phaenomenologica. Romanian Journal for Phenomenology*, IX: 269–86.

Zahavi, D. (1999) "Michel Henry and the phenomenology of the invisible," *Continental Philosophy Review*, 32(3): 223–40.

——(2007) "Subjectivity and immanence in Michel Henry," in Grøn, A., Damgaard, I. and Overgaard, S. (eds) *Subjectivity and Transcendence (Religion in Philosophy and Theology)*, Tübingen: Mohr Siebeck, 133–48.

3

LEARNING TO LET GO

Control and freedom in the *passaggio*

Tim Kjeldsen

In this chapter, I explore the relationship between control and freedom in singing. I begin with two common intuitions, each appealing in itself but *prima facie* at odds with the other. The first is that vocal control and vocal freedom are *interdependent*: control is necessary for freedom and *vice versa*. The second is that control and freedom are, in some sense, *contradictory*: freedom is escape from control, and control limits freedom. We may think this clash can be simply resolved by endeavouring to balance them: too much freedom entails loss of control and *vice versa*. Yet this represents them as competitors, still conflicting with the first intuition that they make each other possible. As a teacher of the Alexander Technique (AT) who works regularly with singers, I have found this is not merely a theoretical issue, but one with which singers struggle practically. Consequently, clarifying the relation between control and freedom in singing is of practical *and* theoretical value.

To begin, I draw on the philosophy of Jean-Paul Sartre. Sartre wrote little about skilled activity, but was profoundly interested in freedom. His thoughts about the latter will prove useful in attempting to resolve the clash. Specifically, I make use of the concept of *internal negation*, which may permit us to understand control and freedom as simultaneously interdependent *and* contradictory. Later, I draw on Maurice Merleau-Ponty's account of skilled activity to qualify and refine Sartre's perspective.[1]

Having explored these theoretical tenets, I expand the discussion with what I take to be an experimental demonstration of my conclusions from a recent study into the AT. The founder of the AT, F.M. Alexander, was not himself a singer, but was a professional voice user, performing monologues, poetry and Shakespearean soliloquies in late 19th-century Australia. His research began in response to his own vocal problems, and he initially promoted his technique as one of vocal and respiratory re-education. Only later did it develop into a more general method, taking the relation between control and freedom in activity as its central subject matter. I argue that the AT demonstrates internal negation in practice.[2]

Finally, I consider the implications of my findings for vocal technique, focusing particularly on the *passaggio*: the transitional phase between vocal registers in changing pitch. The *passaggio* is a primary concern in the Western classical tradition, which esteems an open and even tone production across the singer's full useful range. There are vocal traditions and styles for which this is not a primary value, yet I suspect that there are few for which the relation between control and freedom is of no concern. Negotiating the *passaggio* might therefore be seen as a culturally specific instance of a wider preoccupation.

Internal negation

Internal negation (Sartre 1943: 174–75) is a heavy-duty label for a quotidian phenomenon, which may best be approached in two stages. Firstly, internal negation is a form of internal *relation*. An internal relation is one the terms of which are in some way logically or conceptually dependent on one another.[3] For example, Bill's and Jane's marriage is an *external* relation, each participant retaining his or her identity whether they are married or not. But the relationship of husband and wife that the marriage instantiates is an *internal* one, since Bill could not cease to be Jane's husband without Jane also ceasing to be Bill's wife. An internal negation is one in which the presence or salience of one of its terms depends, in some way, on the absence or withdrawal of the other – a paradigm being the figure/ground relation. Consider the ambiguous Figure 3.1, which can be seen either as a vase or two faces, but not as both at the same time. For the vase to figure, the faces have to become the background, and *vice versa*.[4]

FIGURE 3.1 Ambiguous drawing of vase and faces. © Simon Smith.

Internal negation is central to Sartre's philosophy, embodied in the title of his major work *Being and Nothingness* (1943). "Nothingness" refers to consciousness, which Sartre does not regard as a kind, aspect, or property of being, but rather as its internal negation. Being has what he calls "plenitude": things are just *there*, complete and fully present in themselves. Consciousness, however, is a kind of gap or "fissure" in being, constituted by absences (Sartre 1943: 137–78). As I look at an object on the table in front of me, for it to *be* an object for me, something genuinely other than myself − something "transcendent" − I must apprehend it as having features that are absent from my immediate perception. Spatially, it must have other sides and an interior, and temporally, it must have a history and a future, all of which are absent to me at this moment, but nevertheless constitute it as an object for me.

This view is radically at odds with the Cartesian view of consciousness as a repository of representations. For Sartre, the latter makes a conscious representation just another kind of "thing" existing alongside what it represents. But a representation must not only be *of* something, it must be *for* something (or someone). It follows that, if we have to posit a representation in order to explain our consciousness of things, we will then have to posit a second representation in order to explain our consciousness of the first, initiating an explanatory regress. Sartre's response is to reject the idea that consciousness is any kind of "thing" (and this includes its being a state or process). Rather, it is literally nothing: no-thing. Whenever we try to determine consciousness as a natural object, it promptly becomes an object *for* consciousness, thereby escaping its determination. Consciousness, for Sartre, is always and everywhere pure transcendence (1943: lxi).

Human beings themselves, however, are not pure transcendence. As embodied subjects, we are also material objects like rocks or trees. For Sartre, this makes human beings radically contradictory − a kind of being "which is what it is not and […] is not what it is" (1943: 58). The very kind of being that we are is one that is perpetually negating itself, recreating itself afresh at each moment through acts of consciousness. Sartre calls the conditions of being that are transcended or negated by consciousness "facticity" (1943: 73–79). Facticity includes our physical natures, genetic inheritance and cultural backgrounds, and also such things as our existing skills and abilities: a singer's ability, for example, to perform a *diminuendo* on a high C is part of her facticity. Without facticity there is no transcendence: a singer will evidently not be able to transcend her current range and capacities until she has established them.

This, however, opens Sartre to critique. Merleau-Ponty argues that Sartre's uncompromising dualism of being and consciousness fails to assign an appropriate status to the body.[5] Although Sartre does embrace the bodily nature of consciousness, there remains for him a stark distinction between body-as-object and body-as-subject. As the former, the body is just a fragment of being, existing as a tree or a rock does; as the latter, it is the source of consciousness and the condition of existential freedom. But it does not occupy this latter status in virtue of any properties, innate or acquired, it may have. In the words of the commentator M.C. Dillon, the body-as-subject is, for Sartre, reduced to the "point of entry into the world" of consciousness (1998: 127). This must be so, since to grant the body subjective status in virtue of its properties, would be, for Sartre, to elide the distinction between being and consciousness.

But Merleau-Ponty embraces the elision and builds his philosophy around it. For him, bodily experience is inherently ambiguous (Merleau-Ponty 1962: 98, 230, 458): we are simultaneously both subject and object.[6] Moreover, our subjectivity is bodily, grounded in our innate and acquired habits, skills and capacities, which are "sedimented" within the lived body itself (Merleau-Ponty 1962: 149–50, 249). Thus, the body is not merely the point of entry of consciousness into the world; it possesses its own form of being. Indeed, it is the primordial form of our being, from which "pure" consciousness (transcendence) and "pure" being (immanence) are abstractions.[7]

This difference has implications for Sartre's concept of freedom. Sartre argues that existential freedom is absolute and indivisible; he even says that a slave in chains is as free as his master (1943: 550). Sartre fully acknowledges that a prisoner is not free to walk out of prison, and to say that he is free to wish to do so is to utter a trivial truism (1943: 483–84). Nevertheless, he insists that neither of these constitute his true existential freedom, namely that he is always free to *try* to escape. If he denies the fact of *this* freedom to himself, he is acting in bad faith. For Merleau-Ponty, however, even existential freedom admits of degrees: the bodily sedimentation of habit and skill partly shapes our consciousness at any moment (Dillon 1998: 141). We are not unconditionally free – not even existentially free – to think and try to act just as we like.[8]

From this perspective, our embodied facticity partly constitutes our consciousness: what can count as freedom for a singer – what she can authentically conceive and aspire to – is partly constituted by what she can presently do and how she can do it. This is why singing teachers sometimes have to resort to getting the student to produce sound in a novel way – getting them to bend, dance, or squeal when vocalizing. Repetitive practice is indispensable to vocal technique, not only to train the requisite stamina and flexibility in the muscles, but also because a singer often cannot even imagine what she is aiming for until she produces it, and she cannot produce it until her muscles are engaged appropriately, even by means she cannot initially understand or consciously intend.

Merleau-Ponty's critique transforms Sartre's static dialectic into a developmental one (Dillon 1988: 46): whatever freedom we are able to exercise can enable us to transcend our present facticity, even if only to a small degree, but if we can reproduce the new experiences so created, we create a new facticity that may become a platform for further change.[9] This is why so much depends on how existing vocal technique is established: the more technique is built on the basis of freedom, the more it is open to its own transcendence. This is the point at which the Alexander Technique becomes relevant.

Control, freedom and the Alexander Technique

The Alexander Technique (AT) is a psychophysical discipline popular amongst performing artists, although it can be profitably used by anyone.[10] The AT takes the relationship between control and freedom in activity as its central subject matter. Its benefits for general health, well-being and performance are seen by its practitioners as indirect outcomes of improved control of moment-by-moment bodily activity.[11]

The connections between the AT and vocal technique are direct and profound. This is manifest in two ways. First, the dynamic relation in activity between head and body – a fundamental priority in the AT – powerfully influences both the coordination of the vocal and respiratory mechanisms and the nature of the space in the resonating cavities. Secondly, the dialectic of freedom and control that constitutes all skilled activity is utterly transparent and unavoidable in singing: a harsh and strained voice is extremely hard to listen to. Vocal freedom is, therefore, a requisite in nearly all kinds of vocal performance.

To expand on the above, a case study (Cacciatore, Gurfinkel, Horak and Day 2011) investigated a group of AT teachers and a matched control group in the everyday act of moving from sitting to standing (StS).[12] Force plates measured the changing distribution of weight on the feet, and photoelectric markers on the body measured changing relationships in the spine throughout the movement (Figure 3.2).

The most notable difference between the groups was that during the movement the AT teachers progressively increased the distribution of weight to their feet until all the weight was on the feet at "seat-off," when the bottom left the chair. The researchers call this a "continuous strategy" (Cacciatore *et al.* 2011: 499). This may not seem surprising. What was surprising is that the control group *reduced* the weight on their feet shortly prior to seat-off and then transferred it all in one go (also Figure 3.2). The researchers call this a "sequential strategy."[13]

This can be explained by considering the mechanics of the StS movement. As the torso tips forward at the beginning of the movement, the base of the pelvis tips backwards and upwards, exerting a direct stretch on the hamstrings – which are attached to them – and an indirect one on the calf muscles. The subject must partially release the muscles into that stretch whilst simultaneously retaining sufficient contraction to prevent the torso falling forward. This is known as "eccentric contraction" (Sircar 2008: 120): some fibres in the relevant muscles are "turned off" whilst others continue to fire, the balance between release and contraction modulating throughout the movement. At the same time, the extensor muscles of the lower leg (quadriceps), which will ultimately straighten the legs, are gradually brought into play. The control group appeared to be unable or unwilling to permit the necessary release as the torso moved forward, resulting in the heels being pulled up from the force plate shortly before seat-off, at which point they were obliged to make a sudden transfer of their whole weight to their feet. This correlated with marked spinal distortions that persisted throughout the movement.

This is not just an instance of one group having been trained to do something another group has not. Young children appear to perform this movement instinctively in much the way the AT teachers did (Cacciatore *et al.* 2011: 499). From an AT perspective, the control group's "strategy" is the consequence of "misuse" – cultivated interference with the natural mechanics of the movement. The teachers

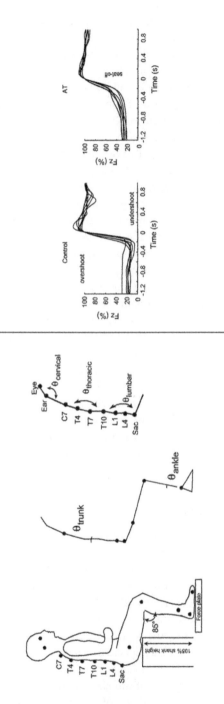

FIGURE 3.2 Measurement of sitting to standing movement, and comparison of weight transference between Alexander teachers (AT) and a control group. On the graph on the right, the horizontal axis represents time taken to perform the movement, with 0 representing the moment of "seat-off." The vertical axis represents the proportion of body weight on the feet. Note the reduction in proportion of body weight on the feet in the control group shortly before seat-off, and then the dramatic increase. Images reprinted from *Gait and Posture*, 34(4), Cacciatore, T.W., Gurfinkel, V.S., Horak, F.B., and Day, B.L., "Prolonged weight-shift and altered spinal coordination during sit-to-stand in practitioners of the Alexander Technique," 496–501, copyright (2011), with permission from Elsevier.

had not so much learned a new way of standing up; as *un*-learned a cultivated misuse. The unlearning of cultivated habits involves learning to relinquish a certain kind of control, one that has become familiar and instinctive (in a colloquial sense), for the sake of allowing something new and unfamiliar to occur which can then be reproduced and consolidated into a new level of control.

What is at stake here is not the mastery of a specific skill but a *generic* competence. Developing the capacity to relinquish existing forms of control as a skill in its own right raises a person's general ability to adapt herself to new and changing demands and requirements. The title of AT theorist Frank Pierce Jones's 1974 pamphlet is "Learning how to learn." In the Sartrean language I have borrowed, the freedom in question is the internal negation of the existing control it transcends.

In adopting this approach as a conscious strategy, a person develops new levels of general competence in which her control of activity is perpetually open to its own self-transcendence. In Alexander's terminology, existing patterns of control become genuine means towards ends, always open to rational reappraisal and modification, rather than fixed patterns with an intrinsic tendency to persist, so to speak, as ends in themselves. Alexander talks of an instinctive competence gradually giving way to a conscious competence. Of course, once acquired in this way, a specific skill can be allowed to operate, so to speak, on semi-autopilot, which received wisdom generally takes to be necessary in performance.[14] Nevertheless, a skill or habit consciously acquired and cultivated is, in Alexander's words, "not truly a habit at all, but an order or series of orders given to the subordinate controls of the body, which orders will be carried out until countermanded" (1996: 74).[15]

This has implications for performance. A performer acquiring and cultivating her skills in this way is not limited to repeating a mechanically acquired pattern in performance, but can transcend her current level of control in the performance itself, allowing something new and uniquely appropriate to the occasion to occur. This is the goal of artistry in any style or tradition. I turn now to explore this dialectic in the context of vocal technique.

Control, freedom and the *passaggio*

The *passaggio* is the phase of transition from one vocal register to another as pitch is raised or lowered. Many untrained singers experience a "break" in the voice at some point in this transition, and much singing training is dedicated to eradicating that break and developing an open and even tone across the full useful range of the voice.

The mechanics of vocal registration are generally well understood.[16] The larynx comprises three main cartilages: the cricoid cartilage is the uppermost part of the trachea, and is broadly circular. Sitting on it is the thyroid cartilage forming a 'v' shape with the point at the front, and open at the back where it attaches to, and pivots on, the cricoid. At the back of the cricoid is a pair of cartilages called the arytenoids that rotate, and come together and apart. A group of muscles, the thyroarytenoids (Figure 3.3), extends from these cartilages to the inside tip of the thyroid. The most medial and inferior muscles of this group are known as *vocalis*, which, as their name

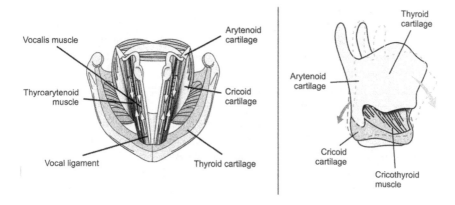

FIGURE 3.3 Thyroarytenoids and cricothyroids. © Simon Smith.

implies, are regarded as the primary muscles of vocalization. On the medial surface of *vocalis* are the vocal folds.

When the arytenoid cartilages come together, the vocal folds approximate, and air passing through them causes them to vibrate, producing tone. Although these muscles themselves can change the pitch of the sound to some degree, the primary mechanism for pitch change involves another pair of muscles, the cricothyroids (Figure 3.3), which connect the bottom front of the thyroid cartilage to the front of the cricoid. These pivot the thyroid forward on the cricoid, stretching the vocal folds. As the folds become longer, tighter and thinner, the pitch is raised.

The thyroarytenoids and the cricothyroids, then, are two distinct mechanisms for producing and modifying tone. They are both involved in normal phonation, although they can be isolated in vocal exercises. However, their relative dominance changes depending upon pitch and the vocal quality the singer desires (and is able to produce). When the thyroarytenoids dominate, the entire medial surfaces of the vocalis muscles, extending a few millimetres deep beneath the folds, are in contact, and the folds themselves normally relatively relaxed. This produces a generally deep and rich tone, full of harmonics: what has historically been called the "chest" voice, or the "heavy" (Wilcox 1935) or "lower" mechanism (Thurman *et al.* 2004). When the cricothyroids are dominant, only the vocal folds themselves, under some tension, are in contact, producing a lighter sound with less harmonic complexity, correspondingly known as the "head" voice, or the "light" or "higher mechanism."[17] The thyroarytenoids and the cricothyroids are antagonists: they pull against one another in most vocalization, and the quality and pitch of the tone results from the interplay. As cricothyroid contraction causes pitch to rise, the thyroarytenoids gradually release, and over a certain number of pitches, the light mechanism becomes dominant. These pitches are the *passaggi*.[18] How much the heavy mechanism releases depends upon the vocal sound required and the capacity of the singer.[19]

The essential skill here is the same as the one exhibited by the AT teachers in the study cited above: one has to retain sufficient tension in one muscle or set of muscle fibres whilst progressively releasing others. The problem faced by singers is rarely that of bringing appropriate muscles into play. More often, it is that of letting go of muscles that need to release *in order* for the appropriate muscles to come into play. In that sense, the singer's problem is a specific instance of that addressed by the AT: the generic ability to let go of the familiar in order to be open to the unfamiliar. As that skill is cultivated, the subsequent skills of engaging appropriate muscles become progressively easier to develop.

Vocal pedagogue Cornelius Reid furnishes an example of the kind of flexible vocal control that is possible, but perhaps rarely achieved. Comparing recordings of Placido Domingo and Franco Corelli singing the "Celeste Aida," he notes that "Domingo only held the B-flat briefly and at one dynamic level, while Corelli not only sang the note with ease, but gradually diminished the sound to a pianissimo," and remarks that "Corelli obviously possessed a freer vocal technique and sang with greater mechanical skill" (Reid 2005: 34). It is interesting to note Reid's conjunction of freedom and mechanical skill. One can, of course, achieve mechanical skill without much freedom. Corelli appears to have mastered the dynamic, dialectical interplay between them, which he was able to exploit for artistic purposes in the moment of performance.

Conclusion: embracing the paradox

I have argued that viewing control and freedom in activity as internal negations of one another resolves the clash of intuitions with which the chapter started. Control and freedom are both interdependent *and* contradictory. This seems somewhat paradoxical, but it is a paradox that may be embraced in practice by cultivating the core capacity to let go of existing forms of control and open oneself to the possibilities that subsequently emerge. Acquiring and cultivating skills in this manner leads to a higher level of competence, which can be consciously exercised even during performance itself.

The experience of allowing the voice to be free, particularly in the higher registers, is an exhilarating one for both performer and audience. One has the experience of getting out of the way, of channelling rather than producing the music, and this can have profound aesthetic, and even spiritual, resonances. One does indeed seem to be transcending one's existing control at such moments. Yet, one has not only to have developed the control in the first place in order to transcend it; one has to respond to the sound almost as one is releasing it, making choices about how to shape what follows according to the needs and possibilities of the moment. In singing, perhaps more than in any other activity, the dialectic between control and freedom is perpetually renewing itself, and this in part is what makes it both so challenging and deeply rewarding.

Acknowledgement

I am greatly indebted to the late Gerald Wragg, and to Angela Durrant, for helping me put the vocal ideas I discuss here into practice.

Notes

1 For similar views, see chapters by Compton and Hall in Stewart (1998).

2 I do not claim that the AT has any kind of monopoly in this area. It just happens to be the relevant discipline with which I am familiar.

3 See Morris (2007: 43–46) for a good explanation of internal relations.

4 Formally, internal negation is negation applied to a component of a proposition, and external negation, to a whole proposition (Slater 1979). In terms of the example: if there is a vase there are no faces (if p then $\sim q$). But in general, the presence of a vase obviously does not depend upon the presence of two faces ($\sim$(if p then q)).

5 Although he does not often speak of Sartre directly in *The Phenomenology of Perception*, virtually the whole work is a sustained critique of *Being and Nothingness*.

6 See also the introductory essay by de Waelhens in Merleau-Ponty (1963: xviii–xxvii).

7 There have been defenses of Sartre against Merleau-Ponty from the outset, some of them arguing that the latter systematically misread the former (de Beauvoir, Stewart and Catalano in Stewart 1998). See also the Introduction to Morris (2010).

8 The core difference between Sartre and Merleau-Ponty, according to Hall (in Stewart 1998: 189–94) is that, for the former, freedom is original: what it is to be a conscious being is to choose oneself. But for the latter, what is original is a field of meaning in which, as embodied beings, we find ourselves and which we do not ourselves choose, but which is nonetheless the necessary condition for freedom. For the former, freedom is absolute: for the latter, it is situated.

9 Merleau-Ponty replaces Sartre's opposition of consciousness and being with a relation of reciprocity between them. This is a rejection of the primacy Sartre gives to internal negation, but I think it relativizes rather than rejects the phenomenon itself.

10 I do not elaborate the methodology of the AT here. For the *locus classicus*, see Alexander (1985); for a scholarly introduction, see Jones (1997); for good popular introductions, see Gelb (2004) and Langstroth and Miller (2007).

11 For current information about AT research, see the websites of the Society of Teachers of the Alexander Technique (STAT) (2014) and the American Society for the Alexander Technique (AMSAT) (2014).

12 The study involved "constrained" movement: each subject was placed in the same position with the same joint angles and required to keep the arms folded to prevent their being used as balancing poles to assist the movement. This enabled the researchers to focus on the bare mechanics of the movement. This was an artificial situation for both groups, but the study showed that the AT teachers' strategy was more adaptable.

13 The researchers, in personal correspondence, were equivocal about whether this ought to be called a "strategy," being perhaps better described as an instinctive reaction to the consequences of a lack of one.

14 See Montero (2010) and Kjeldsen (2011) for a different view.

15 I should note that, in this chapter, I focus exclusively on what might be called the "procedural" dimension of the AT. The AT also has a sophisticated model of the innate mechanisms of postural integration that the procedures essentially incorporate. See the writers cited in note 10.

16 For explanations of the mechanisms of registration, see Vennard (1967: 52–80), Bunch Dayme (2009: 109–17) and Sundberg (1987: 49–92). For recent developments see Roubeau, Henrich and Castellengo (2009) and Thurman, Welch, Theimer and Klitzke (2004). For a good general introduction that incorporates the AT, see Dimon (2011).

17 It is widely accepted that there are four registers, including a very low "vocal fry" and a very high "whistle" register. But the latter are used relatively infrequently.

18 In fact, there are a number of *passaggi*, the first lying roughly between middle C and the F# above it, depending on the type of voice. Indeed, it has been said that every pitch change is a *passaggio*, in that involves some modification of the mechanisms, and this has led some to argue that the voice has, in fact, only one register. Researchers are widely

agreed, though, that there are significant transition points (Roubeau *et al.* 2009; Thurman *et al.* 2004).

19 The more developed the voice, the more pull of the cricothyroids against the thyro-arytenoids needs to be supported by extrinsic suspensory muscles of the larynx, and indeed by the entire postural "support system" of the body (Dimon 2011). This is the mechanical basis of what classical singers call "support."

References

Alexander, F.M. (1985) *The Use of the Self*, London: Gollancz.

——(1996) *Man's Supreme Inheritance*, 3rd edition, London: Mouritz.

American Society for the Alexander Technique (2014) Research, www.amsatonline.org/research.

Bunch Dayme, M. (2009) *The Dynamics of the Singing Voice*, 5th edition, New York: Springer-Verlag.

Cacciatore, T.W., Gurfinkel, V.S., Horak, F.B., and Day, B.L. (2011) "Prolonged weight-shift and altered spinal coordination during sit-to-stand in practitioners of the Alexander Technique," *Gait and Posture,* 34(4): 496–501.

Dillon, M. (1988) *Merleau-Ponty's Ontology*, Bloomington: Indiana University Press.

——(1998) "Sartre on the phenomenal body and Merleau-Ponty's critique," in Stewart, J. (ed.), *The Debate between Sartre and Merleau-Ponty*, Evanston: Northwest University Press, 121–43.

Dimon, T. (2011) *Your Body, Your Voice*, California: North Atlantic Books.

Gelb, M. (2004) *Body Learning*, 4th edition, London: Aurum Press.

Jones, F.P. (1974) *Learning How to Learn: An Operational Definition of the Alexander Technique*, London: Sheldrake Press.

——(1997) *Freedom to Change*, London: Mouritz.

Kjeldsen, T. (2011) "Thinking in activity," Thinking and Singing Conference, Wellcome Institute, London.

Langstroth, D. and Miller, T. (2007) *The Alexander Technique: Freedom in Thought and Action*, Halifax N.S.: Nous Publishing.

Merleau-Ponty, M. (1962) *The Phenomenology of Perception*, trans. C. Smith, London: Routledge

——(1963) *The Structure of Behaviour*, trans. A.L. Fisher. Boston: Beacon Pres.

Montero, B. (2010) "Does bodily awareness interfere with highly skilled movement?" *Inquiry*, 53: 105–22.

Morris, K.J. (2007) *Sartre*, Oxford: Wiley Blackwell.

——(ed.) (2010) *Sartre and the Body*, Basingstoke: Palgrave Macmillan.

Reid, C. (2005) "Vocal science: an evaluation," *Australian Voice*, 11, http://corneliusreid.com.

Roubeau, B., Henrich, N., and Castellengo, M. (2009) "Laryngeal vibratory mechanisms: the notion of vocal register revisited," *Journal of Voice*, 23: 425–38.

Sartre, J-P. (1943) *Being and Nothingness*, New York: Washington Square Press.

Sircar, S. (2008) *Principles of Medical Physiology*, New York: Thieme Medical.

Slater, B. (1979) "Internal and external negations," *Mind*, 88(352): 588–91.

Society of Teachers of the Alexander Technique (2014) Scientific Research, www.stat.org.uk/alexander-technique/research.

Stewart, J. (1998) *The Debate between Sartre and Merleau-Ponty*, Evanston: Northwest University Press.

Sundberg, J. (1987) *The Science of the Singing Voice*, Dekalb, IL: Northern Illinois University Press.

Thurman, L., Welch, G., Theimer, A., and Klitzke, C. (2004) "An alternative, science-based theory of register phenomena," Second International Conference: The Physiology and Acoustics of Singing, Denver, Colorado.

Vennard, W. (1967) *Singing: The Mechanism and the Technic*, New York: Carl Fisher.

Wilcox, J. (1935) *The Living Voice*, New York: Carl Fischer.

4

TRAINING ACTORS' VOICES

Towards an intercultural/interdisciplinary approach

Tara McAllister-Viel

How can current Western voice pedagogy respond to the growing international interest in the field of vocal arts, and contribute to the continuing developments in intercultural performance, and training around the world?[1] What shifting principles and practices of mainstream Western voice training are needed to embody (literally, "put into the body") an intercultural and interdisciplinary approach to vocal training? This chapter attempts to add to ongoing discussions between practitioners and scholars about the future of training actors' voices in a global community. Here, I specifically focus on a series of conversations between master voice trainer, Kristin Linklater, and renowned artistic director of the SITI company, Anne Bogart, throughout several issues of *American Theatre* magazine (2000–2001) as a point of departure for considering ways of interweaving mainstream Western voice pedagogy and a Korean traditional vocal art form called *p'ansori*. Using as a case study my voice classes at the Korean National University of Arts (KNUA), Seoul, Korea, I employ practice-as-research, ethnographic research and traditional scholarly print materials as methodological tools to analyse current Western voice practice and suggest a possible alternative paradigm for training actors' voices.[2]

The question of integration: "Far horizons" and KNUA

In January 2000, I accepted a post teaching Western voice training in the School of Drama at KNUA. I was hired to design and implement voice curricula for Masters of Fine Arts (MFA) and Bachelors of Fine Arts (BFA) degrees within this highly competitive, cosmopolitan acting conservatoire in Seoul. I was asked to teach from Western mainstream canonical voice texts, specifically Linklater's first book *Freeing the Natural Voice* (1976).[3] In that same month, *American Theatre* magazine, a widely read publication for theatre professionals, published an article entitled "Far horizons," in which Linklater had been interviewed as one of eight professionals responding to the question, "Can American artists benefit from leaving the comfort of US training traditions and studying theatre in, or through the lens of, another culture?" (Wren 2000: 38–39). Her reply sparked a very public debate between herself and director Anne Bogart, subsequently published in various issues of *American Theatre* and culminating in an eight-page discussion mediated by David Diamond the following year (Bogart 2000: 3; Linklater 2000: 3; Diamond 2001: 32–38).

In the article that began the debate, Linklater wrote:

> Young actors are too easily tempted to taste the appetizers and desserts of butoh, kathakali, kabuki, Suzuki, Balinese dancing, t'ai chi and the tao of voice instead of getting deep nourishment from the meat and potatoes of our own European-based, verbal traditions. Good actors are inherently versatile – they can pick up ideas from all over the place – but they should be wary of becoming whores with low self-esteem. They and their teachers sell themselves short when they bow down to foreign gods.
>
> *(Wren 2000: 38)*

What interested me about her comments was her focus on Eastern practices and what appeared to be an adversarial relationship created in her comparison between Eastern and Western (European) verbal traditions. Earlier in her career, Linklater appeared to advocate certain Eastern modes of training, specifically "t'ai chi and yoga," for "ridding the body of habitual tensions" as part of the necessary pre-paratory work for developing the actor's voice (1976: 4). By 2006, Linklater's work had elements that were explicitly interwoven with Eastern training modes:

> I must acknowledge that very few of the physical exercises were created by me; I have appropriated and absorbed them from many different sources. [...] Yoga floor exercises have been customized for specific vocal purposes and may be almost unrecognizable as Yoga.
>
> *(2006: 3)*

The binary created between East and West in Linklater's response to the "Far horizons" question is problematic, in part, because traditions considered "Western" may have already "appropriated and absorbed" non-Western praxis.[4]

A decade before, I had graduated with an MFA Acting degree from the Asian/ Experimental Theater programme (Department of Theater and Drama) at the University of Wisconsin – Madison, US.[5] One does not have to leave "the comfort of US training traditions" in order to "study theatre in, or through the lens of, another culture" (Wren 2000: 38). I was an American actor who trained intensively through various traditions simultaneously, specifically taiqiquan, kathakali, kalarippayattu and hatha yoga as well as popular mainstream approaches to voice training – including Linklater, and specifically *Freeing the Natural Voice*. I had spent the majority of my professional acting career integrating these specific modes of training into perfor-mance within my Chicago-based theatre company as well as my freelance work for nationally recognized repertory companies, Shakespearian festivals, film and television. Although I periodically trained overseas, the "meat and potatoes" (Wren 2000: 38) of my training took place in the US.

Linklater's comments in relation to "verbal arts traditions" (Wren 2000: 38) were of particular interest because of the job that lay ahead of me at KNUA.[6] According to the prospectus of the School of Drama at KNUA (2000: 14), educational aims included "an integration of [...] fusion techniques into a complete stylistic synthesis – this synthesis thus being the final phase and the culmination of the students' training." This "integration" included "Linklater voice technique, Alexander movement, Asian martial arts [...] and traditional Korean singing" (2000: 14). While I taught at KNUA, "traditional Korean singing" primarily meant *p'ansori* training that had been adapted for the School of Drama from the School of Traditional Korean Arts, located across the courtyard on the same campus.[7] *P'ansori* is a traditional Korean vocal art which combines *aniri* (spoken voice), *ch'ang* (sung voice) and *pallim* (gesture).[8]

KNUA, a government-sponsored university, was founded in 1993 with the opening of its first school, the School of Music. The School of Drama opened in 1994, followed by four more schools. With the opening of the School of Korean Traditional Arts two years before I arrived at KNUA, the Korean government mandated that actors-in-training at the School of Drama should add two years of traditional Korean singing, primarily *p'ansori*, to their required drama training (KNUA 2004). The government's mandate was not originally intended to design an intercultural/interdisciplinary voice pedagogy, but was part of a larger government scheme to preserve a unique traditional Korean vocal art that was in danger of extinction without government intervention. In 1963, the Korean Government implemented the Intangible Cultural Property scheme and aligned the performing arts, namely *p'ansori* (Intangible Cultural Property Number 5), with nation building (Um 1999). At this same time, Korea was undergoing tremendous change after the Korean War (1950–53).

> As it entered the 1960's, the Korean government endeavored to establish a growing industrial economy. This was particularly true as the incoming regime of Pak Chung-hee introduced a series of five-year development plans. Western culture became dominant as one result of this policy and indigenous traditions continued to fade.
>
> *(Hahn 1990: 36)*

KNUA's founding mission can be understood within this wider socio-historical context. The School prospectus (KNUA 2000: 8) read:

> The launch of the Korean National University of Arts has also served as a much needed catalyst to recapture, after many years of heavy western influence at the expense of traditional Korean artistry, a contemporary national culture and Korean artistic "voice" composed of both external and indigenous methods and traditions.

The prospectus plays on the use of the word "voice." The KNUA curriculum was designed, not simply to train the literal voice of the actor, but as an institutional vehicle for "voicing" Korean "contemporary national culture." This is a political as well as artistic statement. For a country struggling with issues of national identity through a politically turbulent 20th century, "nationalism," or an understanding of what it means to be "Korean" within an ever-shifting landscape, became a main issue. KNUA, in partnership with the Korean government, chose to use pedagogical structure as one means of strengthening a cultural voice.

In the *American Theatre* debates, Linklater raised concerns about American students leaving the US to train overseas. Similarly, the Korean government raised a parallel concern about Korean students leaving Korea to receive their acting tuition in the West.

> The Korean system of higher education has usually included arts education among its courses of study. However, the study of the arts has always been predominantly theoretical and little, if any, practical training has been offered. Accordingly, those young people who desire their careers as artists/practitioners have been forced to seek such training in the United States and Europe. Thus, the need for a high-quality, professional oriented conservatory system – similar to those found overseas – has been long overdue.
>
> *(KNUA 2000: 8)*

Unlike Linklater's (Diamond 2001: 32–33) insistence that American actors "get [their] roots deep enough into this tradition" before they "have earned the right to meet other, international ones," the curriculum at KNUA offered simultaneous study of different traditions throughout the students' time at the school. The KNUA university model seemed to suggest that there was no linear hierarchy in which the student must first learn one tradition before learning others. Linklater's metaphor in which some training is "meat and potatoes" and other training is "desserts" (Wren 2000: 38) separates pedagogy like Western courses in a meal, with priority given to the main course. There are other cultural models or metaphors available for (re)considering the structure of training and its relationship to performance. For instance, in Korea, *hanjeongsik*, 한정식 (literally 한/Korean 정/complete or set menu 식/meal) the entire meal is usually laid out on the table and shared amongst the participants, each person mixing flavours according to their taste. Relocating myself overseas helped me (re)examine the way in which different training traditions could interface, and voice trainers could think and talk about this interaction.

The power relationship of such interactions is controversial. Linklater warns, "If we come to them [non-Western training modes] as if we're going to the street fair – to see what we can pick up to decorate our living rooms – then we're in trouble" (Diamond 2001: 32–33). Bogart agrees: "'boutique' is dangerous [...]. The word I look for in actor training is *rigor*" (Diamond 2001: 34; original emphasis). The way *p'ansori* and Western voice training interacted at KNUA was rigorous. Frequently, my students would finish two hours of *p'ansori* training and come directly to my class for another two hours of Western voice training. However, "rigor" was only one part of structuring this interaction. Integration strategies were needed, as well as ways to avoid reducing art forms to a series of training techniques which "decorated" our emerging approach.

Korean scholar Choi Sun Hee has suggested one can avoid reducing an art to a "mere technique" by placing it back into its historical and cultural context (Choi 2000: 61). Many of my KNUA drama students had not been familiar with *p'ansori* training and culture, but through the School of Traditional Korean Arts, they were exposed to one understanding of *p'ansori* culture in a classroom setting, along with the instructor's personal understanding of *p'ansori* history. This provided some cultural and historical context for the *p'ansori* vocal training. Likewise, Western voice training also needed to be placed in a historical–cultural context. KNUA was one of the first schools in Korea to offer voice training as a separate curriculum within actor training. One of the first questions I fielded from students on my first day of teaching was, "What is 'voice' training and why has it been separated from the acting classes?"

Many of the freshman students had never heard of voice training before, and the mainstream voice texts I brought with me from the US did not necessarily help to define and describe the discipline for them. The content of the texts exemplified the information the authors considered important, but there were other considerations for my students not addressed in these texts. I noticed more than ever before the degree to which US and British culture influenced pedagogy and discipline-specific language, phrases like "voice beautiful" and "outside inwards" (Linklater 1976: 3). Although several authors tried to make the discipline more accessible by targeting the layperson within the books' readerships (Linklater 1976: 1; Rodenburg 1992: ix), the reader would need to be a cultural "insider" to put the work into an understandable context. My Korean students would also need to be fluent in English, with a working vocabulary of the specific teaching languages used in voice texts. At that time, no voice texts had been translated into Korean, although the Head of Acting was in e-mail contact with Linklater to authorize a Korean translation of *Freeing the Natural Voice*.[9]

The basic assumption that the voice can be trained as a separate discipline from acting training and that one can write down that pedagogy in a text for others to teach and learn is a particular kind of pedagogical philosophy. Linklater writes, "In the following chapters I have tried to capture the work that Iris Warren said should never be written down" (1976: 4). *Freeing the Natural Voice* is also designed to fit a certain kind of curriculum, which trains actors for a particular kind of theatre. In the back of our class text, Linklater suggests a "[h]ypothetical four-year actor-training program" (1976: 202–7).[10] Although her approach would fit well with such a proposed four-year acting training programme, it would have to be considerably adapted for the specific curriculum design already in place at KNUA. Linklater suggests that the first year is an "un-doing process" intended to "break down physical and vocal habits." The second year focuses on placing the training within the context of Stanislavsky-style approaches to building a character, exploring "answers to questions such as 'Who am I?' […] 'What do I want?'" In the third year, "singing classes begin now, speech classes (dialects to be lost or acquired, problem [sic] diction etc.), dance […] fighting (fencing, wrestling and whatever is 'in' in Oriental fighting arts) […]." In the fourth year, "as many plays as possible are done before audiences" (Linklater 1976: 202–6).

The singing component suggested in Linklater's curriculum was *p'ansori* and tradi-tional Korean singing at KNUA.[11] I could not teach the "speech" material as a voice and speech teacher because I did not speak Korean and my students usually did not speak English. I taught through in-class Korean/English translators.[12] KNUA students received Korean speech training from a Korean professor in another class and did not need the English language accent/dialect materials I usually taught in my US voice classrooms. Linklater's comment about using whichever "Oriental fighting arts" were in fashion to train actors, sounded a bit dismissive. Asian martial arts training was a rigorous and serious training component at KNUA and manifested itself in the bodies I taught in my voice class, a factor that would shape my curriculum design.[13]

The process of developing an intercultural/interdisciplinary curriculum at KNUA was, in part, one of rethinking assumptions embedded within the principles and practices of mainstream Western voice training. Lo and Gilbert advocate a "strategic way of rethinking the local and context-specific through the global, and vice versa" (2002: 48–49). This led me and my students to experiment with shifting the principles and practices of Western voice for the purposes of our classroom.

Shifting principles: (re)considering assumptions underpinning the practice

The first shift, for me, was to find an understanding of intercultural praxis as a process which could underpin the developing pedagogy. Bonnie Marranca suggests that interculturalism as a practice, theory or worldview is as much a "state of mind" as "a way of working" (Marranca and Dasgupta 1991: 11). The idea that intercultural performance establishes a relationship as well as a particular perspective, or "state of mind," seems to suggest that intercultural practice is continuously changing. Rela-tionships and perspectives are renegotiated through their effect/affect on each other. The lack of stability during continuous renegotiation may be one reason why a *working* definition of "intercultural" is necessary. In my opinion, a research frame-work to develop an intercultural voice pedagogy also needs Lo and Gilbert's (2002: 36) "intentional encounter" in order to create "a more sustained and systematic engagement" with the key issues of interculturalism.

Building intentional encounters between elements of Western voice and *p'ansori* in my class was necessary for a variety of reasons. First, I arrived at KNUA so early in its development that the curriculum was still being realized. Government mandates and the rationale to combine East/West training were clear, but curriculum struc-tures to build learning strategies bridging *p'ansori* with Western voice training into their overall acting training were not yet fully implemented. Second, unintentional encounters such as the random timetabling of *p'ansori* classes and Western voice classes back-to-back, could provide an opportunity for exchange, but we needed a means to identify any benefits from unintentional encounters, and decide if meaning and purpose lay in the exchange. Otherwise, the students would become frustrated and question the purpose of the training.

Through timetabling, the School of Drama unwittingly provided what I call an *environment of transference*; students were transferring knowledge from their *p'ansori* class into my voice class in an attempt to "synthesize" the tremendous amount of training that was required of them. For instance, during class I would sometimes be asked, "When Linklater talks about 'centre,' does she mean *dahnjeon*?"[14] *Dahnjeon* is a term used during *p'ansori* training. A *dahnjeon* generates *ki* (energy) and is part of a larger understanding of the body through Korean traditional medicinal praxis. Here, the students were referring to the lower *dahnjeon*, which my *p'ansori* teacher, Song UHyang, described as the size of a fist located just below the navel and inside the body. It would have been easier for me to dismiss these questions, or to ask the students to set aside their *p'ansori* learning and only focus on the set of skills I was teaching them. Instead, I accepted the context of back-to-back classes and allowed skills to transfer from one class to another. By doing so, I was inviting my students to combine, through empirical learning, one understanding of Western voice "breath support" with *p'ansori* practice (for example, *dahnjeon* breathing).[15]

In our class, Linklater's approach needed to progress alongside *p'ansori* learning as an "intentional encounter" over a length of time in order to create a "sustained and systematic engagement" of the practices both offered. In this way, the students and I could transfer body-voice knowledge from one training mode to another. Sometimes this happened strategically; other times, we experimented through trial and error, discovering how different traditions could work together towards a specific learning outcome. This way of working allowed not only the classroom but also our bodies to become *environments of transference* in which skills encountered each other physically and aurally/orally.

On reflection, the KNUA curriculum design offered two opportunities for intercultural/interdisciplinary voice training. The first opportunity was the kind of adaptations the translators, students and I were developing from the voice pedagogy I brought with me from the US. The second opportunity for intercultural/interdisciplinary work was to integrate this adapted version of the voice pedagogy with KNUA's required two years of adapted *p'ansori* training for actors.

To better understand what my students were experiencing, one month after arriving in Seoul, I began private *p'ansori* training under Human Cultural Treasure Han Nong-Son, for a total of two years until her untimely death. Then, I transferred my training to Human Cultural Treasure Song UHyang. I trained under her for more than a year, and simultaneously studied with *p'ansori* master Bae Il-dong, who was also studying with her at the time.[16] Integrating my *p'ansori* training into my embodied Western voice training was not simply the difficult process of "undoing" as Linklater described it (1976: 202). My learning strategies involved more than interrupting and substituting previously learned muscular response with another, quite different response. Nor was this a kind of "de-education" process, as composer, pianist and traditional Korean arts practitioner Na Hyo-Shin (Na 2002) described – although my *p'ansori* learning experiences were similar to those described by Na. For me, some of my already embodied skills provided a necessary foundation for learning new skills. I did not want to "undo" or "de-educate" my body of these processes.

Through my *p'ansori* lessons and my transference of that learning into my teaching, I began to question some basic assumptions of Western voice training. This was the second shift necessary in order to develop my approach of an intercultural voice pedagogy. Much of my time in those first *p'ansori* lessons was spent devising learning strategies. Often, my *p'ansori* teacher simply could not help me build new learning techniques because my body and previous training was as foreign to her as her body and *p'ansori* training was foreign to me. With each task, I discovered, through trial and error, which existing skills were adaptable and useful and which were not. The more aware I became, not only of my own body and voice, but *her* body and voice, the better my teacher and I were able to communicate. Eventually, we were both looking for, and "reading," a particular set of discipline-specific signs transmitted from her body/voice to my body/voice. A similar phenomenon was happening between me and my students in my classrooms in the transmission of Western voice training. These experiences, upon reflection, generated the following research questions: What previous training is embedded in the bodies of my students through cultural or disciplinary influence? Does one training need to be "undone" before another training can be learned? Is "de-education" desirable, or even possible?

A third shift was to address the body in a cultural context.[17] Influenced by speech science (Kayes 2006; Martin 1991), Western voice training relies on a bio-medical model, the "twinning of science and practice within the modern tradition of voice work" (Boston in Turner 2007: xiii). Teaching from anatomical principles assumes voice exercises are culturally transferable. The assumption that anatomy is "universal" is reinforced in canonical texts (McAllister-Viel 2007; 2009a). Working from a Western scientific approach made it difficult for us to discuss key elements of *p'ansori* training which understood the body through a system of *dahnjeons*, and breath as *ki*. My experience teaching overseas reinforced my understanding that the body is not a stable site for learning. The anatomic principles of the voice are not understood universally, but are acquired and heavily influenced by socio-cultural and environmental factors and discipline-specific training objectives (McAllister-Viel 2007).

When culture has been addressed in canonical texts, the suggestion is that all culture everywhere affects the voice in the same way (Linklater 1976: 1; Berry 1973: 7–8; Lessac 1997: 13–24; Rodenburg 1992: 8; McCallion 1988: 4). Discussions of cultural influence in relation to vocal development have been focused almost exclusively on negative influences that resulted in unhelpful vocal habits. Sociocultural influence has been positioned, at times, within voice discourse as a kind of bad habit that needed to be resolved before the actor, or layperson, could effectively train the voice (McAllister-Viel 2009c: 431–33). The majority of mainstream Western voice training begins with the premise that the student enters training with negative vocal habits learned through environmental and sociocultural influence. Linklater states, "my voice work involves freeing the human being from the constraints that our culture puts on us as we grow up" (Diamond 2001: 33). For her, and many other master voice trainers, socioculturally influenced vocal habits manifest themselves in muscular tension, or body/voice misuse that blocks vocal function and a variety of exercises are offered to reduce or reverse the effects of such influence (McAllister-Viel 2007: 101).

KNUA's approach to developing a sense of "Koreanness" within the curriculum did not seem to share the assumption that Korean culture "limited" vocal use. There seemed to be, instead, an investigation of how culture affected the voice. In my approach I asked, "What if one began voice training with the assumption that sociocultural and environmental influences prepare the body/voice with certain skills necessary for discipline-specific actor training?" In this way, voice pedagogy could strategically use culture as one of the material conditions of training and performance (McAllister-Viel 2009c: 433). My intercultural/interdisciplinary pedagogy would place the students as "experts" (Heathcote and Bolton 1995) of their own culture who, through social vocal training, have already learned certain skills that allow them to "read" meaning in the voice and in sound within their culture.[18] Through ear-training assignments, I attempted to help my students become aware of "off-stage" training which could – through critical examination and devising processes – develop into a sound sign-system in performance.[19]

Teaching at KNUA while studying *p'ansori* and Korean as a Foreign Language offered me another kind of environment of transference – each discipline understood in relation to the other disciplines – allowing me to reflect on aspects of training through the lens of another embodied praxis. This forced me to revisit Linklater's concerns about importing/exporting training. I was an American artist who had left the confines of the US and was training overseas in an Eastern mode of training. I was learning *p'ansori* in Korea, so, in this instance, the indigenous art form was not leaving the country, and yet the art form was leaving its cultural context by "importing" these techniques into my body. Whether or not I was to return to the US and "import" my understanding of *p'ansori* into a US actor training programme, *p'ansori* had already been displaced. "Importing" and "exporting" refer to geographic locations as the sites of learning and not to the site of the body as the place of learning. This is part of the important distinction between "international" and "intercultural" applications of voice when debating intercultural/interdisciplinary approaches to voice training within intercultural discourse (Weber 1991: 27, 29).

The experiences happening in my body, negotiating my Western voice training with my new learning of *p'ansori*, were similar to what I was coming to understand as happening in my students' bodies. How do we discuss what is happening to our bodies and voices? I am calling it "intercultural and interdisciplinary" while continuing to search for articulations that may more closely reflect what I feel and hear. I am taking my understanding of *intercultural* and *intracultural* theatre practice from James Brandon's definitions within a Japanese context (1990: 89–97). Brandon defines *intercultural* theatre in Japan – such as the work of contemporary theatre writer/director Ota Shogo (1939–2007) – as the interaction between Japanese forms, such as Noh, with forms outside of Japan, including Chinese and Korean forms and artists, challenging a simple Eurocentric understanding of intercultural exchange. Unlike Rustom Bharucha's (Fischer-Lichte and Bharucha 2011) definition of *intracultural* as between the many different cultures and languages within an Indian context, Brandon's definition seems closer to Korea's intracultural interaction with its traditional indigenous arts.[20]

Regarding KNUA's curriculum design, perhaps *intercultural* integration happens between contemporary Korean acting training and Western voice training, and *intracultural* integration happens between contemporary Korean acting training and traditional Korean arts, like *p'ansori*. However, such tidy categories do not adequately articulate what I am referring to as an *environment of transference*, or what I think emerges when multiple cultures and disciplines interact in a cosmopolitan training environment like KNUA.

Negotiating embodied acts

The discussion between Linklater and Bogart in "Balancing acts" (Diamond 2001) references several key issues embedded within training practices, one of which is an argument over the place of tension and release in training actors through various techniques. Linklater begins,

> So I believe basic training frees an actor from the constraints of habit, which is always a diminishing, reductive force. I could not train young actors in voice work if they were doing equal amounts of time in Suzuki. Suzuki involves building muscular control, and the work I do involves *giving up* external muscular controls.
>
> *(Diamond 2001: 34; original emphasis)*

Later one panel member returns to this issue and asks Linklater's opinion of American modern dance as a model for training. Linklater responds, "Graham's technique is deadly for actors. Because if you contract in there [*indicating the diaphragm*] you can't breathe" (Diamond 2001: 105). The panel member counters, "With Graham, the emphasis is a lot on contraction, yes, but it's also on release." Linklater responds, "But it's for a different art." Bogart interjects,

> It's not a different art! I think Martha Graham is the most important theatre person of the century. [...] I play a game in my head sometimes: "What would have happened if the Moscow Art Theatre never came to the US in 1922 and '23?" I think, "Maybe Graham would have been our entire theatre!".
>
> *(Diamond 2001: 105)*

Here, the discussion shifted to the appropriateness of integrating different *disciplines*, classified as different art forms with implied differences in training objectives or performance outcomes. This particular part of the discussion was key when integrating the way *p'ansori* approaches muscular contraction as a tense/release cycle. The contraction and release of contraction within the musculature creates a particular kind of sound which is one of the "building elements of the music." Lee Byong Won (Lee 1999) explains,

> A common aesthetic feature of much [Korean] musical performance is the continuous alternation of tension and release as building elements of the music. This alternation may be present not only in the sonic design of the music, but also in the conditions by which the sound is produced, such as performance postures and some characteristic organological structures.

For *p'ansori*, the beauty of the sound comes in part from excessive muscular contraction but for many Western theatre vocalists, tension "murders" the vibrations necessary to create a rich, resonating sound (Linklater 1976: 41). How does one bridge these different training objectives, rooted in traditions that seek different aesthetic outcomes?

I had understood Linklater's voice training to be a psycho-physical approach; indeed, she refers to her training as such throughout her first book. I had also understood my actor training through the Acting programme at the University of Wisconsin – Madison to be psycho-physical. I had depended on the psycho-physical approach in these two training modes as a working actor in Chicago. And I had hoped to solve my curriculum design problem at KNUA by using my experience of integrating psycho-physical Western voice and Asian movement training as a kind of model to integrate Western voice with Korean *p'ansori*.

The practice itself, in this case my reliance on understandings of "psycho-physical" practice, was intimately tied to certain principles that developed from historical, cultural and political contexts. The process of integration was not straightforward or easy, and ultimately led me to reconsider what "psycho-physical" meant in Western voice praxis as differentiated from Eastern modes of training (McAllister-Viel 2007: 103–6; 2009a: 166).

The process of developing KNUA's voice curriculum became the process of re-examining the most fundamental components of learning and teaching an embodied practice. I needed to carefully reconsider which principles and practices could be adapted. I could not simply discard my own training and start over. I do not believe "de-education" is possible or desirable. The principles and practices of Western voice training, including Linklater's approach, were the materials of my voice training, adapted to my needs as a working professional. These exercises had been embedded in my musculature and I had been hired by KNUA, in part, to pass on my understanding of these exercises from my body into the bodies of my students. The exercises had served me well throughout my career and I felt they could also be adapted to serve my students' needs to achieve what I understood as the School of Drama's intercultural/interdisciplinary objectives.

My choice to adapt mainstream Western voice techniques reflected my belief that the exercises were adaptable and useful. However, I had few other pedagogical models for intercultural/interdisciplinary voice training to use as my inspiration. Although there had been calls from mainstream voice trainers for more diversity within current US university acting programmes and voice curricula (Burke 1997: 58, 61–62; Brown 2000: 124–28), there were very few practical alternatives on offer at that time.

My experiences teaching voice in a Korean acting training programme, while undertaking vocal training in *p'ansori* and learning Korean as a Foreign Language, helped me to reexamine current Western voice pedagogy and consider its future within the larger demands of a global community. Theatre discourse in Korea and the US at the start of the 21st century, and particular discussions such as the debates in *American Theatre* magazine, helped guide me through curriculum choice by providing a theoretical basis for the developing practice. On reflection, four main considerations shaped my evolving intercultural/interdisciplinary pedagogy during that time:

- The teaching/learning relationship between in-class translator (if one is needed), student and instructor to realize the specific adaptations of the voice training for a certain cultural context. This aspect of my approach rejected pedagogy as an intact form (e.g., strictly teaching from a textbook) in favour of viewing pedagogy as a changing cultural relationship.
- Understanding the sociocultural influences within my students' bodies as assets to voice training by addressing the body in cultural context.
- Working within an "environment of transference," in which two or more training traditions are studied simultaneously. This "environment" could be the site of a school as students pass from one classroom to the next transferring the skills developed in one classroom into other classrooms. Or, "environment" could refer to the student's own body as the site for transferring skills, using the embodied practice acquired from one tradition to learn the skills of another tradition via student-centred learning strategies.
- Structuring a "dialogue" between practice and theory to help "integrate" practices.

This chapter proposed to extend and refine a discussion about ways Eastern and Western vocal arts can interact and create different intercultural/interdisciplinary approaches. What results, perhaps, is an understanding that working in this way creates, for the practitioner, a radically different point of view of voice and its potential. Learning different traditions side-by-side offers actors-in-training other kinds of body knowledge that can develop different aural/oral experiences in training and in performance. As international interest in vocal arts continues to grow, many other kinds of intentional and unintentional encounters will occur. If these encounters, developing over time, create approaches to training actors' voices, I suspect what will result is a very different kind of actor. This, in turn, can change the way we think, talk about and experience voice in theatre – and theatre in general.

Notes

1 I use "Western voice training" or "Western voice pedagogy" to refer primarily to mainstream, contemporary voice praxis after 1950, found predominately in US and UK drama schools, and popularized by the texts and studio approaches of Kristin Linklater, Arthur Lessac (US), Cicely Berry and Patsy Rodenburg (UK).

2 For practice-as-research methodologies, refer to Chapter 1 in this volume. By practice-as-research I mean using the experiences of the body/voice to critically analyse voice pedagogy. This form of "empirical research," or knowledge-gathering conducted through embodied practice and first-hand experience, establishes a primary relationship to voice training and performance. I simultaneously establish secondary relationships to practice through more traditional scholarly research.

3 An expanded edition was published in 2006.

4 The larger question here, which intercultural discourse periodically problematizes, is: "What is understood as 'Eastern tradition' and 'Western tradition?'" Here, I attempt to define what I mean by Eastern and Western modes of training within the particular contexts of the actor training institutions in which I was a student and teacher: KNUA, University of Wisconsin – Madison and my current position as Head of Voice at East 15 Acting School (UK).

5 When I was a student, the programme was led by Professor Phillip Zarrilli. For a better understanding of this programme and the training it offered, based on the work of A.C. Scott, see Zarrilli (2009: 24–25, 215–16). I returned to train again under Zarrilli at the University of Exeter, UK, during the three years of my Ph.D.

6 For further reflections on ways I adapted Linklater's first book to the learning context at KNUA's School of Drama, see McAllister-Viel (2001).

7 P'ansori (McCune–Reischauer romanization system) is also spelled pansori (using the 2000 revised romanization system by the Korean Ministry of Culture and Tourism). I prefer to use p'ansori because during the time I am referencing in this article (2000–2005) the McCune–Reischauer system was still the dominant system. The introduction of the new system was highly controversial, and while I was in Seoul, the Korea Times refused to adopt it. The majority of sources in this article also use the McCune–Reischauer system.

8 For more definitions and descriptions of p'ansori, see Park (2003), Pihl (1994), Hahn (1990) and Yi (1982).

9 Later, an official Korean translation of the book was completed by Haerry Kim, a former student of Linklater's at Columbia University: www.thelinklatercenter.com/designated-linklater-teachers/designated-teacher-bios/haerry-kim.

10 US universities usually offer four-year undergraduate training courses, but UK universities usually offer three-year undergraduate courses. KNUA offered a four-year undergraduate BFA acting training course.

11 Since 2003, KNUA has provided a Musical Theatre course, which offers students Western-style singing as part of their acting training.

12 There are larger issues here about how intercultural exchange is mediated through language choice and translation. See Lo and Gilbert (2002).

13 I will return to this issue later when I analyse the place of "tension" in modes of training. Also see McAllister-Viel (2007) for how the voice and its potential change when the concept of the body changes.

14 For a greater understanding of dahnjeon as adapted in my KNUA classrooms, see McAllister-Viel (2007; 2009a; 2009b).

15 For more information about the ways I integrated my understandings of Western voice breathing practices and dahnjeon breathing, see McAllister-Viel (2009b).

16 Han Nong-Son and Song UHyang trained together under the same master teacher, so my transferring into Song UHyang's studio offered a kind of continuum of training within the same pedagogical tradition of this strand of p'ansori teaching.

17 I would eventually be influenced by voice trainer Stan Brown's writings on the "cultural voice" (2000; 2001).

18 Here I borrow from Theatre in Education pedagogy, specifically Brian Edmiston's use of Dorothy Heathcote's "Mantle of the Expert" (Heathcote and Bolton 1995), which I learned as a teaching assistant under Edmiston at the University of Wisconsin – Madison (1991–92).
19 For a greater understanding of this portion of the curriculum development, see McAllister-Viel (2009c).
20 For another discussion on the differences between "intercultural" and "intracultural," see Zarrilli, McConachie, Williams and Fisher Sorgenfrei (2006).

References

Berry, C. (1973) *Voice and the Actor*, New York: Wiley.

Bogart, A. (2000) "Culture shock," *American Theatre*, April: 3.

Brandon, J.R. (1990) "Contemporary Japanese theatre: interculturalism and intraculturalism," in Fischer-Lichte, E., Riley, J. and Gissenwehrer, M. (eds) *The Dramatic Touch of Difference*, Tübingen: Narr, 89–97.

Brown, S. (2000) "The cultural voice," *The Voice and Speech Review: Standard Speech*, 1: 17–18.

——(2001) "The cultural voice: an interview with Danny Hoch," *The Voice and Speech Review: The Voice in Violence*, 2: 124–28.

Burke, K. (1997) "On training and pluralism," in Acker, B. and Hampton, M. (eds) *Vocal Vision: Views on Voice by 24 Leading Teachers, Coaches and Directors*, New York: Applause, 57–62.

Choi, S.H. (2000) "Questions for Dr. Zarrilli," *2000 Seoul International Theatre Festival Special Lecture Series – Interculturalism in Staging*, booklet, Seoul: Munye Theatre, 61.

Diamond, D. (2001) "Balancing acts," *American Theatre*, January: 32–38.

Fischer-Lichte, E. and Bharucha, R. (2011) "Textures: online platform for interweaving performance cultures," www.textures-platform.com/wp-content/uploads/2011/08/Dialogue_Fischer-Lichte_and_Bharucha_pdf.pdf.

Hahn, M.Y. (1990) *Kugak: Studies in Korean Traditional Music*, trans. I. Peak and K. Howard (eds), Seoul: Tamgu-Dang Publishing.

Heathcote, D. and Bolton, G. (1995) *Drama for Learning: Dorothy Heathcote's Mantle of the Expert Approach to Education*, New York: Heinemann.

Kayes, G. (2006) "With one voice," *Vocal Process*, www.vocalprocess.net.

KNUA (Korean National University of Arts) (2000) *School of Drama Prospectus*, Seoul: KNUA.

——(2004) *Prospectus*, Seoul: KNUA.

Lee, B.W. (1999) "Tension and release as physical and auditory signs of affect in Korean music," *Association for Korean Music Research Panel: Meaning and Emotion in Korean Music*, Austin, TX.

Lessac, A. (1997) "From beyond wildness to body wisdom, vocal life, and healthful functioning: a joyous struggle for our discipline's future," in Acker, B. and Hampton, M. (eds), *Vocal Vision: Views on Voice by 24 Leading Teachers, Coaches and Directors*, New York: Applause, 13–24.

Linklater, K. (1976) *Freeing the Natural Voice*, New York: Drama Book.

——(2000) "Kristin Linklater responds," *American Theatre*, April: 3.

——(2006) *Freeing the Natural Voice: Imagery and Art in the Practice of Voice and Language*, London: Nick Hern Books.

Lo, J. and Gilbert, H. (2002) "Toward a topography of cross-cultural theatre praxis," *The Drama Review*, 46(3): 31–53.

Marranca, B. and Dasgupta, G. (eds) (1991) *Interculturalism and Performance*, New York: PAJ Publications.

Martin, J. (1991) *The Voice in the Modern Theatre*, London: Routledge.

McAllister-Viel, T. (2001) "Adapting Kristen Linklater's *Freeing the Natural Voice* to KNUA's acting training program," in *K. Linklater's Voice Training and the Materials of Narrative Skill*, Seoul: KNUA Press, 224–32.

——(2007) "Speaking with an international voice?" *Contemporary Theatre Review*, 17(1): 97–106.

——(2009a) "(Re)considering the role of breath in training actors' voices: insights from dahnjeon breathing and the phenomena of breath," *Theatre Topics*, 19(2): 165–80.

——(2009b) "Dahnjeon breathing," in Boston, J. and Cook, R. (eds) *Breath in Action: The Art of Breath in Vocal and Holistic Practice*, London: Jessica Kingsley, 115–30.

——(2009c) "Voicing culture: training Korean actors' voices through the Namdaemun market projects," *Modern Drama*, 52(4): 426–48.

McCallion, M. (1988) *The Voice Book*, London: Faber and Faber.

Na, H.S. (2002) "A field of music" and "Cholla Province," *A Composer's Travel Journal*, www.hyo-shinna.com/Writings/writings.html.

Park, C. (2003) *Voices from the Straw Mat: Toward an Ethnography of Korean Story Singing*, Honolulu: University of Hawai'i Press.

Pihl, M.R. (1994) *The Korean Singer of Tales*, Cambridge, MA: Harvard University Press.

Rodenburg, P. (1992) *The Right to Speak*, London: Routledge.

Turner, C. J. (2007) *Voice and Speech in the Theatre*, J. Boston (ed.), London: Methuen.

Um, H.K. (1999) "Food for body and soul: measuring the dialectics of performance," *Oideion: Performing Arts Online*, July (3), www.iias.nl/oideion/journal/issue03/um/index-a.html.

Weber, C. (1991) "AC/TC currents of theatrical exchange," in Marranca, B. and Dasgupta, G. (eds) *Interculturalism and Performance*, New York: PAJ Publications, 27–37.

Wren, C. (2000) "Far horizons," *American Theatre*, January: 38–39.

Yi, P.H. (1982) "What is pansori?" trans. B. Song, in *The Annotated Pansori*, Seoul: Britannica Corporation.

Zarrilli, P. (2009) *Psychophysical Acting: An Intercultural Approach after Stanislavski*, London: Routledge.

Zarrilli, P., McConachie, B., Williams, G. J. and Fisher Sorgenfrei, C. (2006) *Theatre Histories: An Introduction*, London: Routledge.

5

A SEA OF HONEY

The speaking voice in the Javanese shadow-puppet theatre

Jan Mrázek

A puppet theatre

In central Javanese shadow-puppet theatre – the *wayang kulit* – a single puppeteer composes an all-night performance, which is never the same each time it is performed. He manipulates the puppets, speaks their voices, narrates and cues the musical ensemble, the *gamelan* (Figure 5.1). Music sounds in one form or another throughout the event. The flat, painted, perforated puppets are moved or placed against a white, translucent screen illuminated by a lamp hanging above the puppeteer's head. The spectators may watch the shadows from behind the screen, but most prefer to be on the puppeteer's side, where they can see the colourful puppets, the puppeteer and the musicians. *Wayang* is usually part of a celebration, such as a wedding, Independence Day festivities, or perhaps the opening of a restaurant.

The centrality of puppet theatre to Javanese society, its art world and imagination, may seem strange for someone from another culture. I grew up in Prague, where I was involved with European classical music and theatre. When I "discovered" *wayang*, it was for me, first of all, a great theatre. As I laughed at jokes, was thrilled by action and absorbed in listening and playing music, the pleasure and the thrill were not entirely different from watching a play by Shakespeare or an opera by Smetana, while, at the same time, I was taught by *wayang* to think and feel anew. This is the double experience – of recognition and transformation – that I would like to share in this chapter, focusing specifically on the use of voice.

Whilst my involvement with *wayang* in Java in the 1990s was perhaps a simple case of a young man falling in love with theatre, I rationalized it to the world as research for my dissertation. This chapter is based on my practical study of performance technique and discussion with the late Ki Naryocarito, or Pak Naryo; conversations with performers and *wayang* aficionados; watching many shows over two decades, and performing in some; and various Javanese comments on the use of voice in

FIGURE 5.1 A *wayang* puppet and the puppeteer are having a good laugh during a dialogue. The puppet is being proper, covering his mouth with his hand. (The puppeteer is Ki Hartokocarito of Pulo, Eromoko. Photo by the author.)

wayang.[1] My primary focus has been Javanese performance practice and the thinking behind it, rather than philosophical and mystical discourses that employ *wayang* as a source of metaphorical imagery. I should note that most puppeteers acquire their skills by being part of performances from early childhood. There are few technical manuals or textbooks, and although they are interesting for the researcher, they are not widely read by puppeteers and do not play a dominant role in the tradition.[2]

One of the delights *wayang* taught me was this: what I previously conceptualized as separate arts or media were organically united in *wayang*. One of the most common ways to enjoy Javanese painting, dancing, acting, music, storytelling and poetry, is to watch *wayang*, where the various media are at their most powerful. The painted puppets – often exhibited as immobile and silent museum objects – come alive in performance and are made to speak, scream, act and dance by the puppeteer, to the accompaniment of music and sung poetry – all within the framework of a night-long narrative. Each form of artistic expression enriches the others. The social experience of the performance – people mingle, converse, eat and drink – along with its sights, smells, tastes, movements, energies and rhythms, are an indivisible part of *wayang*, in constant interplay with what happens on the screen.

Like any great storyteller, the puppeteer works magic with his voice. As I write this, I recollect the puppeteer's voice and it makes me shiver: it has the uncanny power, like that of the rat-catcher's flute, to control the feelings of others, to create a particular mood, atmosphere, or the setting for a scene. With his voice – and not just words – the puppeteer transports the listener into a mythical world. He builds palaces, evokes gods and demons, knights and beautiful women, jungles and heavenly gardens. Yet, however great the powers of the voice may be, they are enhanced through interplay with other forms of theatricality, as is the puppeteer's control of their precise effects. In this chapter, I consider how the voice becomes part of the multisensory theatrical performance, to which it contributes its magic, and due to which its powers become enhanced. I discuss how the puppeteer finds the voice for each character, how the voice penetrates the puppet and becomes one with it, and how, being incorporated into music, it is, itself, musical.

Despite the repeated references to magic and uncanny powers, my discussion primarily concerns performance technique and practice. To paraphrase the indignation expressed to me by a famous puppeteer who was rumoured to have made a pact with the devil in exchange for his incredible skills: "Only lazy idiots could make up those stories! I don't have a pact with the devil! I just work hard!" One of my discoveries while studying *wayang* was something I already knew from Western classical music: the "magic" of performance grows in great part from hard work and the mastery of technique. This technical mastery in *wayang* includes the ability to develop and inhabit different characters through the use of voice.

Finding the puppet's voice

We know that it is the puppeteer who speaks, yet we hear the voice of the puppet. Crossing the boundary between the living and the dead, the voice is at the heart of a magical play of identities through which puppetry reveals and plays with the world. Javanese discussions of puppets' voices in *wayang* stress the relation between the voice and the particular puppet/character. The voice must "fit" (*cocok, pantes*) the puppet. Once, Pak Naryo asked me to try to speak in the voice of a certain character. When I failed, he said that it would be much easier for me to do it when I saw the puppet, because I would intuit the voice in such a way that it fitted the puppet.

The idea that a character's voice can be known from the visual appearance of the puppet is common in Javanese literature on *wayang*. For example, in the *Serat Sastramiruda* (1879) – a treatise on *wayang* written as a dialogue between the expert K.P.A. Kusumadilaga and a novice – one function of the lamp above the screen is explained in these terms: "When the puppeteer makes the puppets speak, he can see the face/facial expression of the puppet, in order to make [the voice] fit/resemble the voice of the puppet" (Kusumadilaga 1981: 188). According to a more recent text, intended as a manual for learning to perform *wayang*, "[t]he voice/pitch of the puppet's speech, whether it is big [meaning: low] or small [high], whether it is arrogant/harsh or humble/refined, is judged from the appearance of the puppet's facial expression" (Nojowirongko 1960: 12).

In such texts, the relationship between a puppet and its voice is seen from the perspective of the performing puppeteer (or teacher of the technique): the voice is made in such a way that it fits the puppet. The visual representation of the character thus appears to be primary; it is something from which the voice can be inferred. Pak Naryo used the term *njarwa rasa* which can be roughly translated as "interpreting by feeling." He explained *njarwa rasa* as *negesi watake wayang* ("to divine the character of the puppet-character"). The verb *negesi* (from *teges*, "meaning, sense"), which I translate as "to divine," can be broadly rendered "to learn the meaning of something," as well as to learn the import of esoteric and mysterious signs. As Pak Naryo explained, *njarwa rasa* means to learn to understand the nature (*watak*) of a character from the appearance, especially the face, along with the name of the puppet. The visual appearance is thus only a key, or a part of a key, to understanding the nature of the character, in addition to being a component of its representation. Ultimately, it is the entire character that the puppeteer tries to divine when he produces a voice.

While I was learning a particular scene, Pak Naryo told me that Wisrawa, a refined character and a spiritually potent sage represented by a rather small puppet, speaks on pitch 1, his son, the young king Dhanaraja on pitch 2, and Banendra, a powerful, "macho" warrior represented by a large puppet, on pitch 1.[3] When I asked whether Wisrawa and Banendra have the same voice (since my teacher assigned pitch 1 to both of them, although their appearance is very different), he said that *of course* not: Wisrawa's voice is sweet and fragrant, while Banendra's is firm and heavy.

Javanese texts provide similar information. A standard *wayang* manual published by a school for puppeteers lists fifty-two kinds of voices for either specific characters or character types (for example, a female ogre). Below are a few examples:

> Raden Janaka: Pitch low 6, enunciation calm.
> Raden Gathutkaca: Pitch low 1, enunciation fierce and firm.
> Raden Antareja: Pitch low 1, soothing [like light breeze]/thin and rather small/high, enunciation harsh and firm.
> [...]
> Prabu Kresna: Small [high], patient, enunciation clever, out-going, friendly, joking. In the first scene: pitch 3, calm enunciation. [...]
> Togog: Big [low], enunciation stupid, strong, extremely boasting. [...]
> *(Mudjanattistomo 1977: 71–72)*

There is a short introduction before the list:

> The voice and the enunciation of each single puppet has to be different [from the voices of other puppets], and has to fit the character and the face/ appearance. There are those [kinds of voices] that observe the tuning of the music, but there are also those that do not.
> *(Mudjanattistomo 1977: 70)*

In the above list, the voice is described in terms of pitch and/or the character of the voice. There are only four pitches (in ascending order: 6, 1, 2 and 3) in the list, so one has to rely on the verbal descriptions of the voices. For instance, apart from Prabu Duryudana, Raden Werkudara and Raden Janaka also speak on pitch 6, but the verbal descriptions of their voices differ. The terms that describe the voices allow for variation and interpretation, and this flexibility makes them truer as descriptions of practice. On the other hand, the pitches of particular characters as given in the list may apply to some puppeteers, but not to all – depending on their vocal range. In codifying the pitches, the text fails to capture the freedom, variety and constant "interpretation by feeling" (to use Pak Naryo's words) in performance.

Let us look at a sample from another text, by Probohardjono, published originally in 1952 and intended "for puppeteer students" (1966: 41):

> Prabu Kresna [:] when in the first scene, his voice is large [deep], often approaching the [pitch] large [low] 6, but when in [the later part of the performance], his voice is small [high], like the voice of Samba [Kresna's son].
>
> Ardjuna, Kamadjaja, and others of the same kind: their voices are like Prabu Kresna's in the first scene, but lighter, slower, more refined, and calmer.
>
> Abimanyu [Ardjuna's son] and other refined knights that have black face: their voices are like Ardjuna's, but lighter, rather small [high].
>
> Irawan [Ardjuna's son] and refined knights that have white face: their voices are like Abimanyu's, but lighter, floating.
>
> Prabu Judhistira [Ardjuna's elder brother]: his voice is like Ardjuna's, but light, floating.
>
> Prabu Salja, Prabu Abijasa, Drupada, Matswapati, Bismaka, Basudewa, Dasarata, Bathara Indra and others of the same kind: their voices are medium, in accordance with the [pitch] 2, rising and falling but firm/heavy, and when they are happy, surprised, or angry, their voices are smaller [higher] and the enunciation rather faster.
>
> Wrekudara: his voice is big [low], firm, honest, stiff without curves, in accordance with the pitch 5.
>
> Gathutkatja, Antaredja, and Antasena [sons of Wrekudara] and others of the same kind: their voices are like Wrekudara's, but not stiff and not as firm/heavy.
>
> *(Probohardjono 1966: 44)*

Much of what I said about the earlier text by Mudjanattistomo is also true here, but in some ways, this text by Probohardjono is significantly different. Many voices are described by comparing and contrasting them with the voices of other characters. We encounter the word *sabangsanipun* repeatedly, meaning "of the same kind/ group" (for example, in the second, sixth and eighth items above). This implies that there are groups of characters that have a similar voice. Generally, characters that have similar voices are represented by puppets that share comparable visual characteristics. The vocal affinity may express genealogical kinships or similarity of character when the characters are not blood relatives.

Probohardjono states that "other characters can follow the example-basis above, making [the voices] fit the shapes of the faces [of the puppets]" (1966: 46). The examples in the list, which has only thirty-six items, thus serve as a basis for the voices of characters not included in the list. When characters with voices that are "the same or almost the same" appear together on the screen, "the older character, or the character of higher status, is made to have a larger [lower] voice, so that the difference be clearly heard" (Probohardjono 1966: 46). The author notes that for some characters the voice changes depending on their mood (Salja and his group in our sample) or the particular scene (Kresna in the sample). These are significant points. They extend the meaning of *cocok*; of what and how the voice "fits." The voice has to fit, not just the isolated puppet but the character at a particular dramatic moment. This is something that is more important in practice than it might appear from these Javanese manuals, but Probohardjono does point the student in that direction.

These manuals may sometimes give the impression that the practice is more rigid than it actually is, whereas they aim merely to introduce the student to the basics of the technique. While the list of characters' voices I quoted from Mudjanattistomo presents standardized prescriptions for specific individual characters, Probohardjono's text teaches one to think in terms of relations, similarities and differences; of groups and sub-groups. Probohardjono pays attention to how voice helps to create a character and to articulate relations and distinctions between characters, and he implies that the voice depends on mood and dramatic context. Based on my experience, I suggest that because it is less rigid, and focuses on process rather than product, Probo-hardjono's text is nearer to the working practices of the puppeteer, and how the voice is given afresh to the puppet in each performance. Every performance is different, created in the moment. This includes the specifics of the puppeteer's voice, and his understanding of each character and the relationships among them.

One could develop Probohardjono's discussion further, and consider other aspects of the puppeteer's work with voice; the ever-changing emotions of the characters, the puppeteer's momentary whims and inspirations, jokes that push the boundaries, or moments when the voice breaks in pain, in anger, in violence, or in horseplay, such as when a sudden scream violently startles all characters on the screen. All of these liberties taken by mature performers help make the characters and the per-formance come alive. An essential skill of the puppeteer is to observe what happens around him – everything from people's behaviour, animals' movements, to current films, television, sports and news – and bring the forces, energies, and unpredictability of life into his performances and his voice (see also Mrázek 2005: 180–85).

Incarnation and "twinness"

Let us return to the basic principle that the voice has to fit the puppet. How exactly does it fit? What is the relation between the appearance of the puppet and the voice? The American linguist A.L. Becker writes: "The puppeteer learns to reshape his mouth and alter his entire vocal mechanism systematically to distinguish certain characters and types of characters" (1995: 59). He told me in a conversation that according to his Javanese teacher, the puppeteer shapes his mouth to resemble the mouth of the puppet. Becker also describes the connections between voice qualities and character traits rather than their appearance:

> Pushing the points of articulation of sounds forward in the mouth suggests
> refinement and culture, pushing them back suggests roughness and raw nature.
> Between these two extremes is an unmarked area where the characters most
> like the "us" defined by the dalang speak. Steady, even pitch and rhythm
> suggest control; wide pitch and rhythm variation suggest impulsiveness, a
> dimension of character very important to Javanese. […] Nasality is tied to
> cleverness.
>
> *(1995: 240)*

Javanese puppeteers and authors are not usually explicit about the details of how
exactly the voice correlates with the appearance of the puppet or the character,
perhaps because they intuit the voice of each character, without the need to conceptualize the process. Instead, their emphasis is on the basic fact that the voice fits
the puppet or character. Why is this important to them?

In one of my lessons, Pak Naryo explained that the point of making the voice fit
is that *swarane dhalang manjing wayang*, "the puppeteer's voice enters the puppet."
The old-fashioned word *manjing* (which I translate as "enter") is best-known to the
Javanese from the expression of *curiga manjing warangka, warangka manjing curiga*,
"the *kris* [magically powerful dagger] enters the scabbard, the scabbard enters the
kris," which describes the mystical union of opposites around which the world is
structured; male and female, god and man, earth and sky, lord and servant. *Manjing*
thus implies not only entering, but also an interpenetration and union of opposites.
This suggests that the aim of making the voice fit a puppet is reaching this union
between the puppeteer's voice and the puppet. Pak Naryo said that he liked the
term *nuksma*, used by some people, meaning "to incarnate." It derives from *suksma*,
"soul, spirit," so could be translated – albeit awkwardly – as "to spirit" or "to soul."
Therefore, as the word implies, the goal of making the voice fit the puppet is to
achieve an "incarnation" of the puppeteer's voice into the puppet. The puppeteer's
voice makes the puppet alive, animates it, by entering soul (*anima*) into it. The
voice enters and is united with the puppet like the soul with the body. No wonder
that puppeteers take voice so seriously: it is a matter of life.

The speaking voice is an expression of the human, living physicality of the
puppeteer. The puppet is a material thing that is implicated in the puppeteer's
physicality through voice. As the words *manjing* and *nuksma* suggest, the way that
a puppeteer fits his voice to the puppet – "learns to reshape his mouth and alter his
entire vocal mechanism" (Becker 1995: 59) and controls his breath (*anima*) to achieve
it – involves an intimate relationship between the puppeteer and the puppet. This
is similar to the moment when he holds the puppet in his hand and – as the puppeteer Ki Suryasaputra put it in a conversation – enters his "trembling"; putting his
life and his soul into the puppet, letting his own energy flow into the puppet,
making it alive.[4]

This could be compared to the experience of actors on a stage. The words of the
actor are understood, on some levels at least, as the words of the character they
represent. However, while in actors' theatre the character's body is represented by

the same body that produces the voice, in puppet theatre the body of the character is represented by the puppet, even though it is the puppeteer who speaks, "entering" the words into the puppet. In actors' theatre,

> [j]ointly claimed by the actor and the character, the body on stage is also implicated in the real and the imaginary that underlie the twinness of dramatic fiction [...] the actor's body never ceases asserting itself in its material, physiological presence [...] endowing the character's body with borrowed physicality.
>
> *(Garner 1994: 44)*

By contrast, this "twinness" in puppet theatre is reflected in the duo of the puppet and the puppeteer. The puppet does function in a similar representative capacity to the actor's body; yet, the puppeteer never quite disappears. His body (and his voice), "never ceases asserting itself in its material, physiological presence." It is in the context of this organic bond that the union of the voice and the puppet has to be understood: the speech belongs both to the puppeteer and the puppet, and this ambiguity participates in giving meaning and feeling to what is said; this twinness allows the puppeteer to speak in the puppet's voice.

Voice, music, words and moving pictures

So far, I have offered some observations on the way that a puppet and voice form an organic union of the thingness of the puppet and the puppeteer's "sounding breath of the human voice, which is certainly the most stable-warm imaginable thing in the world of sound" (Mann 1948: 68). Yet, the puppeteer does not only speak in the voices of the characters; he also recites narrative, descriptive passages and chants.

His speech is heard against a continuous flow of soft music. It is punctuated by, or alternates with, louder music and chants that he sings. The puppeteer's voice, on a continuum between speaking and singing, sometimes speaks on a particular pitch, which follows the accompanying music. The puppeteer respects musical timing, pausing to wait for significant points in the music. His voice functions like other voices in the musical texture, becoming part of the music without entirely disappearing into it.

In various ways, the voice coheres with, and is pervaded by, music. The function of music in *wayang*, and Javanese discourse on the issue, are beyond the scope of this chapter, but suffice to say that – as in the case of the voice's connection to the puppet – the emphasis is once again on *cocok*, on making an element fit. In this case, music needs to fit the feeling of a scene or a moment, evoke multiple feelings or changes in feeling which may be gradual or startling, and thus intensify and enrich their expression (Mrázek 2005: 191–268).

The puppeteer's voice is therefore musical in another sense. When I asked one of my teachers, Sumarsam, about the meaning of a few sentences from a descriptive passage used in the scene that traditionally opens every performance, he emphasized that "it is sound-play." Analysing a short excerpt will illustrate the sense of play with sound/voice/*swara*:

> ... panjang punjung pasir wukir loh jinawi gemah ripah kartå tåtå tur raharjå.

First, one finds playful pairs of playful words. (1) *panjang–punjung:* the consonants are the same in each word, but instead of the *a*'s in the first word, there are *u*'s in the second word; (2) *pasir–wukir:* the words rhyme (*-ir*); (3) *gemah–ripah:* rhyme (*-ah*); (4) *kartå–tåtå:* rhyme (*-tå*). Furthermore, there is an interaction between the pairs.[5] For instance, in the first pair, the coupling of *a* in the first word of the pair (*panjang*) with the *u* in the second word (*punjung*), is echoed in the second pair in the first syllables of the words, as the *a* of *pasir* is coupled with the *u* of *wukir* – the sequence of vowels in the first four words is *aa uu ai ui*. There are other musical effects, such as the almost-Dadaist *tåtåtå* of *kartå tåtå*.

The passage above is an excerpt from an elaborate description of a great kingdom. It is narrated during a scene which takes place in a king's reception hall. Poetic words and the quiet accompanying music create a stately atmosphere and evoke the greatness and wisdom of the king, the splendour of his palace and the glory of the realm. It is this special, refined feeling, along with the music and the sound of the puppeteer's voice, that the audience enjoys during this long scene, when, essentially, nothing transpires. The puppeteer half-chants the long passage and the sound-play of the words blends with the sounds of the musical instruments.

Immediately following this, the words from the above excerpt reappear at the beginning of phrases, echoing a fundamental technique of Javanese music: a melodic or rhythmic pattern can be expanded in time, so that the tones of the original pattern sound less frequent and the resulting spaces are filled with ornamentation. The expanded form is often felt to be expressive of a calmer, more sedate mood, appropriate in the situation. The passage is recited, with some variations, in most performances:

> ... **panjang punjung pasir wukir loh jinawi gemah ripah kartå tåtå tur raharjå. Panjang** *dhåwå pocapané,* **punjung** *luhur kawibawané,* **pasir** *samudra,* **wukir** *gunung,* [...] **loh** *tulus ingkang tinandur,* **jinawi** *murah kang sarwo tinuku,* **gemah** *kang lumaku dagang, rainten dalu datan ana pedhoté* [...]; **ripah** *janmå ing måncå kang sami griyå salebeting pråjå* [...]; **kartå** *kawula ing padhusunan pådhå tentrem atiné* [...]; **raharjå** *tebih ing parang mukå* [...].

In the beginning of the passage, the words were paired on a musical basis: *panjang* with *punjung, pasir* with *wukir*. However, the semantic meaning of the words is a part of the play: *panjang* ("long"), *punjung* ("high"); *pasir* ("sea"), *wukir* ("mountains"). Therefore, in addition to the musical pairing, the same pairs make sense on a semantic level: long–high, sea–mountains.

This cooperation of sound and sense can be also seen in another, later scene, in the description of the female court-dancers and other women waiting on the king:

"*ayu-ayu rupané, éndhah-édi busanane, mandul-mandul payudarané.*" The passage has an inherent musicality – note the changing, developing pattern of the dominant vowels *a* and *u* in each phrase, punctuated by the rhyming suffix -*né*. However, it becomes much richer when the semantics of the words comes into play. Broadly translated, the excerpt means: "their forms beautiful, their garment splendid, their breasts rising and falling." The semantic meaning of *mandul-mandul* ("rising and falling [of breasts]") is evoked musically by the pulse in the sound of the word *mandul-mandul*; the rising and falling breasts signified by the word resonate with the alternation between the more open *a* and the more closed, sensually rounded *u* in the sequence *a-u-a-u*.

The image of rising and falling breasts is signified by the sense of the words and musically evoked by their sound in space. The musicality and the meaning of words combine with the visual image on the screen – the two puppets of the female attendants of the king and their shadows. They have naked shoulders and the upper part of their large bosom is visible. In the past, when an oil-lamp served as the source of light (instead of the electric light, which is common today), the light made the shadows appear to be "breathing" – something I was told about and have observed in some rare performances. This multisensory play is comparable to what was discussed in the first section of this chapter: the manner in which the voice of a puppet harmoniously fits the visual characteristics of the puppet. In both cases, the speaking voice and the visual image combine to evoke a richer experience.

This is not a voice

The musical qualities of the speaking voice, the attention given to the particular intonation of speech and the sounds of words, the incarnation of the puppeteer's voice into the puppet, the rigour with which voice is used in *wayang* and closely related to visual images and material objects – these are all part of a larger, multi-sensory, intensely physical performance. Taking the cue from the Javanese emphasis on finding a voice that is *cocok,* that fits the puppet, I have explored how in various ways the voice is made to cohere with different elements of the performance – the puppets, the music, the sound and meaning of words, and ultimately with the whole formed by all these elements – having suggested that the powers of the voice are thereby augmented. I will conclude with an excerpt from an ancient Javanese text, the *Wangbang Wideya*: a description of the puppeteer's "sweet, soft" voice, "mingling" harmoniously with the "sweet and lovely," "caressing" sounds of music, as well as with the aesthetic of the puppets and the "charm" of the puppeteer. It is within this sensual/sensory whole that the voice, incarnated into puppets and integrated with music, is heard in the Javanese theatre.

> [He] sat down and at the same time took out his puppets – how his charm grew. Raden Srenggara-Yuda now began playing the *gender*, and Empu Siwasmreti likewise played the *redep*;[6] the gong sounded caressingly in unison. The *gender* was fairly big, and bore the name Asep-Menyan. Its sound was

> sweet and lovely, mingling with the sweetness of the voice of him like Smara
> [god of love] […] as if a sea of honey were flowing from his mouth. All the
> spectators were smitten with love, and all the palace servants crowded around
> to watch, excitedly coming by way of corridors […]. The audience got
> more and more carried away – they said, "His performance of *wayang* in
> daylight only makes it all the more beautiful, as if he will disappear into thin
> air; it lights up his charming appearance and the fine puppets."
>
> *(Robson 1971: 186–89)*

The above description shows how the puppeteer's voice is heard within a musico-
theatrical performance, but – crucially – within a particular setting, within a world that
responds and is stirred by the performance. We sense the sweetness and sensuality
of the voice in the physical and emotional movement of the audience, as if their hearts
"sounded caressingly in unison," like the gong used in the performance. Moreover,
the description is but an excerpt from a long narrative about the adventures of a
prince. His *wayang* performance is inspired by his desire for a princess; he is moved
and "carried away" by the world, just as his audience is "smitten with love" as they
listen to his voice. He performs *wayang*, sings poetry, paints and demonstrates mastery
of other arts to express his love and to impress and seduce the princess by his display
of sophistication and culture. "The Sanskrit words in his speech [the mark of
sophistication and erudition] were used faultlessly, and he has mastered the meaning
of works of literature – he was certainly an expert in the sacred books," comments
the text's author (Robson 1971: 189).

We can take our cue from this text and reflect on how voice is not only part of
a performance, but equally part of a larger physical, social and culturally specific
space. This particularity can be sensed, for example, when thinking about voice as
conditioned by the distinctions and slippages of particular languages. For instance,
in English, speech is commonly distinguished from singing, and the human "voice"
from the "sound" of musical instruments. Yet, the nuances of such distinctions may
differ depending on language. "The puppeteer's voice" is *swarane dhalang* in Javanese,
but *swara* has a different emphasis and range of meanings than the English "voice."
While "voice" refers primarily to the sound produced by humans with their vocal
apparatus, *swara* is used equally commonly for any noises or sounds, notwithstanding
those produced by animals and objects, including musical instruments. Another
word – *uni* – usually translated as "sound" or "noise," is frequently used to mean
"speech," "the content of a written text," or as a verb – *muni* – it means equally
"to sound" and "to speak." To "read" (*maca*) traditional Javanese poetry is to sing
it, and poetic metres are at the same time rhythmical and melodic. This is not the
place to delve into the semantics of either English or Javanese, and I do not want
to overemphasize and exoticize these differences. Yet, it is worth remembering
them, so as not to treat Western distinctions of voice, instrumental sound, singing
and speech as universals. More generally, and even though I do not argue that
voice and *swara* are *entirely* different, we must not assume that voice is the same as
swara or *uni*; that is, we must not assume that what we think about and perceive as

voice in English is thought about and perceived in exactly the same way in other languages, despite the illusion of transparency produced by translation.

It would be interesting to consider how a form of theatre, or any vocal practice, is shaped by, and enacts the particular distinctions, slippages, values and silences of a language; and how that language reflects the particularity of how people hear and work with voice. After all, as the prince's display of cultural sophistication through vocal performance reminds us, the use of voice is inspired by and expresses a *particular* world. Thus, it needs to be heard and studied anew, in each new place and historical moment, as "same-same but different," as we say in Southeast Asian English(es).

Notes

1 This text draws on a discussion on speech in *wayang* in Mrázek (2005: 269–95).
2 See Sears (1996) and Keeler (2002) for a discussion of the standardization and codification of performance practice, and the influence of texts and educational establishments. For an analysis of Javanese interpretations of *wayang* and their relationship to practice, see Keeler (1987: 243–60).
3 In Javanese music, each pitch in an octave is assigned a number.
4 Ki Suryasaputra, personal communication (interview, 1996), quoted in Mrázek (2005: 152).
5 Vowels are pronounced mostly similar to Italian; *å* is close to Italian *o*, *g* is always hard as in "go," except in *-ng*, which is like in the word "sing." The particular pronunciation matters here, and I distinguish between *a*'s that are pronounced (approximately) as [a] and as [o], by writing them *a* and *å* respectively.
6 *Gender* and *redep* are musical instruments.

References

Becker, A.L. (1995) "Text-building, epistemology, and aesthetics in Javanese shadow theatre," in Becker A.L. (ed.) *Beyond Translation: Essays Toward a Modern Philology*, Ann Arbor: University of Michigan Press, 23–70.

Garner, S.B. Jr. (1994) *Bodied Spaces: Phenomenology and Performance in Contemporary Drama*, Ithaca: Cornell University Press.

Keeler, W. (1987) *Javanese Shadow Plays, Javanese Selves*, Princeton: Princeton University Press.

——(2002) "Wayang kulit in the political margin," in Mrázek, J. (ed.) *Puppet Theater in Contemporary Indonesia: New Approaches to Performance Events*, Ann Arbor: University of Michigan Press, 92–108.

Kusumadilaga, K.P.A. (1981) *Serat Sastramiruda*, Jakarta: Proyek Penerbitan Buku Sastra Indonesia dan Daerah, Departement Pendidikan dan Kebudayaan.

Mann, T. (1948) *Doctor Faustus*, New York: Knopf.

Mrázek, J. (2005) *Phenomenology of a Puppet Theatre: Contemplations on the Art of Javanese Wayang Kulit*, Leiden: KITLV Press.

Mudjanattistomo, R.M. (1977) *Pedhalangan Ngayogyakarta Jilid 1: Gegaran Pamulangan Habirandha*, Ngayogyakarta: Yayasan Habirandha.

Nojowirongko, M.Ng. (1960) *Serat Tuntunan Pedalangan*, Jogjakarta: Departement Pendidikan dan Kebudayaan.

Probohardjono, R.Ngb.S. (1966) *Serat Sulukan Slendro, ingkang Djangkep lan Baku Kangge Njuluki Wajang Purwa, Katambahan Kawruh-Kawruh Padhalangan ingkang Sanget Wigatos*, Sala: Ratna.

Robson, S.O. (1971) *Wangbang Wideya: A Javanese Panji Romance*, The Hague: Nijhoff.

Sears, L.J. (1996) *Shadows of Empire: Colonial Discourse and Javanese Tales*, Durham: Duke University Press.

Part III
Voice in performance

6

NONSENSE

Towards a vocal conceptual compass for art

Mikhail Karikis

Despite its three-dimensionality, its visceral and sensual power, sound is furnished with graphic representations that are mostly flat, boneless and fleshless. The electrification of sound and its visualization through analogue and electronic means have given it a "face" that is mostly abstract and diagrammatic. Even in the case of the human voice, its invisible character resists representation, lending itself to a dynamics of dematerialization. Yet, thinking of sound as such – without a "body," non-material and ghostly – has implications.

Unless we talk about technologically mediated voices, psychoacoustic phenomena or legend – which present mostly expanded conceptions of the body – sound is connected to material things and voices exist within physical bodies. Each time a voice is heard, in the realm of speech or as wordless utterance, it invokes and calls for a body (Chion 1994: 128–31). It is disconcerting to conceptualize human speech without taking into account the body that produces it; such thinking undervalues the embodied "who" that speech emanates from, and keeps only the semantic aspect of the voice. It implies a logocentric way of thinking, which undermines all those vocal sounds we produce that are not destined to language, asserting the hegemony of the disembodied transcendent sign.

In addition, thinking of the voice as disembodied reproduces a kind of model of the body and its products which has political implications. In capitalist societies where economics is an ideology, and political and cultural decisions are taken from a reductive perspective of financial profit and the rules of supply and demand, there is extreme emphasis on the body as a producer, a consumer, or a commodity. As a locus of socio-political complexity and material needs, the body is ultimately annihilated for the sake of a "transcendent" value – its worth in abstract financial terms (Hardt and Negri 2009: 32–38). In contrast, Adriana Cavarero explains that paying attention to the resonant materiality of the voice implies appreciating it as an expression of one distinct embodied individual to another (2005: 197–210). The voice anchors us in the unique singularities of our bodies, challenging logocentrism and confronting the dissolution of the body prescribed by economism. It acts as an anti-metaphysical force, demanding a profound engagement with people, their bodies and genders, cultures and environment.

The voice is a chunk of (audible) stuff. I think of – and work with – voice as a physical, sculptural material, a malleable substance that could be compared to visible, physical things used by sculptors, such as rubber or clay. Voices have textures – they are husky, grainy, sharp, or growly. They also change shape – we stretch our voices to different pitches and volumes, and shape them into different forms (language being one of them). Speaking is a highly coded sound sculpture. When we talk, we generate an intricate combination of sound forms we have learnt to decode and understand. However, the voice produces a much wider variety of sounds than mere language.

Squeaks, shouts, whistles, sighs, gibberish, jargon, cries, yells and so on are produced by people in different environments and are often deictic in their utterance. A focus in my art practice has been to research the production of vocal sounds which are beyond language, exploring the meanings we attach to the "nonsense" sounds we invent. In relation to language, these "nonsense" sounds are somewhat anarchic; they are deserters or rebels, occupying an outsider's position to the rules of syntax and its principles, which govern the structure of language. John Cage stated that he and his friend Norman O. Brown thought of syntax as the "army of language" (1979). In his work *Empty Words* (1979), in which language is progressively hollowed out and musicalized by gradually removing phrases, sentences, words and syllables from a text, to leave only isolated vocal noises and breaths, Cage suggests that transforming language into "nonsense" by breaking the rules that govern it, decommissions the "army of language" and leads to its demilitarization. This implies the power of extra-lingual vocal sounds to act as a force of resistance and pacifism – a force which I wish to mine and which informs my thinking of "nonsense" vocal sounds, guiding my interest in the kind of communities with which I have been collaborating, and influencing the artistic strategies I employ to reappraise conventions that pre-determine human vocal expressive conduct.

Two examples of community-based sound art practice

The two artistic examples I examine in this chapter – *Sounds from Beneath* and *SeaWomen* – are part of a quartet of projects I developed in collaboration with other artists and local communities in England, South Korea and Italy.[1] All four projects take the form of sound and video installations, and feature human action or performances. What connects these projects is my research into how sound and non-verbal vocal production relate to specific work communities, echoing their particular marginalized histories and cultures, and have the power to resist official language and challenge the political forces that institute it.

Sounds from Beneath: *the lament of the unlamented*

The project *Sounds from Beneath* emerged as an artistic response to an invitation by an arts festival in Kent, South East England, to create a site-specific work. It orchestrates an aural reunion of a group of former coal miners in a disused colliery, and discovers a mode of voicing that responds to their professional specificity, charged with the political and historical dimensions of their community and culture.[2]

Kent was a place of intense coal mining activity, where local and migrant miners and their families lived, worked, and partook in the cultural and political life that characterized the mining community. With a rich industrial history from the time when coal played a primary role in British domestic and industrial heating, literally fuelling the socio-political and cultural life of the country, the Kentish landscape is marked by the radical urban, social and economic changes that have taken place in Britain since the mid-1980s. Lush green hills are punctuated by barren and disused collieries, vast shopping malls, former mining villages and their alienated regenerated versions. Since the dismantling of the coal mining industry in England, the Kentish coal mines have stood silent.

Despite the striking muteness of the empty pits, what is still audible – through the spoken memories of old ex-miners – is the generational passage of song and story in the vivid language of the miners, keeping account of their history and tradition, giving voice where official narratives and histories have denied it. Traces of such sounds and memories can still be heard in some village pubs and mining welfare clubs and choirs, where former colliers socialize and sing. But what sounds are specific to this community and how are they to be remembered? Are official language and ceremony adequate memory keepers of the miners, their resistance and culture?

An area of auditory culture where we encounter contrasting modes of vocal production is the expression of grief through official speeches or laments. Defeated by the state, the coal miners did not receive official praise, nor were they ceremonially mourned as they fell in combat with the state's interests. Official praise (through civic speech), and ceremonies (through religious or formal musical rituals) are vocal acts designed to introduce the fallen into the realms of glory and historical memory through language. Speeches have a role to play in managing public grief and suppressing expressions of resentment. In the case of fallen soldiers, who are sent by the state to the battlefield, ceremonies and speeches manage trauma and control rage, which may threaten public order. As vocal acts, they are essentially control strategies of public expressions of grief, giving articulate and restrained shape to sorrow. Civic speeches and formal rituals are experienced communally, overwhelming individual lament in its manifestation of despair, trauma and fury at the cause of harm, and they subdue the potential of lament to lead to reciprocal violence which could subsequently shake the stability of the state and challenge its leadership.

As Gail Holst-Warhaft observes in her study of traditional ritual laments practised by women in Greece and across other parts of the world, lamenting has often been suppressed and antagonized by official authorities due to its open expression of personal anger at the cause of death, and its refusal to acquiesce with the state's demand for men to die in its defence (1992: 121–26). Ethnographic studies and film projects such as Cecilia Mangini's *Stendalì: Suonano Ancora* (1960) indicate that laments operate outside official language; they inhabit the marginal space of dialect and idiom, and include extra-lingual vocal gestures such as shouts, sighs, cries and sobs, as well as vocalizations which imitate animals.[3] Laments present personal narratives that summarize the dead relatives' lives and the emotional impact of their loss. While official national mourning finds expression in articulate vocal acts which assert the state's authority over death, and insist that posthumous glory outweighs private grief, inspiring new generations to fight for a state that glorifies its fallen in a uniform comradeship beyond physical defeat, laments are infused by a logic of care that privileges birth and makes an enemy of the cause of death. Operating beyond official language, laments are examples of vocal production, which not only express the preservative role of love and oppose the military function of the body and destruction of life, they also subvert language itself. They present a demilitarized conception of language, human life and the body.

There is a conflict of interests inherent in any attempt to make official civic speech a memory-keeper of the miners, for it would transform into partisan propaganda either by rendering heroic the miners' resistance to the state or by under-emphasizing its impact. Yet, it also presents the female practice of laments as a model of voicing loss, which exists outside official language and shakes its authority. If there is to be a mode of vocal production that expresses the narrative of accomplishments and disempowerment of the miners, it must transcend official civic speech and gain the subversive dynamics and challenging power of women's laments, while expressing the miners' cultural specificity.

On the issue of identifying the sounds that are specific to the mining community, my field research for *Sounds from Beneath* revealed some stark facts. In my exploration of the region of Kent, I visited local pubs and mining welfare clubs where old miners gather to socialize. In 2010, at the back of Snowdown Colliery Welfare Club, I discovered a choir of elderly former miners who regularly rehearse, in a large barrel-shaped dance-hall, a repertoire that ranges from miners' anthems to Broadway songs – the former singing of past strength and the miner's hardships, the latter offering light entertainment. This vast gap in content and sentiment in the choir's repertoire is a poignant signifier of the alienation and abrupt interruption of the miners' choral tradition, which was entwined with their workplace and the union. Sung outside work and recounting past narratives, the choir's mining songs are temporally disconnected from the present and from the current context of the former miners' lives.

Beyond the choir's mining songs, however, the work of the collier was itself sonorous, as was the working mine with its powerful soundscape of excavating the earth. From the rumble of subterranean explosions to the scratching of shovels, each part of the coal mining process was sonically distinct, making sound practice the by-product of the miner's labour. The soundscape of the mine formed a profession-specific noise composition, which followed the rhythms of the working day. Its noise connected the miners' labour with their worksite, producing an aural signifier of the mining community, identity and profession.

Although mining sounds have stopped resounding in the Kentish collieries, they still exist in the aural memories of former miners. In my search for sounds specific to their community, I collaborated with Snowdown Colliery Choir and invited them to recall and vocalize the sounds they used to hear in the mines. In a subsequent film entitled *Sounds from Beneath*, the choir sing noises that evoke the coal mine standing in the disused Tilmanstone Colliery near Dover. Mechanical clangs, whirring engines, wailing alarms, subterranean blasts, scratching, hissing and whistling vocalized by the men reanimate the empty pits. Detached from their original source and emanating from the aging bodies of the miners in the colliery, these noises re-establish a connection between the labour of mining and the body, site and memory, humans with the earth and machines. Their song presents the men with a reason to come together again and transforms the desolate site into an amphitheatre of communal remembering, forming a subjective and site-specific record of former activity and community. These are not sounds as they used to resound across the mine in the past; they are aural recollections as they exist in the embodied present, marked by the texture of the half-remembered and of time passing. In their abstract vocalizations, their hisses, growls and gasps, the miners unearth a suppressed memory of loss and compose a re-collective lament outside the confines of language, both resisting social inaudibility and resonating beyond the silence of vanished industrial architectures.

Notes on the film Sounds from Beneath

The film *Sounds from Beneath* (Figure 6.1) is edited following a sonic structure. Accompanied by a silent soundtrack which does not direct the viewer's attention to sounds emanating from a specific part of the moving image, the film begins with

FIGURE 6.1 *Sounds from Beneath*, 2011–12, video still. © Mikhail Karikis and Uriel Orlow.

a panoramic view of a yellow horizon blossoming below an ominous charcoal sky and overwhelming a barren foreground. This seemingly distracted gaze lingers for several seconds before an explosive sound abruptly interrupts the silence and blanks the screen; it extinguishes the filmic image to a black sequence until a slow fade-in reveals a close-up of the rugged terrain of the former colliery.

This is what we are here to really look at, and sound is our guide; it choreographs the filmic sequence, directing our visual experience and attention. The next time we hear the same explosive sound, at thirty-four seconds, we see its actual source – a group of elderly former colliers standing in the desolate windswept landscape of the disused colliery, singing noises and rhythms excavated from the depths of their memories and the landscape, echoing a culture and livelihood that are lost but not forgotten.

SeaWomen: an eco-feminist song

While visiting Seoul in South Korea in 2011, I was encouraged by a local to visit the isle of Jeju: a small patch of black volcanic land which belongs to South Korea, and floats in the North Pacific between China and Japan. Since then, Jeju has become the destination of numerous research trips to develop the project *SeaWomen*, a large-scale sound and video installation focusing on the work and aural sub-culture of a vanishing community of native elderly female sea labourers called *haenyeo*.

My first encounter with the *haenyeo* was auditory. Driving along the rocky coast of Jeju, I heard an extraordinary series of sounds wafting out from the sea; interwoven high-pitched whistles resembling bird-calls, or perhaps dolphin or seal noises. The sounds were coming from the horizon, where a small pod of black animated creatures moved in and out of the water. As they swam closer, I realized I was observing humans, having originally thought them to be seals because of their black rubber wetsuits. Their ambiguous creature-like sounds were coupled with a gender ambiguity created by their uniform diving suits and masks. Reaching the coast, their aquatic agility gave way to a limited terrestrial mobility, as they emerged clumsily out of the water revealing their weathered facial features and carrying heavy baskets loaded with shells. Who were these divers, why were they only women, and why were they all elderly? What were the extraordinary sonorities they produced and what was their purpose?

Operating outside the currents of modernization, the *haenyeo* (literally meaning sea women in Korean) are an ancient and fast-diminishing community that now consists predominantly of 60- to 90-year-old women who dive to depths of up to twenty metres with no oxygen supply to catch seafood, collect seaweed, and find pearls. This is a gendered profession, practised only by females. The limited research that exists on the subject and interviews I conducted suggest several reasons for this. A physiological explanation is the distribution of fat in women's bodies, which insulates them better than male bodies against the cold and allows them to stay in the sea for as long as eight hours even during the coldest winter months. Anne Hilty (2013) identifies a cultural reason for the exclusive female engagement in this profession to be the Korean attitude towards exposing the flesh and nudity, which was (and still is) considered to be degrading, and was reserved for poor women of low social status; before the introduction of the rubber wetsuit, the women divers worked half-naked covering mainly their genitals with white cloth. Thus, the profession of the *haenyeo* was a social stigma (Hilty 2013). A socio-political factor which contributed to the growth of this women-only profession, paradoxically, is the sexism in Confucian law, which, until the beginning of the last century prevented these women from working and did not recognize female labour, excluding the *haenyeo* from taxation. Thus, the diving women engaged in a low-status profession and worked against the will of the state, but brought their entire income back home.

I observed *haenyeo* dive up to eighty times a day. Each dive lasts up to two minutes and is punctuated by a combination of sounds, including a high-pitched breathy whistle, shrieks, grunts and sudden wheezing. These are arguably spontaneous non-verbal vocal gestures bursting out of the mouth, which one might mistake for sea mammal or bird calls. The diving women make a living by constantly nego-tiating the limits of that which sustains them: their breath. At once alarming and joyous, their sounds form the rugged edge of an auditory blade that marks the horizon between life and death. But the *haenyeo* come prepared. They are equipped with the *sumbisori* – an ancient breathing technique, which has been practised for centuries, and passed on from one generation to the next.

In a local museum on Jeju Island dedicated to the *haenyeo*, a display caption explains that the physiology of the *sumbisori* entails the control of nitrogen levels, exhaling rapidly the carbon dioxide accumulated in the body, and quickly inhaling fresh oxygen. The lungs of the *haenyeo* shrink from the pressure in the depths, and hungry for air when the diver resurfaces, they expand, causing a violent inhalation and a wheezing gasp. This "official" explanation does not provide any real clarification on the breathing technique of the *haenyeo* and the shape of the women's mouths. Also, it does not confirm my visual observations of the women's oral behaviour; I noticed that they produced certain high-pitched sounds by parting their lips and rolling them over their teeth while exhaling. In addition, my encounter with a born-deaf *haenyeo* on the island, who did not generate the full range of *sumbisori* sounds, led me to question the seemingly direct connection between the women's breathing technique and the sounds they produce, and doubt the pure physiological necessity of the latter.

The *sumbisori* with its aural production is a work skill – a specific craft which a *haenyeo* learns as a young girl and requires years to perfect. Practised only by women and passed on from an older diver to a younger, this is a gender-specific vocal skill that is trans-generationally transmitted, creating an inter-generational aural bond that connects the community and functions as a sonic signifier of professional identity.

Certain *sumbisori* sounds occupy high frequencies above the sonorities of the noise of the sea and are easily identifiable acoustically. The *haenyeo* hear them above water even when their visibility is restricted due to condensation in their masks, fog or high waves. Therefore, when at work in the sea, the sounds of the *haenyeo* could be said to function as aural signals and acoustic location markers that keep each diver within hearing distance and within their group. Also, to the trained ear, each woman's *sumbisori* has a distinctive sound – a unique acoustic signature produced in the individual mouth and body of each diver.

Beyond the function of its sounds, the subtlety of the word *sumbisori* reveals a further layer of meaning. As Jeju *haenyeo* researcher Dr Cha Hye Kyoung (Cha 2012) explained in an interview, the word *sumbisori* – which may literally be translated as the vocal sound of breath – is parallel to that of "overcoming." What did the *haenyeo* "overcome"? Dr Cha explained that in the last century the *haenyeo* community led the anti-Japanese resistance movement on the island and witnessed a large loss of the male population after the end of Japanese rule, when American and South Korean forces massacred those suspected of supporting reunification with North Korea.[4] Any form of commemoration or memory of this event was suppressed by punishment and the destruction of physical sites. It is impossible to verify the sounds the *haenyeo* produced before this incident, but the connection between this traumatic event, its systematic removal from official memory and the dimension of "overcoming" the word *sumbisori* evokes is deeply meaningful. In this light, the sounds of the *sumbisori* become charged with the expression of trauma and suffering. Its sonorities transform into a complex cultural sound-object that is the product of a subculture operating within a particular political, geographical and historical specificity. The *sumbisori* is impregnated with the potential to operate as a vocal marker of a historical event and a non-verbal transmitter of memory, of resistance, and of rising above difficult circumstances.

Recent statistics reveal that the *haenyeo* community, which comprised thirty-thousand women forty years ago, is now on the brink of disappearance.[5] Through interviews with the women divers and local researchers on Jeju Island, I discovered that in the 1970s the *haenyeo* were the leading economic force on the island, creating a social system in which women occupied prominent roles – a glimpse of matriarchy in an otherwise patriarchal Korean society. But the scale of fishing has since changed radically, while the women still insist on traditional and sustainable (and for some, eco-feminist) practices outside capitalist trends and mainstream industrialization. In addition, the *haenyeo* assert that water pollution and the warming of the seas have diminished pearl oysters, sea-life and, by extension, their profits. Reduced proceeds and occupational hazards (such as drowning after getting entangled in stray fishing nets adrift in the Pacific) prevent their profession from being a career choice for the younger generation. Currently, there are no encouraging economic initiatives on a national level that could transform the future of the profession and provide the right incentives for younger women to join it. Consequently, the work of the *haenyeo* and their culture are disappearing.

It is hard to envisage the aural practices of the *haenyeo* community, which form a unique sonic subculture interconnected with skill, without their professional practice. The vanishing sounds of the *sumbisori* (as well as *haenyeo* work songs, the ebbs and flows of their debates, noises of communal cooking and bathing, and other sonic events generated by the divers in and around their camps) make little sense divorced from the women's sustainable work and community. However, as I observed and worked around the *haenyeo*, I realized that their example proposes a model of existence that reverses traditional gender roles, nurtures a deep sense of community, practises egalitarianism and democratic debate, self-organizes collective economics, cultivates a professional identity and celebrates a unique sense of purpose in later age.

As each inhalation is followed by an exhalation, the work practised by the sea women of Jeju is in a state of perpetual incompletion – a dual movement of possession and dispossession, of a "within" and a "without." This is being. Being negotiating a vacuum. Becoming filled and becoming empty. This is what the sound of the *sumbisori* suggests – becoming full of oxygen and life, and letting go of life. Like being pregnant and giving birth, holding the mysteries of labour and life bearing.

In the end, in my search to find the meaning of the whistling "nonsense" sounds I had heard wafting out from the Pacific Ocean surrounding this volcanic island, I heard the diving grandmothers of Jeju making a kind of noise that operates beyond language and is created within a local work context that challenges the mainstream of globalization and mechanization. In their sounds, I heard an ancient craft and a trans-generational bond, a cultural sound-object and an aural transmitter of memory and resistance. I heard an acoustic signature of a community and of a professional identity, its fun and its purpose. The sounds of the *haenyeo* form a trans-vocal sonic composition of a self-organized community. This rich aural subculture is what I heard before I even began to enter the semantic level of their linguistic vocal exchanges and the actual meanings of each word they utter in their local dialect. The profound cultural depth and socio-political dimensions of this sound raise questions about the hegemony of speech within the political realm – this "nonsense" sound *is* politics.

Notes on SeaWomen *the audio-visual installation*

Unlike *Sounds from Beneath*, which orchestrated a vocal performance captured during a day-long filming session and includes little other footage from previous site visits, *SeaWomen* (Figure 6.2) entailed several trips to Jeju Island. It required several weeks of filming and sound recording, which were unrehearsed and followed the work rhythms of the *haenyeo*, the tides and the wind. The visual footage with which I returned was several hours long and had the feel of an ethnographic film, yet I was not on an ethnomusicological field trip. My sound recordings captured previously unrecorded aspects of the women's work noises and aural culture, but often, sonically significant sections did not coincide with visually interesting or informative material. The relationship between sound and moving image was therefore radically different from the way sound challenges the image in *Sounds from Beneath*, forming a close audio-visual connection as well as a conflict. *SeaWomen* required different treatment.

The final work features an immersive twelve-speaker sound environment of Jeju field recordings, composed and divided into distinct aural episodes (*sumbisori* sounds, work songs, the noises of communal bathing, for example), which are distributed across the space in a configuration resembling a large (sonic) ship. In addition, the work consists of a silent film that is not of the same duration as the sound, and is also divided into different chapters (such as the *haenyeo* preparing to go to work on

FIGURE 6.2 *SeaWomen*, 2012, video still. © Mikhail Karikis.

a boat, underwater diving, communal cooking, or women selling seafood on rocks). In its installation, the work mirrors the mystery of my first encounter with the *haenyeo*; it choreographs a spatial experience in which the women's intriguing soundscape is heard before the viewer discovers the moving images that may anchor the sounds to the women's bodies. Sound and film operate in close proximity, inform one another and collaborate to produce an overall audio-visual experience. Yet, they are independent from each other; sound and image are out of synch, rupturing any expectation of ethnographic "facts" or documentary "truths" by making the observer aware of the disconnection inherent in the constructed representation of another's culture.

Notes

1 The quartet of projects includes *Xenon: An Exploded Opera* (2010–11), commissioned by the Whitstable Biennale, UK; *Sounds from Beneath* (2010–12), presented at Manifesta 9: The European Biennial of Contemporary Art (2011); *SeaWomen* (2012), exhibited in *Aquatopia* at Tate St Ives (2013–14), among other museums; *Children of Unquiet* (2013–14), produced at the Devil's Valley in Tuscany, Italy and featured at the 19th Biennale of Sydney (2014). See also Connor, Gregos, Jones and Reynolds (2011) and Hilty, Karikis, Smyth and Toop (2013).
2 An excerpt can be viewed online: https://vimeo.com/49149095. My blog (Karikis 2010) contains further information on the making of *Sounds from Beneath*.

3 See: www.youtube.com/watch?v=vziV5npthaI.
4 This event is commemorated on Jeju Island as the April 3 Massacre, part of the Jeju Uprising which lasted from 3 April 1948 until May 1949. See Johnson (2004: 99–101).
5 The official numbers of active sea women on Jeju Island vary, but statistics are unanimous in presenting the dramatic decrease of their population. A recent article in *The Guardian* states a drop of 21,500 sea women in the last forty years, with 4,500 remaining divers (Radnor 2014).

References

Cage, J. (1979) *Empty Words*, Middleton, CT: Wesleyan.
Cavarero, A. (2005) *For More than One Voice: Toward a Philosophy of Vocal Expression*, trans. P.A. Kottman, Stanford: Stanford University Press.
Cha, H.K. (2012) Unpublished interview conducted by Mikhail Karikis.
Chion, M. (1994) *Audio-Vision: Sound on Screen*, trans. C. Gorbman, New York: Columbia University Press.
Connor, S., Gregos, K., Jones, S. and Reynolds, L. (2011) *Sounds from Beneath: Mikhail Karikis and Uriel Orlow*, London and Brussels: future perfect and Sub Rosa.
Hardt, M. and Negri, A. (2009) *Commonwealth*, Cambridge, MA: Harvard University Press.
Hilty, A. (2013) "Social enterprise and the indigenous model of mutual aid societies: a case study of Jeju Island," paper presented at UNITAR Jeju International Training Centre, Jeju Island, Republic of Korea.
Hilty, A., Karikis, M., Smyth, C. and Toop, D. (2013) *SeaWomen*, London: future perfect.
Holst-Warhaft, G. (1992) *Dangerous Voices: Women's Laments and Greek Literature*, New York: Routledge.
Johnson, C. (2004) *Blowback: The Costs and Consequences of American Empire*, New York: Owl Books.
Karikis, M. (2010) "Singing sounds from beneath," *Xenon: An Exploded Opera by Mikhail Karikis*, http://mikhailkarikis.blogspot.nl/2010/05/singing-sounds-from-beneath.html.
Mangini, C. (dir.) (1960) *Stendalì: Suonano Ancora*, www.youtube.com/watch?v=vziV5npthaI.
Radnor, A. (2014) "Picture of the week: the sea woman of Jeju, by Jean Chung," *The Guardian*, www.theguardian.com/artanddesign/2014/jul/04/sea-woman-jeju-jean-chung-photography.

7

PERFORMING THE *ENTRE-DEUX*

The capture of speech in (dis)embodied voices[1]

Piersandra Di Matteo

> The voice responds to what is said,
> but it cannot be responsible for it
> [*La voix répond à ce qui se dit,*
> *mais elle ne peut pas en répondre*]
>
> (Lacan 2004: 318)

Capturing speech

To speak of the word uttered and listened to is to conjure up theatre and the spotlight, the place where the spoken word is staged, the place devoted to the staging of speech. The theatrical metaphor permeates the discourse of Michel De Certeau and all his reflections on language (the language of possession – mystical and glossolalic – inherent in pedestrian rhetoric). The *capture of speech* is used by De Certeau (1998) to come to grips with the topological dimension of the event of language and its political nature. It signals a commencement, a cue for pronunciation that sets up and circumscribes *a space for speaking* wherein what matters is not principally the communicative content, or *who* is speaking, but rather the posture taken in speaking and the *place* from which something is spoken.

The topology of speech – with which the actor is most crucially concerned – makes it necessary to analyse the speaking subject and the modalities and morphologies of his or her presence, penetrating into the *sense effects* produced by the performer's utterance. The effort is to come to grips with the performer's representation as a "speaking I." But this horizon seeks to move into the body of discourse and into its spatial configurations and resonances, turning to the concreteness of the subject's flesh, of his or her phonatory organs – the larynx, the vocal cords, the lungs, the diaphragm and the mouth. The *capture of speech* thus makes it necessary to pay heed to the paradoxical dimension of voice, situated in the *entre-deux* between body and language, at once here and elsewhere, and at the same time at the intersection (chiasmus) with the world (the scene).

This *entre-deux* contemplates the interstices of speech with discourse as a *vocalic entity*;[2] an entity that desacralizes the Western idea of a devocalized *logos* (Cavarero 2005) and focuses on the *grain of the voice*, the "materiality of the body which emerges from the throat [...] where the phonic metal hardens and takes shape" (Barthes 1985: 255). The quivering of a throat in the flesh is the bodily wellspring from which flows the tactility and urgency of breathing. These are forces anterior to the construction of language; forces which resound in the child's preverbal echolalia but subside through language acquisition (Heller-Roazen 2008).

To look at theatre from the perspective of the capture of speech is to also take into account a space textured with preverbal sounds, tics, the sounds of the body and the glottis, as well as with borborygmi, hemming and hawing, coughing, muffled grumblings and stammers. These are ways by which to pierce through and puncture language with "tattoos on the process of phonation" (De Certeau 1986: 50), which on this level have nothing to do with the articulation of meaning. The voice – understood not as a signifying power but as sound – is enriched by the respiratory and bodily sources active in the language, and by encoding specific dimensions of corporeality, it traces words back to the physical events which give them life. The voice is thus always written by the body. Closely bound up with the place of utterance, the voice is the art of guiding the body. As a result of rhythmic-nervous excitement, the vibrations of the vocal folds produce sound emissions from the nasal–oral cavity, in close connection with the entire body. Every gesture, including vocal gesture, is supported by posture, which is muscular, visceral and related to the bodily orifices. The primary of these is the mouth, a mobile resonator that can change form, so as to enable the emissions to undergo timbre morphing. Yet sound also depends, among other things, on the labouring of the epiglottis, on the contractions of the diaphragm and on the way the tongue slaps against the teeth.

The voice spreads through the air and penetrates the ear, the monitoring centre that channels the rhythms of the sound vibrations and the distances between them. To listen to a voice is to perceive a body in motion, with its cavities, its mucous membrane and cartilage, its intra-muscular play, the empty and full spaces in the passage from the inside to the outside and *vice versa*. The voice implies *hearing*: it *is* hearing. According to Jean-Luc Nancy (2007: 9), who distinguishes listening, hearing and understanding, listening can be regarded as our understanding of the *spacing* of resonance: listening is therefore at the same time a referral (*renvoi*) between bodies.

In the *entre-deux* between body and language

Reflecting on the "absolute performative," in the footsteps of J.L. Austin's speech–act theory, Paolo Virno argues that "the ceremony of voice, or taking the floor to speak, makes the speaker visible as *bearer* of the power of speech";[3] to this, he adds that "the voice [...], by symbolizing the power of speech, ensures that the particular living body in which this power inheres is fully exposed to the gaze of others"

(2003: 44). It is precisely on this "power of speech" and on this "being exposed" that I intend to dwell, analysing some theatrical cases drawn from the history of the Socìetas Raffaello Sanzio. In so doing, I proceed from an assumption Mladen Dolar sets out in *A Voice and Nothing More*:

> What language and the body have in common is the voice, but the voice is part neither of language nor of the body. The voice stems from the body, but is not its part, and it upholds language without belonging to it, yet, in this paradoxical topology, this is the only point they share.
>
> *(2006: 73)*

The voice – both as a bodily *event* and as the *exposition* of that event – is the gesture which exhibits the relational uniqueness of being, which each time restages itself towards the other. As an *event* that *from one moment to the next* is now, an event at once here and lost somewhere else, the voice also makes possible the unsettling experience of *listening to oneself*, recalling the perceptive chiasmus that places the voice at the same time inside and outside the subject. A well-known argument has been made by Barthes in this regard, underscoring that the familiar antipathy we sense upon hearing our own voice is connected with the fact that the voice, "reaching us after traversing the masses and cavities of our own anatomy, [...] affords us a distorted image of ourselves" (1985: 255).

But the topological paradox Dolar is talking about refers to something more specific:

> The voice is the flesh of the soul, its ineradicable materiality, by which the soul can never be rid of the body; it depends on this inner object which is but the ineffaceable trace of externality and heterogeneity, but by virtue of which the body can also never quite simply be the body, it is a truncated body, a body cloven by the impossible rift between an interior and an exterior. The voice embodies the very impossibility of this division, and acts as its operator.
>
> *(2006: 71)*

It is precisely the complex nature of the "impossibility of this division" that resounds in the questions that Norie Neumark articulates:

> How do voices relate to bodies and subjectivity – how do voices speak to, from and of embodied subjects? What happens to embodied voice when it is mediated? How do voices speak of alterity – performing intersubjectively, and sounding out the physical, affective, signifying and psychic spaces between subjects?
>
> *(Neumark, Gibson and van Leeuwen 2010: xv)*

Starting out from these premises, the performances I analyse make explicit this ineradicable materiality where the voice lies: in an interspace *between* flesh and emptiness, between the corporeality of speech and discourse, between anatomy and culture, the subject and the other. These are cases that do not enact a "normal voice," but in a way bear a connection to the idea of dysfunction or the limit-points of a "clinical" voice. That point can be argued in light of the reflections offered by Gilles Deleuze, especially in the introduction to his last collection of essays (1997). Here Deleuze, having established a close link between language and delirium, frees the notion of *delirium* from the ideological trap-lines of the pathological, taking us on a foray into literature as that which lies at the limit of language, where language shows itself to be capable of leading to a *barbaric point*, with the creation of *a foreign language within your own language*, "a foreign language as a whole in turn being toppled or pushed to a limit, to an outside or reserve side that consists of Visions and Auditions that no longer belong to any language" (1997: 5). In this respect, in the machinery of speech, these cases are not mere deficiencies but are a part of the information conveyed through that machinery, testifying to the body's inherent role in the making of language, as well as to the rootedness of language within the body.

It is useful, by way of a contextual framing, to recall that over the course of 20th-century theatre, voice assumed a role of primary importance in breaking the conventions of text and representation. As emerges from the collection of essays *Teatri di Voce* (Amara and Di Matteo 2010), this development unfolded along two main lines. On the one hand, there is the work done by the line of theatre directors and trainers who have explored the idea of "vocal exercise," understood as an essential debate between the actor and the character in preparation and training; this can be appreciated in the work of Stanislavskij and Copeau, as well as in Decroux's "vocal mime," Grotowski and Odin Teatret. On the other hand – building on the work of Antonin Artaud, and running parallel to that of German expressionists and the *Der Sturm* group in the *Wortkunst* and the *Workunstwerk* – was the genealogy of practices that instead developed through a series of experiences, including the shout of the Living Theatre, the anti-Oedipal *desiring machines* of Carmelo Bene's *phone* theatre, and the experimentation on language, voice and speech in the theatre of the Socìetas Raffaello Sanzio.

The Socìetas Raffaello Sanzio, conventionally defined as visual theatre, reinvestigates the biological, physiological and conceptual value of language. It is a theatre whose primary achievement I would locate in problematizing, with sustained and equal emphasis, our being bearers of discourse; the topology of (the actor's) speech; the unveiling of the rhetorical devices of language; the word's sound-thought and its acoustical deception; and discourse as a sound clot, as expectoration, internal chomping on the word, pure emission of sound raised to the *false language* that within itself condenses all of the earth's peoples in a telluric scream, the alphabet dissolved into a blot or transformed into a shapeless object.

What is the invention of the *Generalissima* language if not a way to reset our preconstructed language to zero so as to enable the *faculté de langage* to emerge? *Generalissima* is an artificial language coined in 1984 by the Socìetas Raffaello Sanzio, and recently adapted to a changed iconographic, thematic and gestural context for the 2014 performance titled *Uso Umano di Esseri Umani* (The Human

Use of Human Beings). *Generalissima* was forged by combining a crossover study done on Creole languages that came into being in the 18th and 19th centuries – pidgins created by the child slaves transported to the Caribbean, the Hawai'ian islands, the Antilles, the areas around the Indian Ocean where people were coerced into mixed communities – with the *Ars Magna*, a universal language that Raimondo Lullo conceived in the 14th century on a numerological basis. *Generalissima* – composed of four hundred all-embracing terms sorted into semantic groups – is a layered language that slides along a series of increasingly abstract levels of comprehension: it is structured on four cognitive "leaps," starting out from everyday language and growing increasingly abstract until it reaches the highest and purest level – composed of only four words (*Agone*, *Apotema*, *Meteora*, *Blok*). *Generalissima* is intended to exhaustively account for all phenomena, using a progressive and ever-more-essential process of reduction. The language set out in this way can reduce all phenomena, even the most mysterious, to articulations dominated by language (Calchi-Novati 2009: 59–62).

Emblematic in this respect is the *intra-phonic* or *controversial* technique the Socìetas Raffaello Sanzio deployed in the 1987 performance *I Miserabili* (*Les Misérables*). This technique is based, not on sending the voice *out*, but on drawing it *in*; the voice ends up being significantly hampered in revealing itself semantically, partly because of the actors' constricting poses (such as having a noose coiled around the neck). A significant character in this logo-clasm is the "word eater," caught in the attempt to swallow a long monologue. The *controversial* vocal technique was used in ancient Egypt to distinguish truth from lying on the basis of intonation alone, and its use is a way to shift the focus *from what* is uttered *to how* it is uttered: it is a way to shift our attention to tonality and prosody, understood as a prerequisite to the vocal utopia of speaking. This has more to do with the primal act of making sounds than with communicating specific words.

The body without the organ (without vocal cords)

In the subsequent phase, *Epopea della Polvere* (Epic of the Dust, 1992–99) – a cycle aimed at deconstructing the "traditions of Western drama" – the Socìetas Raffaello Sanzio set out to deactivate all textual representation, questioning the idea of theatrical tradition as the staging of a preexisting theatrical text. From the outset, this theatre reclaimed the right to abandon the customary meaning of language. These theatrical experiments unhinge every practice by which the dramatic text is illustrated, and, for this reason, the spectator is not placed before a chromatic layout, luminescent and made plastic with presences subjected to a "mimetic regime." Rather, this theatre starts out from a quest for a presence (be it a human figure, an animal, a light, a machine) that is primarily corporeal: "the body as a pure communicable entity" (Castellucci 1997a: 23).[4] In this sense, Romeo Castellucci, founding director of the company, claimed that "matter [...] is the ultimate reality that sees its extremes in the breath of a newborn and the flesh of a cadaver" (Castellucci *et al.* 2001: 271).

In Shakespeare's plays and in Aeschylus's *Oresteia*, the word *exits* the stage cut up by the scalpel of philological dissection so as to open a clearing for itself in the truth of the body. In *Amleto: La Veemente Esteriorità della Morte di un Mollusco* (Hamlet: The Vehement Externalism of a Mollusc's Death, 1992), the explosion of the scene's matrixed corporeality coincides with the working out of strategies by which the verbal uttering of an autistic Hamlet is led back to an almost aphasic language. *Amleto* densifies a score of signs, gestures, sound events and noises through which the Shakespearean verbal dictate is derailed towards a plurivocality resounding with the echo of a text that no longer exists. Words are transformed into matter, absorbed by all the elements of action, whether they be the lacerating or microscopic gestures or shrieks of the only actor on stage, his long silences, deafening revolver shots, the phantom parents' tomb-box, or the lighting produced within eyeshot by the electrical generators. Unequivocal in this regard are the words spoken by Castellucci:

> The word had this bulkiness, corresponding to the weight of a body, but we didn't take this as a reason to work on effacing the text. On the contrary, we worked for depth until the text could be reabsorbed. Where the text has been effaced, it comes back in a phantasmic form, the form of an unconscious dream, of aesthetic choice.
>
> *(2000: 100)*

The text is molecularized, in collusion with a series of corporeal manifestations: bubbling with saliva and spitting, burping and choking up, breaking wind and even simulating diarrhoea by using "a large clyster syringe loaded with a mixture of water, barley and flour" (Castellucci et al. 2001: 38). The voice, characterized by agrammatical markers, is embedded in the superarticulatory space of the infantile echolalia rooted in the biological. Hamlet keeps quiet, screams, emits sounds and a few scattered words, and finally sings the *Victimae Paschali Laudes*, a Gregorian chant still recited in the solemnness of Easter. Despite the deep difficulties autistic subjects experience in articulating themselves in meaningful ways, they can often utter entire sequences by memory, sometimes prayers, manifesting themselves as phonological eruptions with which the silence is broken (Ramaglia and Pezzana 2004: 12–27). In his dying scene, Hamlet loudly utters his salvific song, compulsive and litaneutical. His sudden ability to articulate, his familiarity with voids between phonemes, reveals the speaking subject's *potentia loquendi* as an act by which the language is set on new foundations: it is resurrected. Virno (2003) sets up a relation between religious modes of pronouncement and the child's egocentric language, with its peculiar traits, those on which depend the formation of self-consciousness and the principle of individuation, both indissolubly bound up with the processes of vocalization. It all happens through a voice which starts out by whispering, mumbling, swallowing and stuttering – a voice deformed into a salivary lump by coughing, laryngeal flooding and internal mastication of the word – and which is then articulated in an automatic, disembodied giving forth with words. What comes into shape here is the linguistic tension of the siege universe into which Hamlet, autistic and aphasic, has withdrawn.

In *Orestea (una Commedia Organica?)* (Oresteia [an Organic Comedy?], 1995), this somatic dimension of discourse is fleshed out and layered through technological instrumentations making it possible to musically and conceptually enter into words, modifying their pitch and intensity, the rhythm and duration of the syllables, the tics, the nuances of timbre and cadences. The strategy consists in defining characters through the acoustics of their verbal emissions, which from a dramaturgical stand-point, take on substantial weight. Instruments with which to synthesize voices deform the emitted sound to make it seem as if the speaking was done by the characters' wraiths: Athena's voice is the summational outcome of compounding the voices of a child, a woman and an old man. The voice of the Coryphaeus Rabbit is that of a eunuch, and that of Clytemnestra is made masculine by drastically altering its pitch.

In another pivotal work from *Epopea della Polvere*, *Giulio Cesare* (Julius Caesar, 1997), which draws on Shakespeare and Roman historians, the voice presents itself as a vector of *linguistic erosion*. It enacts tactics that scalp the dramatic text with vocal blows, to the point where the textual material is reduced to stigmata on the body:

> Hammering, hammering, hammering the text until it expands: The text needs to be heated up by hammering it in the reading of it, and this hammering opens some pathways that on a first reading, a specialistic reading, or an intellectual reading cannot be opened. Only through obsession is it possible to open otherwise noncommunicating paths.
>
> *(Castellucci* et al. *2001: 272)*

This hammering – also intended to derail "the name of the Father" (the Author) with its normative import (the dramatic text) – is literally embodied in the characters " … vskij" and Mark Antony, who in the performance face each other in a stance of clear mutual engagement. These are icastic images of a true drama of the voice. The entire performance is a take on the theme of power, when cloaked by the word's persuasive force. The topology of speech (of the actor), the pre-eminence of the language and of its corporeal machines, and the relation between rhetoric and acting are set in a polarity having the form of a cast and a print. At the centre of this polarity lies the body with its locutionary organs in a prominent role.

Giulio Cesare opens with the character " … vskij" – a diminutive name alluding to Stanislavskij. An explicit relation is set up between the forefather of Western theatre and Cicero, the master of rhetoric, embodied on stage by an overweight actor whose face is hidden behind a latex mask that erases his facial features. This deformed physiognomy is revealed only once another mask, with a duck beak, is removed. This allusion to the relationship between classic rhetoric and theatre highlights that in method and composition, the classical rhetorical happenings pertaining to *the action* are assimilated into acting, with the rhetorician proposing a modulated use of the voice with alternating tones, timbres and rhythmic registers associated with a system of gestures, postures and behaviours. In *Giulio Cesare*, the text (the diegesis, the logic of events as they unfold) is eroded and made to coincide with "the mode of doing, of acting in front of and for the others" (Castellucci 1997b). In this rebuttal, Castellucci shows how the semantic sphere in (Shakespearian) texts can be rhythmicized, working exclusively towards an *intractable act* that absorbs the word's corporeal material so as to thwart it.[5]

The character " ... vskij" inserts an endoscope up his nasal cavity towards the glottis. The path taken by the endoscope is projected onto a circular screen so that the audience can follow the journey of the voice, all the way back to the vocal folds. The large circular projection behind the figure marks the physical origin of the voice caught in the act of the spoken dialogue among Flavius, Marullus and the cobbler – a voice issuing from a single source, but not monological in form. The spectator is confronted with the tautological entity of a voice overlapped with the visible vibrations from the oral cavity, with its obscene shape (literally a *boccascena*). The suggestion of the vagina is quite evident in its philological matrix: *os, oris*, which in Latin means "orifice," "mouth," "origin." Here the actor is the "*uterus expositus* of the theatrical word" (Castellucci 1990: 25), and it is the biological and anatomical source of the voice that has itself become the main character.

Later on in the performance, Mark Antony enters and makes his way to a marmoreal podium, a rhetorician's pulpit, on which the word "*Ars*" is engraved. Dalmazio Masini, who embodies Mark Antony, has had a laryngectomy. His speaking is affected by painful syncopations in his breathing, producing an anxious rhythm marked by tired pauses. This alternative phonatory technique challenges his speech both acoustically and semantically. Here, the voice produced by a laryngeal mutilation is an oesophageal pulsation. Shakespeare's famous funeral oration literally coincides with the body speaking from the gut. This tattooed speech affects an oration with a *vocal delinquency* (De Certeau 1996: 33). It is uttered without the throat; it issues from a "wound," the only organ capable of bearing the story of the body of Julius Caesar transfixed by "speechless mouths."[6] The Shakespearean text is picked apart until the textual matter is reduced to its pithiest, to the soma, so as to make it possible to authentically dive into the dramatic and rhetorical matter of speech.

This throatless speaking, with its accompanying gesturing, becomes the exoskeleton of rhetorical persuasion, while the discourse issuing from *a body without its organ* (the vocal cords; see Artaud 1976) becomes the banner signifying "an abjection of meaning," a body possessed of its own eloquence (De Certeau 1996: 30). This word, insufflated with breathing and entrails, digs into the corporeal roots of the human element, in its organic and pulsational matrix, carnally symbolized in "an 'I' overcome by the corpse" (Kristeva 1982: 25). In a negative theology of the voice, the hole through which Mark Antony's breathing might pass makes it possible to spy " ... vskij"'s throat, inverted in its absence.

The iconical mirror-image force of these two speeches, one being the cast for the other, prompted a revisitation of the complex original version of the performance, under the title *Giulio Cesare: Pezzi Staccati* (Julius Caesar: Spared Parts, 2014). In this partial reenactment, the speeches by " ... vskij" and Mark Antony are delivered with the actors facing each other directly, like two living nuclei. This version was first staged in the Aula Magna of the Bologna Academy of Fine Arts, a neoclassical Jesuit church whose walls are lined with an army of copies of Greek sculptures and neoclassical fragments, including a copy of Michelangelo's head of David and of parts of his Laocoön Group.[7] This performance is envisaged to abide in places closely resonant with the work's foundation, the drama of the voice in its rhetorical articulation.

A gurgling object voice

Focusing now on Castellucci's latest performances, this final case study takes on the themes and questions dealt with previously, but drives them to extremes. Having delved into the somatic voice "emanating from a body yet not quite being 'disembodied'" (Neumark, Gibson and van Leeuwen 2010: xvii), a voice caught between rhetorical signification and visceral pulsation, I now turn to an example of a voice-object located in the very heart of the body; uncontrollable, like a parasite, a foreign intruder represented as an object of "spectral autonomy" detached from the body (Dolar 2006: 70).

To this end, I will put another work by Castellucci under the magnifying glass. *The Four Seasons Restaurant* debuted at the Avignon Festival in 2012 and is the first of two recent productions drawing inspiration from the work of the German romantic poet Friedrich Hölderlin.[8] The first part of this production, which has also become a free-standing piece called *Giudizio Possibilità Essere* (Judgment Possibility Being, 2013), is set in a real gymnasium with climbing frames, basketball hoops and gymnastics equipment. The spectators are gathered on the high-jump mat in such a way that this place for athletics, a setting not (conventionally) suitable for theatre, is made into a space where the sense proper to the poet's words can resound in their displaced heresy and beauty.

The loud sound of a black hole recorded by NASA fills the stage while its textual description is projected. The following scene stages the act of cutting off tongues, a voluntary action done by ten female characters who seem to live in the gymnasium of a boarding school for girls. They perform this ritual mutilation either alone or in small groups, with gasping and recoiling gestures. A dog comes in and eats the severed tongues off the floor; these are actual pieces of meat that the actresses hold in their mouths and cut using actual large scissors. As Joe Kelleher suggests, this "singular act of decision (*decidere*: to cut off) involves a cutting away of each of us, an absolute separation of this from that, which cannot after be mended" (2014: 9). The echo of a bouncing ball is heard, and immediately, these young women, dressed in Amish outfits, set out to stage Hölderlin's unfinished dramatic poem "The Death of Empedocles." They are represented as capable of articulating intelligible speech by way of their "tongueless mouths." In a domain of explicit fictional credibility, the "tongueless speaking mouth" refers to the human speech apparatus, bringing out the paradoxical relation between the terms *language* (as poetry) and *tongue* (a particular manner of speaking). The poetic words are reborn and voiced through an extremely formalized score of gestures inspired by paintings and sculptures from the history of Western art. The girls deliver the dialogues of the play from the flesh of their throats, but we know that, symbolically, these vocalized words are sent forth from mutilated mouths (see "Aglossostomography" in Heller-Roazen 2008).

The characters in the play (Pausanias, Panthea, Critias, Hermocrates and the citizens of Agrigento) are distributed among the actresses, but by turns, when they crow wearing golden laurels, they embody Empedocles, speaking his text. Empedocles is Hölderlin's philosopher king, who at first is venerated but then falls from grace. Accused of having emulated the gods, he finally – like a deity – recedes from view, eschewing the mediation of politics and vanishing into Mount Etna.[9] This multivocal and scattered vocalization literally entrusts the scene to the figure of Empedocles as a subject who "*off-centered*, abandons his limited 'egoity' and sinks into the 'abyss' of the object, assuming an *aorgic* form" that coincides with the absolute fusion of nature in the crater of the volcano (Bodei 1994: 37).

While this presumptive gymnasium fills up with southern banners, pistols and Kalashnikovs (setting up an *analogon* between arms and language, a theme that weaves its way through the entire performance), the lines of text are uttered from the actresses' fleshy throats, announcing the presence of the body which bears the verses and situates them in the *vocalic space* "by echoing forward away from the body while also granting that body a sense of individuation" (LaBelle 2010: 149). As the action unfolds, something renders the psycho-acoustic temperature of the discourse ambiguous. The actresses begin to lip-sync their own voices, now being sent forth from a speaker, invisible to the spectator's gaze, hidden in their clothes but facing outward, as if the sounds originated from their bodies. In this auto-dubbing, the voice seems to issue from the figures moving their lips, but the sound of their voices – slightly unsynchronized – retains an unknown metallic and inorganic quality. The gap between the voice, the articulation of speech and the voice's singular belonging to the figure's body – an inappreciable time-shift – is made visible and audible. This device gives rise to an indecipherable perceptual confusion: Who is speaking? Where is the voice coming from, if it seems to originate precisely from that specific body with its tonal intonation, rhythm, timbre and cadence, appearing to coincide with the figure by which it is born?

An escalation of expropriation is then triggered. Following a series of statements, the actresses exchange voices with one another. One woman's voice comes from another who lip-syncs the words. At this point, the voice enacts a new quality of bodily presence, while revealing the difference between speaking the words and uttering them. The question of the capture of speech takes on a conspicuous role: the voices have hitherto been familiar to that body, in that a clear relationship of embodied belonging was established, but in the act of substitution and exchange, they convey a homely *habitus*. What matters is not just that the voice emanates *acoustically* from that body without coming *from* that body (or belonging to it) but that this shift winds up showing, contrariwise, what Cavarero (2005) considers to be the embodied "uniqueness" of every voice. No matter what the *content* of the utterance is, the vocalic relationality inevitably reveals the singularity by which individuals address one another.

In another passage, there is a voice with no moving lips. The actresses keep their mouths closed, yet the voice still comes from their "bodies" (through the hidden devices). The spectators witness a voice represented as if nobody were speaking: another occluded speaking mouth. But there is no sinking into the body and the entrails, only an ambiguous and uncanny image of (dis)embodiment. Therein lies the crucial point, since in addition to the voices not seeming to correspond to a speaking mouth, and the actresses not being represented as conveyers of language, the voice comes across as a spectral sound emanating and resonating from within that figure as an external/internal object.

After a collective "birthing," a ritual where the characters are each generated from one another, the girls take their clothes off, resembling the scene depicted in Masaccio's *The Expulsion from the Garden of Eden*, but with an inversion of meaning. Their clothes are on the floor. The spectators now witness a totally disembodied object voice: a gurgling voice coming from the speaking clothes. The girls' spatialized voice on the stage depicts a *dysprosody*, lacking any physical support, enacting a pure vocal pulsation with its hallucinatory charge. The appearance of an external ghostlike presence inhabits the scene, inflecting the gradual process by which the phonatory organs are undocked from the horizon of enunciation, and revealing a disincorporation of the voice as it proceeds in a de-objectifying process.

From Dolar's Lacanian perspective, the spectator can be said to be frontally facing "the properly traumatic dimension of the human voice, the human voice not as the sublime, ethereal medium for expressing the depth of human subjectivity, but the human voice as a foreign intruder" (2006: 70). Here, the bearer of language is totally *out of place*. The degrees of disembodiment reveal its obscene dimension and traumatic presence freely floating about. The women enact the disorienting experience of being *transformed into objects* by an autonomized voice, completely ghostly, revealing all its monstrous ungovernability as something Other than the voice. The problem lies not in the question of who the voice's fleshy owner might be, but in the fact that the voice does not belong to anyone. The voice offers resistance even at source, and it is structurally revealed to lie in the dimension of a loss. In other words, in *The Four Seasons Restaurant* and in *Giudizio Possibilità Essere*, a transformation can be witnessed whereby the voice of one subject becomes the voice of another, turning into the Other of the voice.

The "diapason subject" (Nancy 2007: 16–17), a repeating ringer of allusions and resonances, transitorily becomes an emblem denoting the *parasite parolier* (Lacan 2005: 95) – the wordsmith that Jacques Lacan speaks of in analysing the Joycean symptom – only to turn into a fading and expropriated subject. We can say, with Slavoj Žižek, that "here we encounter the Lacanian distinction between reality and the Real: this spectral voice which we hear in our interior reality, although it has no place in external reality, is the Real at its purest" (2009: 193).

A few closing thoughts

In the cases previously analysed, the core of the performative dimension coincides with a physiological event that moves along the body's inside/outside threshold and probes the ineradicable materiality of the voice even when it crosses out the subject as speaker. One cannot but appreciate that the voice in the *capture of speech* presents itself as a tactic by which to demystify the fictional vector of the *dramatis personae*, the traditional notion of the character as a bearer of discourse, all the while undermining the figure of the dramatic author (the Authority). It is a way to put an end to the hierarchical priority of the dramatic text in theatrical projects, a way to reclaim a space for discourse capable of embracing a "wandering of semantics" (De Certeau 1984: 102). Here, the words of the text collapse, not into nonsense, but into the bodies and into the "vocalic space" as theorized by Steven Connor (2000: 12). Speech, not easily graspable, is marked by moments of impediment in the flow of discourse. These moments are then understood as events that inform the body's performance, finding their place in the intermediate range between the exhibition of the act of speaking and the activation of the hermeneutic circle (the meaning of that which is said).

In *Giulio Cesare*, the voice is the tool for a spatialized semantic dissemination *into* the body, a manifestation of the *disconnect* between the utterance and that which is uttered, between the phonetic organs and the *fact of speaking*, which is the breaking of silence in the act of stating something. But in *The Four Seasons Restaurant*, the speaking subject is materialized by an autonomized *object voice*: this is the traumatic dimension of a *purely phantom-like* presence that reveals a subject caught in a de-objectifying implosion. The journey of the voice detached from the body visibly marks a substantial and *inalienable undecidability* between embodiment and disembodiment.

The voice as the vector of a "dismembering-memberment" figures out a problem pertaining to the *figurability* of the subject itself, in the sense that it provides a representation, not of the subject, but of the limits of the representation that can be made of the subject. What is at stake in this *phonetic skin* (Stahmer 2012) and the somatic voice is the rupture of the *intensive unity* of the body, a rupture caused by voices as *a perturbation of intimacy*, undercutting the very possibility of experiencing one's self as a whole.

Notes

1 This chapter builds on a lecture delivered at the conference *History of Sound in Theatre (from the 19th to the 21st Century): Acoustics and Auralities*, CRIalt/Université de Montréal–CNRS/ARIAS (November 2012).

2 *Vocalic* is used throughout this text as a term of art: it is an adjectival form referring not to vowels (its standard meaning in phonetics) but to vocality in the sense clarified by Paul Zumthor as a set of activities and values that define voice independently of language. Cavarero problematizes, on a philosophical and political level, the physical and pulsational values of *vocality* associated with the concepts of *poetico* and *semiotic chôra* introduced in Kristeva (1984).

3 All translations, unless otherwise indicated, are the author's.

4 Parts of this text are edited and republished in Castellucci *et al.* (2001: 84–90).

5 See *Giulio Cesare* in Castellucci *et al.* (2001: 163–226), especially "Cacofonia per una messa in scena: Giulio Cesare" (205–12) and "La retorica" (218–19).

6 See Castellucci, "Profeta di una voce nuova, o Cose udite," in Castellucci *et al.* (2001: 208). On the relationship between the voice, cutting and wounds, see Connor (2006).

Jesper Svenbro (in Grottanelli and Parise 1984: 231–52) discusses the body and ancient Greek sacrificial rituals in connection with the foundation of poetic rhythm.

7 The performance *Giulio Cesare: Spezzi Staccati* is as a segment within the project *E la Volpe Disse al Corvo: Corso di Linguistica Generale* (And the Fox Said to the Crow: Course in General Linguistics), dedicated by the city of Bologna to Romeo Castellucci (January–May 2014) and curated by the author. See also Sack (2014).

8 The other work, not discussed here, is the 2013 *Hyperion: Briefe eines Terroristen* (Hyperion: Letters of a Terrorist), Schaubühne, Berlin/F.I.N.D. Festival.

9 Romeo Castellucci comments: "This amputation is carried out as a voluntary act: cutting off your tongue, excluding it […] it is no longer possible to get the tongue (language) back […] however, [the women] will do it with 'another tongue/language,' the language of poetry" (Castellucci and Tilmann 2012).

References

Amara, L. and Di Matteo, P. (eds) (2010) *Teatri di Voce, Culture Teatrali*, 20.

Artaud, A. (1976) "To have done with the judgment of God," in Sontag, S. (ed.) *Selected Writings*, Berkeley: University of California Press.

Barthes, R. (1985) *The Responsibility of Forms: Critical Essays on Music, Art, and Representation*, New York: Hill and Wang.

Bodei, R. (1994) "Hölderlin: la filosofia e il tragico," in *Sul Tragico*, Milan: Feltrinelli.

Calchi-Novati, G. (2009) "Language under attack: the iconoclastic theatre of Sòcietas Raffaello Sanzio," *Theatre Research International*, 34(1): 50–65.

Castellucci, R. (1990) "L'attore è l'inesperto, il forestiero," in *Disputa Sulla Natura del Teatro*, Cesena: Edizioni Casa del Bello Estremo.

——(1997a) "L'iconoclastia della scena e il ritorno del corpo: la potenza carnale del teatro," in Carillo, G. (ed.) *Teatro*, Naples: Cronopio.

——(1997b) "Ingannando l'attesa: sul Giulio Cesare della Sòcietas Raffaello Sanzio," in Giacchè, P. (ed.) *Linea d'ombra*, N.123: 52–55.

——(2000), "Intervista," in Chinzari, S. and Ruffini, P. (eds) *Nuova Scena Italiana: Il Teatro dell'Ultima Generazione*, Roma: Castelvecchi.

Castellucci, C., Castellucci, R., and Guidi, C. (eds) (2001) *Epopea della Polvere: II Teatro della Sòcietas Raffaello Sanzio, 1992–1999*, Milan: Ubulibri.

Castellucci, R. and Tilmann, C. (2012) "Conversation between Christina Tilmann of the Berliner Festspiele and Romeo Castellucci," *Berliner Festspiele/Foreign Affairs*, August 15.

Cavarero, A. (2005) *For More than One Voice: Toward a Philosophy of Vocal Expression*, trans. P.A. Kottman, Stanford: Stanford University Press.

Connor, S. (2000) *Dumbstruck: A Cultural History of Ventriloquism*, Oxford: Oxford University Press.

——(2006) "Phonophobia: the dumb devil of stammering," www.stevenconnor.com/phonophobia/.

De Certeau, M. (1984) *The Practice of Everyday Life*, trans. S. Rendall, Berkeley: University of California Press.

——(1986) *Heterologies: Discourse on the Other*, trans. B. Massumi, Minneapolis: University of Minnesota Press.

——(1996) "Vocal utopia: glossolalias," *Representations*, 0(56): 29–47.

——(1998) *The Capture of Speech and Other Political Writings*, trans. T. Conley, Minneapolis: University of Minnesota Press.

Deleuze, G. (1997) *Essays Critical and Clinical*, trans. D.W. Smith and M.A. Greco, Minneapolis: University of Minnesota Press.

Dolar, M. (2006) *A Voice and Nothing More*, Cambridge, MA: MIT Press.

Grottanelli, C., and Parise, N.F. (eds) (1984) *Sacrificio e Società nel Mondo Antico*, Rome and Bari: Laterza.

Heller-Roazen, D. (2008) *Echolalias: On the Forgetting of Language*, New York: Zone Books.

Kelleher, J. (2014) "Giudizio Possibilità Essere/Judgment Possibility Being," in Castellucci, R. and Di Matteo, P. (eds) *Canto del Cigno*, Mantova: Corraini.

Kristeva, J. (1982) *Powers of Horror: An Essay on Abjection*, trans. L.S. Roudiez, New York: Columbia University Press.

——(1984) *Revolution in Poetic Language*, trans. M. Waller, New York: Columbia University Press.

LaBelle, B. (2010) "Raw orality: sound poetry and live bodies," in Neumark, N., Gibson, R., and van Leeuwen, T. (eds) *Voice: Vocal Aesthetics in Digital Arts and Media*, Cambridge, MA: MIT Press, 147–71.

Lacan, J. (2004) *Le Séminaire, Livre X: L'Angoisse, 1962–1963*, Paris: Seuil.

——(2005) *Le Séminaire, Livre XXIII: Le Sinthome, 1975–1976*, Paris: Seuil.

Nancy, J-L. (2007) *Listening*, trans. C. Mandell, New York: Fordham University Press.

Neumark, N., Gibson, R., and van Leeuwen, T. (eds) (2010) *Voice: Vocal Aesthetics in Digital Arts and Media*, Cambridge, MA: MIT Press.

Ramaglia, G. and Pezzana, C. (2004) *Capire l'Autismo*, Rome: Carocci.

Sack, D. (2014) "Giulio Cesare: pezzi staccati/Julius Caesar: detached parts," in Castellucci, R. and Di Matteo, P. (eds) *Canto del Cigno*, Mantua: Corraini.

Stahmer, A. (ed.) (2012) *Parole #2: Phonetic Skin/Phonetische Haut*, Cologne and Berlin: Salon Verlag – Errant Bodies Press.

Virno, P. (2003) *Quando il Verbo si Fa Carne: Linguaggio e Natura Umana*, Turin: Bollati Boringhieri.

Žižek, S. (2009) *The Parallax View*, Cambridge, MA: MIT Press.

8

SENSING VOICE

Materiality and the lived body in singing and listening philosophy

Nina Sun Eidsheim

Prelude

In 2007 I received an invitation to a recital that would take place in my bathroom. The Southern California-based soprano and performance artist, Juliana Snapper, offered to come to my home and present an underwater concert in my tub. My reaction? "Crazy," I thought. "Why go to the trouble of singing in an element so far from ideal?" I scoffed at the idea, and failed to take the artist up on her offer. But her endeavour lingered in my thoughts, caught there like a snag, returning often to my mind with no apparent purpose. After a year of mulling it over, I finally realized that what I had dismissed for its hopeless impracticality might, precisely because it was impractical, offer fresh perspectives on singing and listening by resituating those familiar activities in vastly unfamiliar territory.

Introduction

What *is* familiar to those who study Western music is that which can be written down. Common methods of musical representation and analysis evidence Western culture's preoccupation with what notation can capture and preserve. Traditional Western scores emphasize music's measurable parameters such as pitch, rhythm and duration. Even in contemporary works and studies, where traditional scores are not wholly relevant, sound waves, time lines, algorithms, diagrams and charts maintain the traditional tendency to quantify music. Consequently, the abstractly yet fixedly *notated* overshadows the ever-shifting *experience* of music. In vocal studies, this orientation plays out as a privileging of dramatic, structural and semiotic content (libretto, score and socio-historical context) over the distinct quality, or timbre, of each individual voice in each performance of each work. Generally, Western music studies favour the idealized and abstract at the expense of the sensible, unrepeatable experience.[1]

Conceiving the voice as a generic vehicle for words, pitches and duration results in the neglect of key vocal and sonic dimensions that are not traditionally notated. By considering the underwater singing practices of Juliana Snapper (1972–), this chapter points the way towards those aspects of music that are inaccessible to standard notation but available to all our perceiving senses. Snapper's work opens a window on the physical and sensory properties of singers' and listeners' bodies; on the spaces and materials in which sound disperses; and on these aspects' collective indispensability to singing and listening *as experiences*. Because sensory readings of singing and listening reach for dimensions of voice and sound that are difficult, if not impossible, to account for with conventional analytical methods, multi-sensory perspectives may enrich the analysis of musical sound in general, and vocal practices in particular.

In musicology – the scholarly perspective from which this piece is written – great strides have been made towards a thorough consideration of the body's role in musical experience.[2] Scholars working outside musicology have made significant progress in considering how the full spectrum of sensory experience contributes to our interpretation of sound and music, but less has been done to specifically address musical repertoire.[3]

A growing number of fields now consider the qualities of sounds themselves, not merely their iconographies. As Feld and Brenneis recognize,

> Sound has come to have a particular resonance in many disciplines over the past decade. Social theorists, historians, literary researchers, folklorists and scholars in science and technology studies and visual, performative and cultural studies provide a wide range of substantively rich accounts and epistemologically provocative models for how researchers can take sound seriously.
>
> *(2004: 461)*

Recent work reflects on the soundscapes of everyday life and the spaces we inhabit,[4] the recovery of sound and soundscapes across time,[5] the science of sound[6] and listening practices.[7] This chapter aims to extend these works' perspectives on sound, listening and singing, in ways that may both challenge and relate to musicology while contributing to the general body of sensory scholarship.

In what follows, I approach the sound of voice from a sensory perspective that transcends audition, focusing on sound's transduction through various types of matter and examining the body's physical relationship with sound.[8] I begin by narrating Juliana Snapper's journey towards her underwater singing endeavour, the *Five Fathoms Opera Project* begun in 2007, positioning it within her catalogue of vocal work. Focusing on the interactive component of the *Opera Project*, I describe her underwater practice by recounting a workshop in which I participated, led by the artist herself, and by drawing on conversations about her practice. Incorporating feminist philosophies on the materiality of the body, I reveal the ways in which examining voice and listening with all the intermingling senses may help us to understand that the experience of sound is temporal – arising and coagulating only to pass all too quickly. Thus a musical experience is not some*thing* that can be captured in notation, but an open-ended and pluralistic negotiation with sound in all its physicality. Such a negotiation will also involve the images, myths and ideologies that shape how people think of sound in a given time and locale. In short, examining a vocal practice that displaces singing from its habitual environment, the air, reveals deficiencies in traditional musical approaches to sound, and offers avenues through which to reconsider the ontological status of materials within which we sing and hear.

Pushing the limits of voice and body

Snapper's work experiments with (or perhaps against) the limits of her voice and body, challenging her physical abilities as well as her imagination. The venues for her underwater operas range from bathtubs to Olympic-sized pools.[9] Performing in an unfamiliar element forces the vocalist to confront, through trial and error, the processes involved in singing on the most fundamental level: how do I get air? Do I emit the sound from my mouth or vibrate it through my bones into the water? How can I share the sound with my audience?

As a classical singer who trained for most of her life in order to gain complete control of her voice, Snapper began a journey towards unsettling that foundation. She wanted to complicate her performing relationship with her instrument, her voice, by pulling the rug out from underneath herself, so to speak, implementing techniques that would undo her hard-earned control. She found that "the operatic instrument is actually incredibly tough" and difficult to disturb. "I started really delving into this idea of the prepared body with Ron [Athey]," says Snapper, recalling their collaborative explorations that would culminate in *The Judas Cradle* (2005–7):

> We had a hell of a time trying to get my voice to break down under stress. We had me folding over jungle gym bars and contorting every which way before discovering that hanging upside down, with a slight arch to the back will undo the vocal mechanism over the course of several minutes.
>
> *(Kumerdej 2008)*

Through rigorous experimentation, Snapper located the point at which she, as a singer, lost control, allowing her voice to take over as an autonomous, driven and determined entity. Her own voice hastened her to places where her knowledge of singing and her artistic imagination could not take her. She discovered that allowing the physicality of her instrument, rather than pre-written instructions or pre-conceived ideas, to dictate the sound of her performance led her to new possibilities. Meditating on the human capability to misuse other people's bodies, *The Judas Cradle* is a sadomasochistic drama with a musical collage of opera (Monteverdi, Puccini), prelinguistic sounds, and baroque costumes and staging. Opera, as well as the heterosexual, gendered body, is parodied through excess. Following *The Judas*

Cradle tour, Snapper took her voice on the ultimate ride, embarking on a series of underwater experiments. If singing upside down limited her vocal control, singing underwater would instantly jettison twenty-five years of training. Any rules had yet to be discovered.

Flood and Rapture

Snapper began her underwater project in aghast response to an environmental disaster, which was met with reactions ranging from the apocalyptic to the utterly indifferent. Watching Hurricane Katrina on television from the West Coast, Snapper bore horrified witness to an emerging awareness of our changing climate, as fear of flooding and drought turned to a full-on politics of disaster. She watched Evangelical Christians absorb climate change into their idea of the Rapture: the Biblical end of time in the form of melting glaciers and rising sea levels. A Judeo-Christian perspective is predisposed towards a linear sense of time and the "progressive" inevitability of events. The end of the world is thus inexorable, and often depicted as an uncontrollable flood – not as a gateway to cleansing and renewal, as with Noah's Ark, but as an eternal doom, an irreversible watery state. The element from which we ascended billions of years ago, that we depend on for survival, enjoy in recreation and use as a means of transportation, is also the unstoppable punishment that will obliterate humanity from the earth. Therefore, even as scientists search for clues to the beginnings of civilization, others predict the end of time, wondering: What are the signs? What deeds might trigger events of such magnitude? And how should we act when we are faced with the Rapture?

Outraged by Evangelical views of the supposedly "inevitable" suffering wrought by Katrina, and appalled at the inertia of the unaffected populace who, dry and warm in their living rooms, watched the flood unfolding, Snapper began to reflect on water's relationship with society. Had people lost touch with water, its potential, and what it represents? Were they numbed by a media culture that profited from fear? Snapper describes her hope that opera, if ejected from the opera house and steeped in water, could infuse souls:

> [T]he idea that water [always] represents emotions in some fundamental way is all over our language. The idea of being flooded with emotion, or storms of rage, or raining tears. It's very raw. [Water is a] technology that gets people feeling in a new way. My hope is to use that technology in a way that is more fresh and more immediate and really actually *can* work on people listening – which I think less and less happens in the *opera house*. I think we need to take it out of the opera house and bring bodies together. [...] Maybe opera can help us to bind in new ways, to feel what we're feeling.
> *(Vestinavesti 2009)*

Because water can represent extreme emotion, Snapper believes that to connect with water is to foster our engagement with our feelings. She views underwater singing as a medium through which to address a society distanced from itself and from emotion, paralyzed by the prospect of the end of time. Additionally, for Snapper, singing underwater is an adaptive strategy for basic and artistic survival, post-Apocalypse. She wonders: instead of accepting watery engulfment as the conclusion of our story, could one *adapt* to this new state? Snapper says: "I am interested in what it means to accept the end of things – instead of trying to keep things that are dear to us alive at any cost" (Kumerdej 2008). Thus, the *Five Fathoms Opera Project* (hereafter *FF*), was born from the idea of adapting singing to the condition of the end of time and, through this adaptation, *defying* the end of time as proposed by Evangelical Christian leaders.[10]

At the beginning of the version entitled "You Who Will Emerge from the Flood," Snapper enters the pool area in a costume, designed by Susan Matheson, that looks like a beautiful, yet eerie, transformation of seaweed into dress. Two men, with swords longer than themselves, escort her, later a full chorus comes on the scene, and the drama unfolds by the side of the pool, in the water, on an underwater stage, and on a video projection. Metaphorically, this is an expression of human creativity that defies the end of time. Seen in this context, one way of reading *FF* is as a thorough undermining of the attitude exhibited by the Evangelical Christians who viewed Katrina as divine punishment for homosexual activity.[11]

Spilling the truth

Several striking elements indicate a continuum between Snapper's *The Judas Cradle* (hereafter *JC*) and *FF*. The unusual vocalizations that characterize both pieces arise from severe corporeal transformations. In *JC*, Athey's glossolalia spills out of him because God's presence has overtaken his body; Snapper's trained voice breaks because she is hanging upside down.[12] In *FF*, Snapper's entire vocal repertoire and sonority are transformed by her aquatic immersion. Whether by utilizing glossolalia in a queer masochistic performance; by challenging the body in order to break through operatic training; or by defying the end of time by learning how to sing underwater, Snapper and Athey play with subverting regimes of body and mind, not by escaping or averting them, but by facing them in order to pervert them. Both pieces are also extreme responses to various manifestations of control exerted through terror. The Judas Cradle was a medieval European torture device, a pyramid-shaped apparatus onto which victims were lowered for penetration inflicted by their own body weight.

FF is also a response to horrific events. The title combines an adaptation of a Shakespearian song – sung by the spirit Ariel to a shipwrecked prince in *The Tempest* – with a quote from Bertholt Brecht's poem trio, *An die Nachgeborenen* (To Those Born Late) (see Brecht and Hennenberg 1984). Set to music by Hanns Eisler, Brecht's poetry is addressed to survivors of world-annihilating tragedy, asking them to remember those who caused the tragedy with understanding. This song is performed twice during *FF*. Both pieces are perversions of dominant narratives that significantly influence how the world appears to be configured. In *FF*,

Snapper teaches that even after the flood, promised by Judeo-Christianity to destroy the world, humans can find the strength to survive, even to make music. In *JC*, she exaggerates conventional Western narratives of male and female sexuality, to demonstrate how those narratives cruelly demand impossible confinements of the human body. Moreover, there are unavoidable parallels between the Judas Cradle and the similarly antique "no-touch torture" technique of waterboarding. The latter is frequently discussed in the early 21st century, as the US government's so-called "anti-terror" programme continues to use waterboarding to obtain confessions. *FF* is also a response to Judeo-Christian tales of the ultimate punishment – annihilation. In fact, both pieces offer intense critiques of Christian values. The masochistic aspects of *JC* draw on a long history of Christian martyrdom, in which we find repeated re-embodiments of Jesus' hanging, pierced, dismembered body.

Perhaps hoping to shed the undesirable trappings of her inherited Judeo-Christian culture, in *JC* and *FF* Snapper forcibly divorces herself from the hyperbolic discipline of the operatic body. Opera, along with ballet, is arguably one of the most extreme of the arts which involve the "regimentation of the female body to attain an ideal" (Jones 2006: 167). While in *JC* both performing and listening bodies are sonically and metaphorically penetrated through a "(masochistic) enactment of pain" (Jones 2006: 167), the setting of *FF* enacts the ultimate cradle, the embrace of oceanic depths, celebrated and feared since the beginning of history. Notably, in many Western myths, the ocean is personified with the mutated female forms of sirens and mermaids. Thus, in a connection to which I return below, the flood, the Apocalypse, is associated with the female in Western mythology. Snapper knows that her work is unavoidably received within such contexts, and so deliberately alludes to multiple penetrations of the female/oceanic body, that enable it to absorb and exude sound.

Situating Snapper's compositional and vocal practice in *Five Fathoms Deep Opera Project*

While it may seem natural to locate Snapper within the lineage of extended vocal technique, Snapper understands her endeavour as a *breakdown* rather than an extension of vocal technique. Snapper likens the process of breaking down her instrument to the "preparation" of instruments investigated by experimental composers in the 1950s, such as John Cage and Peter Yates. To "prepare" a piano or guitar is to distort the instrument's usual capabilities by inserting alien objects, causing the instrument to create new, distinctive sounds. Similarly, Snapper distorts the sound of the operatic voice by penetrating, mutilating, or inhibiting the human body. In *JC,* Snapper's vocal body is temporarily deformed by being tied upside down; and in *FF*, being underwater prevents her from drawing breath. As a practice, "preparation" evidences a desire to interrupt and disturb traditional human relationships with instruments and their histories, as well as curiosity and adventurousness about sound. We might also imagine Snapper's vocal "preparation" as a way to remark upon, negotiate and play with the boundaries between nature and culture: between the female voice historically understood as uncontrollable or "natural," and the operatic voice as refined and controlled.

Despite Snapper's breakdown of her instrument in pursuit of new sonorities, at the core of her work is a committed – if fraught – relationship to operatic technique and tradition:

> It is an amazing feeling to sing operatically. All of this power gushing from your center! I trust it beyond any other means of communication. It is totalizing, erotic, uncanny. Every part of you is active, your insides are turned out. That's why I center my work within operatic singing [...] and explore the limits of the voice by directly addressing my body.
>
> *(in Sule 2010)*

To Snapper, there is nothing more uncanny than operatic vocal technique, except possibly the form of opera itself. This idea raises another relationship that foregrounds a fantastical aspect of Snapper's practice: the metaphorical juxtaposition of this arguably most artificial of vocal forms, opera, with dolphins' and whales' sonorous communications within bodies of water.[13] In this relationship, it is important for Snapper that she never becomes comfortable with singing in her newly chosen element, whether upside down or underwater. To her, the newness of the element, for both herself and the audience, enables the old operatic media to be transformative.

Beyond the obvious parallel of the marine environment, Snapper's work has much in common with that of other late-20th-century composers who explored the sonic possibilities of aquatics. The composers with whom I see Snapper most closely aligning herself are not those who splash and drip, foregrounding the sounds *of* water, but rather those who work with sound *in* water.[14] Major composers who deal with the acoustic environment offered by water include John Cage with Lou Harrison (*Double Music*, 1941), Max Neuhaus (*Whistle Music*, 1971) and Michel Redolfi (various works since 1981).[15] With Cage and Harrison, Snapper shares the notion of changing the sounds of a familiar source by immersing it in water. With Neuhaus, she shares the desire to eject music from concert spaces and institutions, and to showcase the sonorous possibilities of traditionally "non-musical" environments. With Redolfi, Snapper shares a fascination with adapting instruments, performers and listeners to an aquatic medium. However, Snapper is the first to concentrate on *singing* underwater. Among Redolfi's approximately two hundred underwater pieces, for which he has tried to perfect various custom-built instruments (mostly based on percussive principles), only one piece was created for a soprano. But whereas Redolfi (2008) is disturbed by the bubbles resultant from air-based instruments underwater, and therefore avoids such instruments altogether, for Snapper, causing bubbles is part of the performative experience, and the idiosyncratic sounds of bursting bubbles form an aspect of the music.

Snapper sees herself as extending and dialoguing with the operatic form – as part of its monodramatic lineage. She views her work as a continuation of the one-character opera tradition. In her own scholarship, Snapper (forthcoming) identifies

Arnold Schoenberg's *Erwartung* (1909) as prompting a flurry of postwar single-voice dramatic works, such as Francis Poulenc's *La Voix Humaine* (1958), Peter Maxwell Davies's *The Medium* (1981), and Luciano Berio's and Cathy Berberian's *Visage* (1961). In the interest of exploring media and sonorities, these monodramas were carried out as both live performances and tape pieces, in all of which the feminine body acts out madness operatically. While mostly featuring women, the mad figure might also be a feminine man, or a man rendered effeminate by his madness – for example, in Davies's *Eight Songs for a Mad King* (1969).

Snapper sees this repertoire as "hysterical" because of the extreme extent to which it "re-arranges the body of the singer" in ways that affect vocal quality (Sule 2010). This rearrangement "extends outward from [the performer's] body" – affecting the other musicians' and the audience's empathetic bodies, "rearranging" our ingrained notions of music as an ineffable experience. As we may be lulled into believing that we are completely disconnected from the broadcast suffering that we watch from the comfort of our homes, so we can persuade ourselves that music, fleeting and seemingly intangible, causes no lasting consequences. Snapper attempts to rearrange these beliefs through what she calls "hystericism" – alluding not to an illness, like the hysteria historically assigned to women who did not align with prescribed gender roles, but to an approach to technique that deliberately harnesses physical responses to terror in a musico-dramatic operation. While her performances are not *about* hystericism, her objective is to "harness the technology of hystericism" – to redirect the kinds of energy that propagate a growing culture of fear (Sule 2010).

Through hystericism, Snapper addresses ways in which women are silenced, prevented from using their voices in ways that seem proper and natural to them; the ways this silencing plays out in emotionally lonely places; and her personal experiences as a woman with a fundamental distrust of language. After Snapper lost the ability to speak for a period of some weeks at age 19, her relationship to verbal discourse, and to social expectations grounded in language, became a deeply distrustful one. While she could articulate words during this period, she could not form sentences or sing lyrics. This resulted in an inability to explain herself (and how can a 19-year-old explain that she has suddenly lost her grasp of language?). Though she attempted to communicate with her eyes and with non-verbal sounds, she loathed the powerlessness that came with being half-mute. Snapper views her vocal compositions, consisting largely of wordless, gestural music, as a reaction to her own abandonment by language.

Singing underwater

As she gradually adjusts to new, self-imposed, linguistical and physical constraints, Snapper's practice in *FF* involves continually pushing her body towards a moment of surprise. She first experimented at home, in the bathtub. Her first performances, too, were in bathtubs. "Once I got the hang of, well I am still getting a hang of it," Snapper shares, "I started working with movement, different depths, different apertures" (interview December 2008) (Figure 8.1).

FIGURE 8.1 Snapper performing *Five Fathoms Deep My Father Lies* at P.S.1 Contemporary Art Center/MoMA, New York City, 15 March 2008. (Photo by Marina Ancona.)

When she described her process to me, we agreed that the best way for her to demonstrate being overwhelmed by a new environment was to take me through a comparative experience. So, in the spring of 2010, I took a group of graduate students to the Standard Hotel in downtown Los Angeles. We gathered in their rooftop bar with fire-truck-red waterbeds and a large saline swimming pool, one of Snapper's many performance venues.

Once we were in the water, Snapper took us through some exercises. The first formed us into pairs; one person gently held the other underwater, while the person underwater made sounds. I was paired with Natalia (Figure 8.2), who shouted – but with my ears above water I did not hear her voice.

We tried another strategy: one person made sounds underwater while the rest of us put our heads and ears in. This enabled us to hear him. We found that the deeper into the water we descended, the more difficult it was to sing high notes. Fast tempi were also difficult to maintain; Natalia's attempt resulted in muddled sounds. Surprisingly, while sung sounds generally did not seem very loud, small internal throat sounds were incredibly powerful. They boomed, beamed and spread, and were almost overbearing. These exercises demonstrate the extent to which the medium in which sound waves flow affects their characteristics: their speed, direction and so on. It also shows that in order to register sound, the

FIGURE 8.2 The author with Natalia Bieletto (under water). Aquaopera #4/Los Angeles, 28 April 2010. (Photo by Jillian Rogers.)

listening body (including the head) must be immersed in the material through which the sound flows.

The next exercise linked the six of us together by the arms; three participants stood in a line, with their backs against three others. We sang in a drone-like manner, playing with our voices above the water, at its surface, slowly descending into it. We felt the sonic vibrations largely through direct contact with each other's bodies. Of course, sound also passed through the air and the water, but because the most immediate path was from one body to another, this was the sensation that overpowered us.

We ended the day gathered around the poolside fireplace and discussed how different singing felt in a liquid environment. We had found that aural experience is predicated on our physical contact with sound waves through shared media, in this case water and air, flesh and bone. We noted that the shared medium makes a great deal of difference to how we experience the voice, and that the sound ultimately heard depends partly on what is sung, partly on the medium through which it passes and how our bodies interact with that medium. In other words, we discovered that sound is a multi-sensory experience, tactile as well as aural.

Snapper's workshop revealed that music-making involves more than traditional theories and notation can capture. Therefore, although some of us were singers with decades of training, we felt that little of our experience could effectively apply or even seem relevant underwater. We wondered: Why did singing and listening underwater feel so different from the same experiences in air? And how might this difference relate to a consideration of voice, listening and community?

The sensing body in relation to the material world

Singing in water sounds so different from the way it sounds in air, largely because, as Julian Henriques notes, unlike transverse waves of light, longitudinal waves of sound require a medium through which to propagate (2010: 66). Hence, the speed at which sound waves travel depends on the density and compressibility of the medium through which they pass. Consequently, sound cannot travel through a vacuum.[16] Because higher densities and compressions engender slower speeds – and, relative to air, water is very dense but nearly incompressible – the speed of sound in water is generally about four times faster than the speed of sound in air, with slight variations depending on several factors. These factors include water quality (distilled or salted, warm or cool), and hydrostatic pressure (which in turn depends on the distance below the surface at which an object sounds).[17] That is why Natalia's up-tempo tune sounded muddled underwater. Snapper, therefore, chooses slower tempi for underwater music than for music sung in air.

The specific relationship between our material bodies and the materials in which we immerse ourselves also affects how we experience sounds. In its unfamiliarity, listening underwater brings the relationship between sound, matter and eardrum – which in air we take for granted – into relief. Because the density of the human eardrum is very similar to that of water, the eardrum does not provide the resistance necessary to translate underwater vibrations into tympanic movements, that is, into sound that eardrums can register. However, because our skull bones *are* dense enough to convey the sound, the skull bones, rather than the eardrums, capture most of the sounds that humans do manage to register underwater. As a result, the sound resonates in the body, going directly to the inner ear and circumventing the eardrum. Like air and water, the eardrum and skull bones are media through which sound passes, and by which its character is affected.

The part of the body that registers sound also plays a role in its apparent directionality. For example, our ability to hear in "stereo" – two distinct signals, left and right – is the result of sound entering our bodies from two directions (two ears). In contrast, when the inner ear registers sound via the skull bones, the sound seems to be omnidirectional rather than stereo.[18] Because the sound waves vibrate the bones of the listener's body, her perception is that her own body created the sound. The sound becomes a "state" or "quality" of the listener's body – in Stefan Helmreich's description, a "soundstate" (2007: 624). In effect, at an underwater performance, where the audience and performers are immersed, the singer's body, the water and the audiences' bodies become one vibrating mass, a single pulsating speaker.[19]

Snapper's fascinating displacement of singing to the underwater realm reminds us of the physical realities of sound, and shows us that the medium through which sound travels configures the music we experience as much, if not more, than the performed pitches, rhythms, harmonies or textures – parameters usually favoured in Western musical analyses. By accentuating the role of the body and the environment in the experience of music, Snapper proves that the longstanding narratives of sound's ineffable "ethereality" and music's quantitative abstraction hinge on concrete events occurring within material bodies.

Sensing voice

An approach to sound as materially bound offers points of departure from the mechanistic, scientific and utilitarian metaphors prevalent in Western discourse, as from metaphors grounded in visually oriented epistemologies (e.g., sound waves, X-rays, sonograms) (Rodgers 2010). Instead, multi-sensory perspectives recognize sounds as affective and open-ended processes. Snapper's practice offers such perspectives, working from the premise that sounds come into being as evental processes of touch and movement. She grounds her vocal practice in a materialistic epistemology centred on the human body and its surroundings that nonetheless refuses to treat them as stable, *a priori* entities encapsulated by given scientific laws. Thus, her undertaking joins a rich chain of feminist work on the materiality of the human body, and its configuration within social and cultural frameworks.

Through the idiosyncratic vocal practice that I at first dismissed, Snapper effectively addresses familiar ideas about gender, nature and culture, and begs us to reflect on the material and embodied aspects of sound, music making and the reception of music. She challenges notions of the female body's dangerous ambiguity that have survived across millennia, geographies and cultures in stories of sirens' and mermaids' seductive and enveloping voices. By descending into water with excessive performative expressions, costumes, set designs and vocal sounds, and inviting her audience with her, Snapper confronts head-on the pervasive cross-cultural ambivalence about the female body. Moreover, literally and figuratively, the underwater female body and its material form symbolize the feminine embrace and the allure of humans' complete dependency on the woman's body while *in utero*.[20]

"To be present in the world," writes Simone de Beauvoir, "implies strictly that there exists a body which is at once a material thing in the world and a point of view towards the world" (1974: 7). De Beauvoir recognized that it is impossible to locate a body outside its performative representation of culture. In other words, she recognized that material in a "natural" state is a phantasm to which we do not have unmediated access. Rather, the materiality to which we do have access is produced by, and reinstantiates, ideas and representations which are unavoidably subject to power relations. In a response to feminist scholarship on the relationship between materiality, performativity and "nature" in the question of sex and gender, Toril Moi (1999) offers the image of the *lived body* (replacing categories of both sex and gender) as a means of illustrating the involvement of our bodily characteristics in the formation of a *lived* sense of ourselves. This lived body is embedded in, and subject to, cultural forces at a foundational level. It is this body, whose perceptual system has been "tuned" by a given culture, that is the perceiving conduit of sound.

By highlighting the material aspects of sound and their reception, Snapper reminds us that *what* we hear depends as much on our materiality, physicality, cultural and social histories, as it does on so-called objective measurements (decibel level, sound-wave count, or score), which are themselves mere images. Indeed, the experience of sound is a triangulation of events wherein physical impulses (sonic vibrations), our bodies' encultured capacity to receive these vibrations, and how we have been taught to understand them are at constant play and subject to negotiation. In the experience of sound, what becomes clear is not a stable explanation of what sound or music *is*. Instead, we are guided to understand that each such account is a composite manifestation of our understanding of sound at a given moment in time and place.

Snapper's idiosyncratic vocal practice stimulates us to consider how music as a material endeavour with physical consequences – through which our own and others' bodies are engaged and impacted – contributes to a modern sense of subjectivity and inter-subjectivity. In such light, music can no longer be dealt with at arm's length. Indeed, if, as T.S. Eliot's classic phrase succinctly captures it, "you are the music while the music lasts," Snapper's practice is a resounding reminder of why analyses of sound and music, albeit continuously negotiated and defined, cannot be divorced from a socio-historically bound consideration of its material condition and sensuous pulsation.

Acknowledgements

This research is funded in part by a grant from the UCLA Center for the Study of Women. This piece was originally published in *The Senses & Society* 6(2) © Nina Eidsheim, July 2011, "Sensing voice: materiality and the lived voice in singing and listening," Berg Publishers, by permission of Bloomsbury Publishing plc. An expanded and updated version will be included in Eidsheim (forthcoming).

Notes

1 See Cavarero for a discussion of voice and logos (2005: 1–78) and a nuanced critique of Derrida's notion of voice and presence (213–41).
2 Including Becker (2004), Cusick (1999), Dunn and Jones (1994), Gordon (2004), Le Guin (2006), Poizat (1992) and Szendy and Nancy (2008).
3 Including Calame-Griaule (1986), Connor (2004), Dyson (2009), Helmreich (2007), Henriques (2010), Ihde (1976), Kahn (1999), Koestenbaum (1993), Massumi (2002), Nancy (2007), Rodgers (2010) and Serres (2009).
4 Bull (2000), DeNora (2000), Fox (2004) and LaBelle (2010).
5 Corbin (1998), Kahn (1999) and Thompson (2004).
6 Gouk (1999) and Thompson (2004).
7 Erlmann (2004), Helmreich (2007), Hirschkind (2006), Sterne (2003) and Szendy and Nancy (2008).
8 Some foundational and influential examples of sensory enquiries include Corbin (1998), Howes (2005), Seremetakis (1996) and Stoller (1997).
9 See Eidsheim (forthcoming) for a complete list of Snapper's underwater projects.
10 The project as a whole is entitled the *Five Fathoms Opera Project*. The workshop version I participated in with my students is called "Aquaopera #4/Los Angeles." Currently, there

are two additional performances under the *Five Fathoms Opera Project* umbrella, "Five Fathoms Deep My Father Lies" and "You Who Will Emerge from the Flood." The latter is the title of the large-scale show with choir for which Andrew Infanti composed some of the music.

11 Conceived and performed by Ron Athey and Juliana Snapper, sound design by Amanda Piasecki and costume design by Susan Mattheson. Jones discusses the queer performative ethics of the piece (2006).

12 Raised as a fundamentalist Pentecostal minister's son, Athey often talks about his childhood ability to speak in tongues. See "Biography" on www.ronathey.com.

13 Snapper's performances have thus far been staged in pools rather than in the ocean. For obvious reasons, singing underwater is much more risky than playing an instrument. Working with researchers from the Scripps Institute of Oceanography, Snapper is gradually developing a practice suited to the ocean. To learn about underwater sound pollution, see McCarthy (2004).

14 For a discussion of some music dealing with water without immersion, see Kahn (1999: 245–88).

15 Cage himself traces his use of water to much later. In 1973, at UCLA, he accompanied water ballet swimmers and sought to find a way to cue them while underwater (Kahn 1999: 249).

16 For histories of underwater acoustics, see Hersey (1977), Medwin (2005), Schlee (1973) and Urick (1983).

17 For detailed information on the speed of sound in liquid, see Medwin (2005).

18 Kittler (1999) posits that the stereo spatialization of cranial interiors only became possible with headphones.

19 The late composer and sound artist Maryanne Amacher worked with expanding our ways of hearing sound by purposefully using the physicality of the body beyond the eardrum for transmission.

20 It is interesting to observe that sharing the medium of water (versus air) seems to be perceived as "more material," and to incite stronger visceral feelings. This is perhaps why policies regarding the sharing of aquatic spaces have often been enforced (for example, gender and race segregation in pools).

References

Becker, J.O. (2004) *Deep Listeners: Music, Emotion, and Trancing*, Bloomington: Indiana University Press.

Brecht, B. and Hennenberg, F. (1984) *Das grosse Brecht-Liederbuch*, Frankfurt am Main: Suhrkamp.

Bull, M. (2000) *Sounding Out the City: Personal Stereos and the Management of Everyday Life*, Oxford and New York: Berg.

Calame-Griaule, G. (1986) "Voice and the Dogon world," in King, N.F.C.a.N. (ed.) *Notebooks in Cultural Analysis*, Durham: Duke University Press.

Cavarero, A. (2005) *For More than One Voice: Toward a Philosophy of Vocal Expression*, trans. P.A. Kottman, Stanford: Stanford University Press.

Connor, S. (2004) "Edison's teeth: touching hearing," in Erlmann, V. (ed.) *Hearing Cultures: Essays on Sound, Listening, and Modernity*, Oxford: Berg.

Corbin, A. (1998) *Village Bells: Sound and Meaning in the 19th-Century French Countryside*, New York: Columbia University Press.

Cusick, S.G. (1999) "On musical performances of gender and sex," in Barkin, E. and Hamessley, L. (eds) *Audible Traces: Gender, Identity and Music*, Los Angeles: Carciofoli Verlagshaus.

de Beauvoir, S. (1974) *The Second Sex*, New York: Vintage Books.

DeNora, T. (2000) *Music in Everyday Life*, Cambridge and New York: Cambridge University Press.

Dunn, L.C. and Jones, N.A. (eds) (1994) *Embodied Voices: Representing Female Vocality in Western Culture*, Cambridge and New York: Cambridge University Press.

Dyson, F. (2009) *Sounding New Media: Immersion and Embodiment in the Arts and Culture*, Berkeley: University of California Press.

Eidsheim, N.S. (forthcoming) *Sensing Sound: Singing and Listening as Vibrational Practice*, Durham: Duke University Press.

Erlmann, V. (ed.) (2004) *Hearing Cultures: Essays on Sound, Listening, and Modernity*, Oxford and New York: Berg.

Feld, S. and Brenneis, D. (2004) "Doing anthropology in sound," *American Ethnologist*, 31(4): 461–74.

Fox, A.A. (2004) *Real Country: Music and Language in Working-Class Culture*, Durham: Duke University Press.

Gordon, B. (2004) *Monteverdi's Unruly Women: The Power of Song in Early Modern Italy*, Cambridge and New York: Cambridge University Press.

Gouk, P. (1999) *Music, Science, and Natural Magic in Seventeenth-Century England*, New Haven: Yale University Press.

Helmreich, S. (2007) "An anthropologist underwater: immersive soundscapes, submarine cyborgs, and transductive ethnography," *American Ethnologist*, 34(4): 621–41.

Henriques, J. (2010) "The vibrations of affect and their propagation on a night out on Kingston's dancehall scene," *Body & Society*, 16(1): 57–89.

Hersey, J.B. (1977) "A chronicle of man's use of ocean acoustics," *Oceanus*, 20(2): 8–21.

Hirschkind, C. (2006) *The Ethical Soundscape: Cassette Sermons and Islamic Counterpublics*, New York: Columbia University Press.

Howes, D. (2005) *Empire of the Sense: The Sensual Culture Reader*, Oxford: Berg.

Ihde, D. (1976) *Listening and Voice: A Phenomenology of Sound*, Athens: Ohio University Press.

Jones, A. (2006) "Holy body: erotic ethics in Ron Athey and Juliana Snapper's Judas Cradle," *TDR/The Drama Review*, 50(1(T189)): 159–69.

Kahn, D. (1999) *Noise, Water, Meat: A History of Sound in the Arts*, Cambridge, MA: MIT Press.

Kittler, F.A. (1999) *Gramophone, Film, Typewriter*, Stanford: Stanford University Press.

Koestenbaum, W. (1993) *The Queen's Throat: Opera, Homosexuality, and the Mystery of Desire*, New York: Poseidon Press.

Kumerdej, M. (2008) "Soprano Juliana Snapper's underwater sirensong" [*Sopranistko Juliana Snapper pod vodo, Sirenine podvodne arije*], *Delo*, 28 June, 24–26.

LaBelle, B. (2010) *Acoustic Territories: Sound Culture and Everyday Life*, New York: Continuum.

Le Guin, E. (2006) *Boccherini's Body: An Essay in Carnal Musicology*, Berkeley: University of California Press.

Massumi, B. (2002) *Parables for the Virtual: Movement, Affect, Sensation*, Durham: Duke University Press.

McCarthy, E. (2004) *International Regulation of Underwater Sound: Establishing Rules and Standards to Address Ocean Noise Pollution*, Boston: Kluwer Academic Publishers.

Medwin, H. (2005) *Sounds in the Sea: From Ocean Acoustics to Acoustical Oceanography*, Cambridge and New York: Cambridge University Press.

Moi, T. (1999) *What Is a Woman? And Other Essays*, Oxford and New York: Oxford University Press.

Nancy, J.-L. (2007) *Listening*, trans. C. Mandell, New York: Fordham University Press.

Poizat, M. (1992) *The Angel's Cry: Beyond the Pleasure Principle in Opera*, Ithaca: Cornell University Press.

Redolfi, M. (2008) "Underwater music facts, interview with Kevin McGuinness, Walt Disney Studio Home Entertainment," *Redolfi-Music*, www.redolfi-music.com/eau/UnderwaterMusicFaqs.pdf.

Rodgers, T. (2010) *Synthesizing Sound: Metaphor in Audio-Technical Discourse and Synthesis History*, Ph.D. Thesis, Montreal: McGill University.

Schlee, S. (1973) *The Edge of an Unfamiliar World: A History of Oceanography*, New York: Dutton.

Seremetakis, C.N. (1996) *The Senses Still: Perception and Memory as Material Culture in Modernity*, Chicago: University of Chicago Press.

Serres, M. (2009) *The Five Senses: A Philosophy of Mingled Bodies (I)*, London and New York: Continuum.

Snapper, J. (forthcoming) (untitled), Ph.D. Thesis, San Diego: University of California.

Sterne, J. (2003) *The Audible Past: Cultural Origins of Sound Reproduction*, Durham: Duke University Press.

Stoller, P. (1997) *Sensuous Scholarship*, Philadelphia: University of Pennsylvania Press.

Sule, K. (2010) "A hundred paragraphs on the skin," trans. K. Sule, *Wysokie Obcasy*, 23 October.

Szendy, P. and Nancy, J.-L. (2008) *Listen: A History of Our Ears*, New York: Fordham University Press.

Thompson, E.A. (2004) *The Soundscape of Modernity: Architectural Acoustics and the Culture of Listening in America, 1900–1933*, Cambridge, MA: MIT Press.

Urick, R.J. (1983) *Principles of Underwater Sound*, 3rd edition, New York: McGraw-Hill.

Vestinavesti. (2009) "Interview with Juliana Snapper," *YouTube*, www.youtube.com/watch?v=gqDz6UCT5ws&feature=PlayList&p=06C40068B70D736D&playnext_from=PL&playnext=1&index=5.

9

LAMENTING (WITH THE) "OTHERS," "LAMENTING OUR FAILURE TO LAMENT"?

An auto-ethnographic account of the vocal expression of loss[1]

Marios Chatziprokopiou

On the 9th April 2010, my father's death made it necessary for me to return home to Greece from Brazil, where I was preparing to conduct the second of a series of fieldwork expeditions to the Krahô Indians' Territory (Tocantins State). Shortly after having assisted in a lament ritual for the deceased 14-year-old Renaldo Krahô, I found myself among the members of my own family in Greece, mourning my father, this time in silence. Then, a few weeks later, the 23rd April 2010 officially signalled the beginning of the financial crisis in Greece.

Moved and inspired by these three successive events, I began a performance project in public spaces, whose fifth and last instalment took place during the massive riots in Syntagma Square, Athens, in June 2011. For the project, I used the leftover *collyva* and the Greek Orthodox communion wine from my father's "forty days" memorial service, integrating the sound recording of the Krahô people's wailing voices as a sort of borrowed, imported lament.[2] To briefly outline the action, I embodied the persona of a *Euzonas* (national guard) lying in a "coffin" made out of cardboard, remaining silent while passers-by were invited to answer the question: "What does this country kill in you?" Although encouraged to vocalize their responses, the participants' "offerings," in their vast majority were manuscripts and drawings placed next to my body as grave goods or written dirges. At the end of the piece, I stood up and read peoples' writings aloud. Then, I burnt my personal belongings and, with my face and hands covered by ash, switched to the persona of a migrant, holding the coffin that was then transformed into a piece of luggage.

Beyond the context of the Greek crisis, my main source of inspiration for this piece has been my experience as a witness of the lamenting voice, in both its presence and absence. Despite their multiple differences, the excessive lament for the young Renaldo and my inability to lament my own father led me to interrogate the conditions of the latter and to wonder if – and how – I could translate an ethnographic *and* a private experience of loss into a live art piece. I sought to address a more generalized sense of mourning relating to a precise historical moment.[3] Keeping this initial enquiry as a common thread, this chapter revisits my tripartite trajectory from being an aspiring ethnographer of ritual lament, to performing myself as a family member in mourning, and finally to "reinventing" a kind of contemporary "meta-lament" through performance art. Each part also denotes the mobility and continuous relocation of my own narrative voice.

My writing does not aim to provide answers or unify these distinct voices into a single or uniform narrative, but rather to raise a series of open questions: What could be the vocal expression of collective mourning today, both in my native society and in a remote one, within the context of globalization? Given that current cultural norms in the Greek social context tend to suppress the overt vocalization of pain, to what extent can silence act as an alternative vocality of mourning? Moreover, is there a clear opposition between the lament of the "Others" and "our failure to lament"? Furthermore, could performance art *instigate* lament, and what form of vocality would this contemporary "meta-lament" take? How can such a performative "meta-lament" facilitate – through voice, words or images – the expression of pain related to collective loss, in the fugitive environment of the city, involving passers-by and casting them as contemporary "mourners"? Finally, what happens when this action is inserted in a context already overwhelmed by voices, and is addressed to people assembling there for the specific occasion of a protest?

Auto-ethnography: "between self-reflexivity and self-absorption"[4]

Drawing on the tension between the sonorous excess of a ritual lament and the silence of a "de-ritualized" urban funeral, my analysis negotiates several challenges. Firstly, silence is understood here as a manifestation of vocality that establishes dynamic, antiphonic tensions with vocal excess – rather than reading it as an essentialized opposite. Secondly, I do not presume that binaries, as used here, correspond to a deeper, inevitably hierarchical, opposition between the two contexts. Such an ethnocentric understanding would define a boundary between the abstract category of "Others," who still maintain their "ancestral" voice through which they can voice their pain, and the abstract category of "us," those who are alienated and silenced by the burden of social norms. Without erasing cultural differences, I consider both situations as particular fragments of time occurring within specific cultural contexts that, albeit different, partake in the same globalized world.[5]

These fragments of time are unavoidably presented through the filter of my own embodied position(s), without any claim to scientific "objectivity." Any pragmatic assessment would reveal that they were also framed by a vertiginous series of transatlantic flights, imbued by the fuzz that this gives to perception and rendered tangible only through the following – and somewhat impressionist – jeg-lagged narrative. This choice is inspired by the auto-ethnographic and auto-reflexive turn in the field of anthropology, especially by studies on death and mourning that connect the personal with the social, and poetry with analytical rigour.

I am particularly inspired by Nadia Seremetakis (1991) who studied lament rituals in her native region of Inner Mani, and Neni Panourgiá (1995) who researched urban ways of dying in contemporary Athens, focusing on her own family. Beyond these voices from Greek ethnography, I also build on Renato Rosaldo (2004: 170–71), who argued that he became able to understand how the members of the Ilonkot tribe he was studying connected rage with grief only after his wife passed away, as well as on Ruth Behar (1991) who explained how she had to suspend her long-term ethnography on death and memory in rural Spain in order to mourn her beloved grandfather in Miami. Considering the journey itself as a micro-lens through which further analysis can be facilitated, this chapter also draws on Shahram Khosravi's (2007) conception of auto-ethnography, as applied to the way he theorized his life-experience as an "illegal traveller" in order to analyse the performance of borders. Finally, following the writings of anthropologists such as Johannes Fabian (1999: 24–31) and Bernard Müller (2013: 75–82), my view of the fieldwork experience is not that of a mere collection of data but of a perfor-mance-in-progress that can legitimately be described and analysed together with a private moment and a live-art piece.[6]

At the same time, I have to agree with Panourgiá that although "the study of death offers an exemplary opportunity for embarking on a self-reflexive anthro-pology," there is a risk of trepidation in the thin line "between self-reflexivity and self-absorption" (1995: 9). Conscious of negotiating these poles of the self, this chapter does not aspire to offer an auto-referential commentary on biographical data. Rather, my trajectory is used as a micro-narrative that allows a broader exploration into divergent modalities of the lamenting voice: from its emergence or disappearance, to the possibilities of its artistic reinvention. In this light, it seems necessary to provide a discursive framework on lament before moving to the auto-ethnographic description and analysis.

Lament: from vocal excess to silence

The ritual lament – a verbal, vocal and corporeal expression of sorrow that occurs during funereal ceremonies – is inherently connected to an acoustics of vocal excess. From an etymological point of view (Hofman 1989: 132), the Greek word for lament, *thrênos* (θρήνος), *derives from the ancient verb thrêomai* (to scream loudly), which is the root of the modern Greek substantive *thóryvos* (noise), but also the verb *throïzo* (to sough). Such vocal excess has been one of the most persistent fac-tors in the prohibition or banishment of lament in different historical and cultural contexts. In the *Laws*, Plato argues that through their passionate musical modes and excessive corporeality, laments create contagious feelings that can feminize and derange a citizen's soul and mind (Alexiou 1974: 28).

In her contemporary ethnography of death rituals based in the Southern Greek region of Mani, Seremetakis (1991) thoroughly analysed the persistent tension between the traditions of ritual lament and the Orthodox church, and between modern medical and/or secular attitudes towards human loss. Seremetakis underlines the importance of acoustic violence as manifested through the lamenting voice, but also the screaming voice (*skoúximo*). For her, "'screaming [for] the dead' counters the isolation of death" in the sense that "the voice of the mourner supplements the silence of the corpse" (1991: 101, 97). As she explains, "the acoustics of death embodied in 'screaming' and lamenting and the presence or 'appearance' (fanérosi) of kin construct the 'good death.' The silent death is the asocial 'bad death' without kin support" (Seremetakis 1991: 97).

This crucial role of vocal excess does not imply its essentialized opposition to silence, but works in an antiphonic relation to it during the lament. For Seremetakis, antiphony is a multi-levelled function that characterizes the "internal acoustic organization of lament," articulated between "linguistic and extralinguistic media, between poetry and prose, music and screaming," but which also has broader social, juridical and political meanings (1991: 100). Silence, performed by the voiceless chorus of men, has its particular role in this co-articulation of different sonorities: "The gender dichotomies of the lament session, in which women are vocal, emotionally demonstrative in public, and the men are silent, inhibited, and spatially separate, can also be understood as a further antiphonic dynamic" (Seremetakis 1991: 104).

By valorizing the physical absence of voice, this broad conceptualization of antiphony can also be useful in our understanding of contemporary performance art and activism dealing with loss, within which my own live art can be contextualized. Through a brief overview of key examples, we can see that in some cases silence is associated with the lack of expression, while in several others it can become a powerful tool that undoes dominant uses of language. For instance, the AIDS activists of ACT UP state in their logo that silence equals death, while Diamanda Galás, a member of ACT UP, but also a musician and performer highly influenced by Maniot laments, recalls in her art the acoustic violence of the latter through a masterful and extreme reinvention that pushes the human voice to a liminal sonority.[7]

On the other hand, activists such as The Women in Black expand the concept of silence by re-appropriating women's deprivation of speech in the Mediterranean, using it as a subversive way of collectively expressing feelings of anti-nationalistic and anti-sexist mourning.[8] As Athena Athanasiou has shown, these activists create "potentials of disquieting silence, one that deconstructs, if only partially, temporarily and incalculably, the mandated silences constitutive to the master narratives of ethnocentrism and phallogocentrism" (2010: 221). In the same register, performance artist Leda Papakonstandinou reinvents the poetics of lament in contemporary urban centres by paying silent tribute to those that remain unmourned in contemporary Greece. In the 2007 piece *In The Name Of*, her voiceless mourning can be read as a symbolic vocalization of resistance to the silenced and concealed losses she aims to undo. Drawing on my earlier conceptualization of antiphony, I propose to understand these divergent "meta-laments" not as essentialized oppositions but as realities and potentialities that operate on a dynamic continuum between the excess and the absence of voice. In the rest of this chapter, I explore the vocal expression of loss through my personal experience as a witness and/or a performer, with the above continuum as the theoretical basis.

Lamenting (with the) "Others"

26th February 2010. Brazil, Tocantins State, Krahôlandia Indigenous Land, Village Pedra Branca. 7:00 a.m. 14-year-old Renaldo Krahô has been killed by his cousin of the same age, during a game with guns that the two teenagers had thought unloaded. Three weeks earlier, within the context of a Franco-Brazilian academic exchange, I had started preliminary fieldwork focusing on the rich tradition of Krahô ritual songs.[9] The Krahô are members of the broader Timbira tribe. They still speak their mother-tongue (Gê, a sub-category of the Macro-Gê linguistic trunk) but are also often fluent in Portuguese. Today they reside in the Central Brazilian savannah, in the North-Eastern part of the state of Tocantins.[10]

As soon as I was informed about the death, I went to the teenager's house, mute with shock. Renaldo was lying in the middle of the room covered by sheets. The Krahô believe that the soul (*Karô*) can return to the body a few hours after death (Melatti 1978: 108–9), but for Renaldo this moment had already passed, and so his hair had been cut and his body washed. Several women were sitting around the corpse forming a circle. At some point, after the sad, but sober, speeches given by two elder relatives of Renaldo, his *inxê* (which might be rendered "mother") started to remove her son's eyelashes, covered him with another sheet, and massaged the fingers of his right hand.[11] Then, she broke into a passionate yet stylized weeping. To my ears, it seemed as if a basic melodic line was repeated and each time intensified, building – through the syllabic prolongation – towards a high-pitched scream, finally turning into a sob, heavy breathing and breathlessness.[12]

The other women started weeping along with her in low voices, in a sort of murmur that gradually became more intense. At some point, the women removed the sheets covering the body and began its ritual adornment. The boy was now laid on the ground, decorated with red paint and white bird feathers. With a shuddering cry, one of the wailing women fell onto the corpse. Some of her fellows, sitting on the floor, held her in their arms. Several male relatives had also joined the circle of tears, wails and sobs. As the night advanced, people from other villages arrived and gathered at the house. Five of the village elders also came in. Guided by the *padré*, the person seen as the "spiritual leader" of the village, they began to intone a song with a constant and rigorous rhythm, vigorously marked by the stamping of the right foot. They formed a rectangle in front of the wailers' circle, while on the other side an increasing number of women were standing, with their knees slightly bent, shaking their arms back and forth. To my ears, constituted by classical music education and Balkan and Mediterranean influences, it seemed like these women were supporting the singers by holding a drone.

Although I did not intend to record, given the nature of the situation, Luis Pinto Caco Xen, one of the elders that I was closer to, urged me to do so: "Where is your camera? Take it and film, so that we do not forget how the Krahô cry, so that our young people can learn." Thus, I took a few shots, until I felt Renaldo's *inxê* stop weeping and stare at me. It was already dark – the space was now filled with candlelight – but the cold light of a lantern was accentuating the paleness of

Renaldo's visage. As the night advanced, songs and wails made the room quake. One woman was passing through offering *cachaça*;[13] "to sustain the night," she said. At some point, I tried to join the drone, timidly, and to my relief, I was warmly encouraged by Luis to continue.

At the first light of dawn, I found that the ritual lamentation was still ongoing, but I decided to go to the place where Renaldo would be buried. There, a group of men were digging a hole. The dead body was placed in the hole. We added some tree trunks on top, then soil, then some more trunks and palm leaves, and finally filled up the hole with dirt. All around, women were crying, more than ever, but still retaining the same persistent melodic line. Renaldo's *inxê* was standing there in silent despair, her eyes dried of tears, her gaze frozen. When I went back to the village, the ritual lament still sounded from inside the house. During the following two days spent in Pedra Branca, I would occasionally hear an aged neighbour, a close uncle of the deceased, utter a shout or form of yodel in front of his house, alone in his pain.[14]

"Lamenting our failure to lament"?

My planned return to Krahôlandia did not materialize. Only a few weeks later, I received a phone call from my home in Greece. After several months of ongoing problems, my father's health had taken a turn for the worse. The phone signal was terrible as – from the other side of the ocean – my father told me: "I called to say goodbye." Hardly audible, high-pitched, almost unrecognizable, his disembodied, interrupted voice sounded like a death rattle.

After a journey of thirty-six hours, I arrived at Thessaloniki airport on the night of the 9th April. From my brother's surprisingly tender hug, I realized that my father had already passed away; it had happened that very morning. So, shortly after assisting in the wake for Renaldo, I found myself in mourning among the members of my own family, this time in silence, away from the body of the deceased. As my mother would later admit, she was putting in an immense effort not to start weeping and screaming; in other words, in order not to lose control. The pressure to perform the social role of the decent widow, contained in her muteness, was carried to such an extreme that one of her very close friends asked: "Why do you remain silent, when your entire face is crying out?" Listening to my mother's memories from that occasion, she confessed that she was not silent when, several months earlier, my father had suffered from a severe crisis that led her to believe he had passed away. Completely alone with her partner, my mother remembers she had screamed so loudly that she was terrified by her own voice. Comparing this lonely howl of terror to her social muteness during the funeral, I understand that on the latter occasion – although her "entire face was crying out" – my mother had to respect dominant urban ethics and acceptable attitudes concerning death and the vocal expression of loss.

When asked later, my mother told me that she felt quite guilty for not having a proper wake, but this was a decision made by the funeral directors, "for technical reasons." Almost two decades ago, the bodies of my two grandmothers had been waked inside our house through the night. Although not a ritual lament, this was the occasion for family and friends to gather around their beloved deceased and to recall their lives, not only with tears, but also sometimes with laughter. This time, the decision reflected common practices in contemporary Greek urban contexts. In most apartments in big cities, it is now rare to hold a wake around the corpse, while in some buildings this is officially prohibited. Although my family house is situated in the suburbs and quite isolated, this generalized unofficial rule has also been partially applied.

My father's body only entered the house the following day, shortly before being transported to the church. After the Christian Orthodox service, followed by the funeral orations of the priest and of close colleagues of my father, I recited one of his last poems, *Apokálypse* (revelation, but also apocalypse). "Lamenting our failure to lament," my only possible farewell to the deceased was made through his own lyrical voice, as I took the responsibility to try and keep it alive. Echoing the title, the poem sounded like an apocalyptic vision of my father's entire life, and death. Was this a kind of self-made, written lament, through which I was able to express my own loss vocally? As I write these words, my father's last verses still make me shiver:

> And suddenly
> one morning
> the body naked like the sob
> thrown supine on the autopsy table.
>
> *(Chatziprokopiou 2004: 10; my translation)*

Following the innumerable salutations of friends and relatives, all wishing us courage and strength, we went to the graveyard. It was one of the first days of spring. Standing in the sunshine, watching the coffin enter the grave, I held my mother's shuddering body. Devastated by a night of voiceless crying, my mother stood there in silent despair, her eyes dried of tears, her gaze frozen. After the funeral meal, exhausted, I faded into a deep sleep. When, three days later, I returned with my mother and siblings to the graveyard for the first memorial service, my sister asked me to perform what is a common ritual act in that occasion. Following her instructions, I broke a plate on the grave marble.[15] Then, we all left.

The need for a "meta-lament"

Deprived of the acoustics of "screaming" and lamenting, Seremetakis explains that the "silent death" is considered in Mani as asocial and "bad." Expanding her point on the emotional consequences of that "silent death," Seremetakis describes the terror she experienced as a witness of an urban *kidhía* (funeral) in Athens and concludes that "the Athenian *kidhía* disclosed the extent to which emotional affect could be determined by ritual; that fear of death and the dead could be constructed performatively" (1991: 166). Conversely, Panourgiá – focusing on the urban ways of dying in Athens – confessed that when she chanced upon a funeral in Mani, she was terrified precisely because of its vocal excess, by its acoustic violence: "The voices of the women, the deep wailing and crying, still ring in my ears" (1995: 125).

Although such a reaction could coincide with generalized Western attitudes towards death in contemporary urban centres, Panourgiá is careful not to infer an easy binary that would oppose Seremetakis's supposed "folklorization" to her own "modernization." Instead, Panourgiá argues that the key factor determining our horror of death is familiarity: "What is familiar, no matter how frightening, is manageable and containable, as it rests within a known and accessible frame of reference" (1995: 125). Panourgiá's assumption is totally reasonable, and anticipated by the fact that her fieldwork was conducted among her family. However, are we justified in ascribing general validity to this assumption? Is it true that the "familiar" is always "manageable and containable," especially at the moment of death?

In relation to my previous narration, when I was back home among my bereaved family, I did not feel that things could be more manageable or containable because of my familiarity with the context. On the contrary, my own deep lack of familiarity with death was further enhanced precisely by the fact that this unfamiliar occurrence took place at *my* home. Combined with my long absence, the vertigo of consecutive flights, and the lack of an all-night-long wake around the body of the deceased father, this lack of familiarity made me feel even more alienated. The numb silence of my relatives, or my mother's muffled cry, sounded unbearable to me. At the same time, the voices of the Krahô lamenters were still ringing in my ears; not in a terrifying, but in a consoling way.

I am not suggesting that having only spent three weeks with them, I felt comfortable among the Krahô, and terrified back home. This would be a completely exoticizing, if not hilariously dilettante, declaration. On the contrary, the fieldwork had made me aware of the complexity and the strains of conducting immersive research among an indigenous community. In many ways, the notion of cultural difference, whose foundations I had been taught to contest during my anti-structuralist anthropological training, made itself tangibly present during that period, articulated in the incessant repetition of the term *cupén* (the white, the non-Indian), in contradiction to *mehin* (the native, the Krahô): sometimes the sole words I was able to catch, immersed as I was in the soundscape of the language I was trying to learn.

And yet, on the night of Renaldo's wake, even if only for those few moments during which I was encouraged to join the singers and support the drone, it seemed that these barriers had been temporarily suspended through the harmonic coexistence of voices-in-tune. Reflecting back on that moment, I now realize that insistently vibrating in my body during my first night back home, these remote voices were articulated, not in an irreconcilable contrast, but in an antiphonic dynamic with the unspoken, silenced pain of my family. It is from this viewpoint that I now perceive why the experience of lamenting with the Krahô cannot be an absolute alterity that would further highlight our "failure to lament" (in contemporary urban centres of the West). Conversely, I propose that, if I learned anything by joining – even fugitively – the cry of the "Others," it is how to lend a more attentive ear to the muffled screams of mourning – both theirs and ours – and let myself be surprised by their deafening potential. Or even, to transform them into live art.

Lamenting voice as a potentiality

The final instalment of my performance project took place on the 28th June 2011, in Syntagma Square, Athens. Thousands of people had assembled there in a 48-hour protest against a new set of austerity measures. Focusing on the soundscape, I can still recall the intermittent, menacing flash-bangs, the ambulance sirens, the voices of the crowd singing, shouting or screaming, chanting slogans or speaking, or drowned in unstoppable coughing. The tangible materiality of the acoustic situation clearly defined the vocal dimension of the performance. Immersed within the voices of the protesters, it seemed pointless to use the recording of the Krahô lament.

Three of us performed, our faces covered by oxygen masks and pulverized Maalox. Starting around 6:00 p.m., dressed like the national guards that stand to attention in front of the Parliament on the left and right sides of a cenotaph (the Monument to the Unknown Soldier), we stepped down the stairs in the direction of the lower part of the Square.[16] Looking at our action, most people demonstrated their approval through overt praise and applause. Moving through the protesters, we reached the centre of the Square and stood there, mirroring the guards. We took it in turns to lie in the "coffin," our simulacrum of the cenotaph, filled-up with texts and images that symbolized *what this country kills in us* (Figure 9.1). Next to the "coffin," people could read a set of instructions that invited them to express their own losses.

FIGURE 9.1 *What Does This Country Kill in You?*, Athens 2011. © Stephanos Mangriotis.

From the perspective of lying prostrate on the ground, the soundscape of the riot seemed like an enveloping dome. The police stun-grenades and the chorus of human voices – sounding in anger or despair – intermingled with songs performed as part of a series of concerts put on in support of the demonstration. Our actions were inserted into the hubbub of the protest, and at the same time dispersed among it; we had the feeling of a "sonic vortex" around us. In the midst of the tumult, protesters were pausing for a moment to write down or draw their responses. Some of them even came to hug us, without uttering a word. Around 8:00 p.m., the atmosphere filled up with tear-gas and more stun-grenades exploded, while the overall situation seemed to be getting out of control. Protesters started fainting. Somebody fell into the "coffin," while the ambulance stretcher also needed space to pass through. Given this urgency, we quickly put people's responses in our "luggage" and stopped. Unlike previous versions of this piece, the recorded Krahô lament was not used, people did not express their losses vocally, and even their written laments were not vocalized. The vocal *ends* of our performance, in both senses of the word *end*, lay suspended (Phelan and Lane 1998).

Should we understand this final silence as a "failure to lament"? A cry, drowned in the tear-gas and atmosphere of Syntagma Square?[17] Given the theoretical premise of this chapter, and through my witnessing of the lamenting voice as described and analysed above, the absence of voice can operate not only in contrast to, but also in an antiphonic dynamic with, its excess. This chapter aimed to unfold the vocal expression of loss in its complexity; Renaldo's *inxê* gazing voicelessly at the grave-side, or stopping her weeping in order to look penetratingly at my camera; my mother's screams, those piercing, and those muffled. Despite the cultural norms of my social context, I found a way to lament my father through his own, written, lyrical voice. Perhaps there is never a complete "failure to lament," predetermined by external contexts: humans in pain do have the agency to express vocally their personal and/or collective losses by the means they dispose at a specific moment and occasion.

What Does this Country Kill in You? has been my own (performative) means at the specific occasion of its creation. My purpose was not to imitate the voices and silences described in this chapter, but to create an *antiphonic* response to them. The suspended vocalization during the final performance should not be seen as a "failure to lament." On the contrary, I propose that the voiceless action of people putting their losses into words itself created an antiphonic, critical dynamic within the hubbub of the protest. In turn, the "coffin" became a sort of cenotaph that contained people's suffering, and hosted that collective poem-*in-situ*, as a sort of embodied page. How could we listen to that page? Based on my own experience of addressing my father's loss through the pages he left to us, as a concluding note to this chapter, I would like to push further the concept of antiphony, and propose that this can also include the written word, in its potentiality to become voice. Thus, I suggest that the responses of the silent participants, albeit unheard, can still function as containers and/or springboards of lamenting vocality. Perhaps, one day, other people will decide to vocalize these written traces of our performance and, through an antiphonic act, turn the debris of our individual losses into collective, and potentially transformative, laments.

Notes

1 The phrase "lamenting our failure to lament" is a direct reference to Holst-Warhaft (1992: 158). A first version of this chapter was presented at the *Inside/Outside Europe: On Performance, Identities and Ruptures* Symposium, University of Winchester, 2013. I thank Marilena Zaroulia and Philip Hager for their invitation and feedback. This chapter is dedicated to Hypatia Vourloumis and Eirini Efstathiou, my dearest friends and fellow performers at Syntagma Square.

2 The forty-days memorial (*sarandámera*) is a highly important practice in the Greek Orthodox Church. Usually held on the Sunday that is closest to the fortieth day after the death, this timing echoes Christ's stay on earth for forty days after the Resurrection. During this occasion, the family of the deceased distributes *collyva,* a wheat-based food that symbolizes everlasting life.

3 This interrogation follows the Freudian conceptualization of mourning as related not only to a human loss but also to an ideal (Freud 1957).

4 Panourgiá (1995: 9).

5 This point of view is suggested by my Krahô interlocutors. For instance, probably guessing my exoticizing expectations regarding the vocal traditions of his tribe, a young man at the village had made me aware that "the globalization has already passed from here. The BBC and Globo made documentaries on us. We also watch TV as everybody does."

6 Fabian (1999: 24–31) suggests that "participant observation itself can never be a series of questions and answers that are being accumulated, but rather a nexus of performances in which the ethnographer acts […] as an 'ethnodramaturg.'" Müller (2013: 75–82) invites anthropologists "to take on the role of co-creators of a social situation and draw the appropriate consequences in terms of their methodology."

7 AIDS Coalition to Unleash Power (ACT UP) is an international direct action advocacy group working to impact the lives of people with AIDS through legislation, medical research and policy. Diamanda Galás is an American avant-garde composer, vocalist, pianist, organist, performance artist, painter and ACT-UP activist, whose works largely concentrate on the topics of AIDS, mental illness, despair, injustice, condemnation and loss of dignity.

8 Women in Black is a world-wide network of women committed to peace with justice and actively opposed to injustice, war, militarism and other forms of violence.

9 My stay in Brazil was financed by CAPES (Coordenação de Aperfeiçoamento de Pessoal de Nível Superior). I am indebted to Professor Armindo Jorge de Carvalho de Bião (1950–2013), without whose support my fieldwork would have been impossible, along with Professor Francisco Serrafim who encouraged me to focus on the Krahô.

10 For an introduction to the Krahô, see http://pib.socioambiental.org/en/povo/kraho.

11 The use of this term is actually a catachresis, aiming to iron out the original complexity of the native term; *inxê* is not equivalent to the Western notion of motherhood. The Krahô people maintain a complex kinship, closely related to a detailed system of naming and determined by both consanguinity and affinity.

12 For a comparative study of the vocal attributes of ritual wailing among tribes of the Gê linguistic trunk, see Urban (1988: 385–400). Urban defines four crying signal types that he calls *icons of crying.* These are: "(1) the 'cry break,' (2) the voiced inhalation, (3) the creaky voice, and (4) the falsetto vowel" (1998: 389). All things considered, these vocal features could apply to the Krahô ritual wailing I assisted in.

13 This is an extremely popular type of Brazilian rum, made from sugar cane.

14 For a study of the Krahô funeral system, see Cunha (1978).

15 Breaking a plate on the tomb is still a common practice in Greece. In some places, its symbolism is to "frighten" Charon (the figure that in Greece incarnates death). According to

a similar belief, the *collyva* of this memorial service have to be sugar-free, "in order not to sweeten Death."

16 Walking in Syntagma Square the night before our performance, and having already decided on using this image with my colleagues, I saw a stencil tagged on the trunk of a tree with the same motive: a national guard with a tear-gas mask and Maalox.

17 This breathlessness evokes both the quality of the Krahô's lamenting voices and their word for the dead: *ratëk*, he who does not have any more *khwôk* (air) entering his *itotok* (heart). The resonance with the equivalent Greek word is startling: *ksepsichó*, to be out of breath, to die, to lose the soul, the *psyche*, which is derived from the verb *psícho*: to blow, to give breath.

References

Alexiou, M. (1974) *The Ritual Lament in Greek Tradition*, Cambridge: Cambridge University Press.

Athanasiou, A. (2010) "Undoing language: gender dissent and the disquiet of silence," in Canakis, C., Kantsa, V., and Yannakopoulos, K. (eds) *Language and Sexuality (Through and) Beyond Gender*, Newcastle upon Tyne: Cambridge Scholars Publishing, 219–46.

Behar, R. (1991) "Death and memory: from Santa Maria del Monte to Miami Beach," *Cultural Anthropology*, 6(3): 346–84.

Chatziprokopiou, M. (2004) *Tá Sínnefa tou Ararát*, Thessaloniki: Gutenberg-Dardanos.

Cunha, M. (1978) *Os Mortos e os Outros: Uma Análise do Sistema Funerário e da Noção de Pessoa entre os Indios Krahó*, São Paulo: Hucitec.

Fabian, J. (1999) "Theater and anthropology," *Theatricality and Culture Research in African Literatures*, 30(4): 24–31.

Freud, S. (1957) "Mourning and melancholia," in Strachey, J. (ed.) *The Standard Edition of the Complete Psychological Works of Sigmund Freud, 14*, London: Hogarth Press, 243–58.

Hofman, J. (1989) *Etymoligisches Wörterbuch des Griechischen*, trans. A.D. Papanikolaou, Athens: Papadimas.

Holst-Warhaft, G. (1992) *Dangerous Voices: Women's Laments and Greek Literature*, New York: Routledge.

Khosravi, S. (2007) "The 'illegal' traveller: an auto-ethnography of borders," *Social Anthropology*, 15(3): 321–34.

Melatti, J.C. (1978) *Ritos de uma Tribo Timbira*, São Paulo: Ática.

Müller, B. (2013) "Le terrain: un théâtre anthropologique," *Revue Communications*, 92: 75–83.

Panourgiá, N. (1995) *Fragments of Death, Fables of Identity: An Athenian Anthropography*, Wisconsin: University of Wisconsin Press.

Phelan, P. and Lane, J. (eds) (1998) *The Ends of Performance*, New York: NYU Press.

Rosaldo, R. (2004) "Grief and a headhunter's rage," in Robben A.C.G.M. (ed.) *Death, Mourning, and Burial: A Cross-Cultural Reader*, Malden: Blackwell, 167–78.

Seremetakis, N.C. (1991) *The Last Word: Women, Death and Divination in Inner Mani*, Chicago and London: University of Chicago Press.

Urban, G. (1988) "Ritual wailing in Amerindian Brazil," *American Anthropologist, New Series*, 90(2): 385–400.

10

ENCHANTED VOICES

Voice in Australian sound art

Norie Neumark

> The overall effect of enchantment is a mood of fullness, plenitude or liveliness, a sense of having had one's nerves or circulation or concentration powers tuned up or recharged …
>
> (Bennett 2001: 5)

Enchantment and wonder, where we are "caught up and carried away" (Bennett 2001: 5), are modes to which sound art is particularly attuned, enlivening the senses of its makers and its listeners, tuning us up and into the world. In sound artworks, voice in particular – uncanny and affective, alluring and disturbing, caressing and musical – has the potential to make the enchantment of the modern world audible. As political theorist Jane Bennett argues through her aesthetic and affective understanding of the ethics of enchantment, to *sense* the enchantment and wonder of the modern world is vital to reanimate the engagement necessary to motivate generous ethical behaviour.

To address here the full spectrum of enchanted voices in Australian sound art is impossible;[1] I have chosen instead to engage in conversations with a number of artists whose work – including radiophonic works, installations and performances – is intensely and viscerally present in my memory. Although these artists work in different ways with voice, I would suggest that they all provoke us to listen to the enchantments of everyday life and the world around us, shifting our sense and our senses:

> [T]o be enchanted is to be both charmed and disturbed: charmed by a fascinating repetition of sounds or images, disturbed to find that, although your sense-perception has become intensified, your background sense of order has flown out the door.
>
> *(Bennett 2001: 34)*

For this chapter, Robyn Ravlich (1949–), Sherre DeLys (1958–), Jon Rose (1951–) and Hollis Taylor (1951–), and Sonia Leber (1959–) and David Chesworth (1958–) generously collaborated in email conversations with me. I have tried to make a space for their own voices to emerge in these edited conversations and to convey a sense of the wondrous complexities, specificities and multiplicities of the voices that animate their work.

Because of the crucial role of the ABC (Australian Broadcasting Corporation) in Australian audio art, I begin with Robyn Ravlich, whose involvement with ABC radio spanned thirty-five years. She was one of the producers and presenters for the innovative audio arts programmes *Surface Tension* and *The Listening Room*, which opened up the "auditory imagination" that Don Ihde has described as "mak[ing] the invisible *present* [...] hear[ing] the *otherness* revealed by voice [and] listening to the *voiced* character of the sounds of the World" (2007: 51, 147).[2] Ravlich's own work, beautiful, lyrical and alluring, is finely tuned to the intimate and poetic possibilities of radiophonic work and the voices it brings forth, as she described it to me, to "caress the ear."

NEUMARK: In many of your pieces you move around particular spaces which are meaningful to the people you are interviewing – this produces a very moving, located and distinctive quality of voice in yourself and the people you talk to, and brings those spaces alive for listeners. Could you talk about that please?

RAVLICH: I often prefer location recordings for interviews. If recorded in a studio setting, for instance, my interview with Norah Guthrie would have lacked the poignancy of recording amidst the archives of her late father Woody Guthrie, where she revealed treasure after treasure amongst his unpublished song lyrics, diaries and drawings; her voice catching in moments of deep emotion and tears flowing between us (Ravlich 2012). Similarly, in the basement of the Louvre's Musée de la Mode et du Textile, curator Lydia Kamitsis pulled out drawer after drawer of regal and worn shoes from centuries past, her voice capturing the rapture of reliving their histories.

NEUMARK: Could you talk particularly about *The Graveyard Gate* (1994), which for me is a stunning example, not just of your sensitivity to the performative potential of voices in location, but also the importance of silence and space in radiophonic work?

RAVLICH: I like to place myself in the landscape in many of my own radio features, no more so than for *The Graveyard Gate*, an excursion through Sydney's Rookwood necropolis, the largest cemetery in the southern hemisphere. I made multiple visits to the cemetery, recording discursive interviews and conversations with artists, a gravedigger, mourners and cemetery managers from different traditions, wandering around plots, tombstones and vaults whose characters and stories were related with verve and great affection. By recording on location I was able to make a performance of my voice and others, eliciting dramatic tales of nocturnal parties and pranks, sad stories of infant mortality and fascinating rituals of a local Gypsy clan. Above all, the talk was not a continuous stream – pauses were left as we walked, leaving our footsteps to speak with their own voice or as an under layer to studio recordings of close-miked actors reading epitaphs and poetic fragments (Ravlich 2010).

NEUMARK: Has your relationship with, and understanding of, voice changed over the years, through your listening and your own practice – any key moments?

RAVLICH: As a teenager, I was captivated by a broadcast of *The Human Voice* by Jean Cocteau, a monologue in which a woman rides a rollercoaster from joy to anguish as she's rejected by her lover in a phone call. I sensed the voice's power and urgency, so in creating my feature *Starry Night*, I sought and found the same hair-raising range in the voice of American art historian Al Boime, who "rendered" the Van Gogh iconic painting so graphically he seemed swept by force into its cypress tree and swirling sky beyond. He was immersed in a compelling inner vision, which was channelled in his voice, creating riveting listening. Later, I asked him to "read" *The Raft of the Medusa,* Géricault's epic painting of a maritime disaster, a metaphor for me of the terrible fate experienced by victims of the Bosnian war and the Rwandan genocide. His rich, rising, choking voice evoked horrors of an unending journey into depravity and despair as a faint beacon of hope glimmered on the far horizon.

NEUMARK: You spoke to me earlier of the "melismatic dance" of voice, can you say more?

RAVLICH: I do like colour and movement in voice as I come from a background of performing my poetry and some performance art. I'm attracted to musical characteristics in the voice, such as melody and melisma. In natural spoken speech – in interviews – I like to hear changes in the voice as they reflect changes in how the person is thinking and feeling.

NEUMARK: And non-human voices?

RAVLICH: I'm mindful that voices are not only human; that such creatures as birds and animals contribute their own beautiful languages and speaking modes in the field recordings that I like to use judiciously where appropriate. The "voice" of the rusting iron gate that I used as a repeating motif in *The Graveyard Gate* was very much about grain, colour and the weft of time. My short feature *Water's Voice* played with language, which was by its nature fluid as well as using the expressive sounds of water lapping, flooding, gurgling and bubbling. I was inspired by a chapter on "Water's Voice" in Gaston Bachelard's *Water and Dreams* but found myself in new territory when I interviewed linguist Bill Palmer, who helped me realize how many of our words for things in the watery domain employed the liquid sounds of water, including "liquescence," "aqua," "fluvial," "flow," "flood," "sprinkle," "trickle," "drop" and "plop." Working with the skilled actor Anna Volska in the radio studio, it became possible to imaginatively play with watery sounding words, which I then wove into a collage of water sounds to suggest a language of water.

Listening to Ravlich's captivating sonorous work and words, I realize how much our "deep and powerful attachments" to the world are rendered "palpable and audible" (Bennett 2001: 4)[3] by a poet's ear, as it enables her to hear and produce the musical voices of people and things.[4] Musical voices are at heart enchanting, for, as Bennett notes, the word *enchant* resounds with the French, *chanter*, to sing: "To 'en-chant': to surround with song or incantation; hence, to cast a spell with sounds, to make full under the sway of a magical refrain, to carry away on a sonorous stream" (2001: 6).

Such is the intense and spellbinding power of the work of Sherre DeLys, who worked on *The Listening Room*, while also maintaining her own sound art practice, collaborating on installations and with musicians. DeLys's work is animated by a distinctive, ever surprising and always captivating "musical approach to voice."

NEUMARK: For me, one of your pieces that works with voice in a most poetic and musical way is *If* (DeLys 2008). Can you talk about the process of making that work?

DELYS: I was at The Children's Hospital in Sydney making a sound installation when I met the young patient Andrew Salter. Andrew has a lively energy that called for movement, and I like walking to keep the conversation grounded in the body. "Let's go for a walk," I say, and we soon find ourselves in the garden where I ask, "What if you were a plant at The Children's Hospital?" "If I were a plant at The Children's Hospital and I saw the kids go past, I'd think to myself, 'I'm lucky to be a plant, seeing all these sick kids go by and I'm fit as a fiddle. I might be turned into a fiddle, but I'll be fit AS a fiddle.'" It's not only in Andrew's words, it's in his lively vocal rhythms, and his curious inflections that we hear his talent for empathy. As we walk around the hospital grounds we play a call-and-response game, with me asking Andrew to imagine himself as the creatures we encounter. "If I was a bird," "If I were a fish" – his voicing of empathy perhaps priming us for empathic listening. And then when we reach the aviary, Andrew coos with the pigeons, a moving communication born of his intense regard for our connection with the natural world.

NEUMARK: There is an affect here that you intensify through the play with his voice, and others' in the production ... Can you elaborate on that process?

DELYS: For me, studio production can enhance the voice's ability to move us, to mobilize the body and mind towards sentiment. Listening back as Andrew thinks an answer aloud, the tentative way he stretches out the word *a-a-and* becomes music, a held note. The different ways he articulates the repeated word *if* contain universes of emotion – now suggesting promise, now questioning and so on. So, in the studio we sample and loop selected words. With tape rolling,

I ask cellist Ion Pearce to transcribe the pitch and rhythm of vocal lines we've created, and I record him working out pitches by trial and error, striving to mimic Andrew's voice with his own and with the cello, going beyond his vocal range, reaching for connection. My interest in voice is never purely musical, but always to do with voice's relational capacities. Arranging these voices, one reaching out for another, the sense of connection took shape along with the music.

NEUMARK: Your work is stunning in bringing out a sense of what musicality of voice is and, unexpectedly, can be. Can you say more about that?

DELYS: During the *John Cage 2012 Centenary,* Rick Moody challenged me and musician Chris Abrahams to use his lecture, a performed essay on Cage and his masterwork *4'33",* as the basis for a radio composition. Rick's text was to be "one element in the music of the thing" and his voice "just an instrument" (DeLys 2013).

We started by recording four minutes and thirty-three seconds of silence, then cut that 4'33" audio track into many short pieces, distributing them randomly throughout Rick's recorded lecture. Cage composed *4'33"* in 1952. I liked the idea that our 4'33" of silence would be deployed in a manner appropriate to our more sped-up era. I imagined the silences, which cropped up in the middle of sentences and even words, as prompts to return, again and again, to awareness of one's own thoughts, feelings and sensations – a form of listening to one's own voice. In any case, the short silences rupture the grammar, offering instead the durational sense of silence and non-silence, thus liberating Rick's voice from the confines of discursive meaning to become musical. Later, we noticed the intervention had unwittingly created an effect similar to Cage's *Lecture on Nothing.*

NEUMARK: In that work, it seems to me that you *inhabit* Cage's work, in Nicolas Bourriaud's sense (2002: 18). Could you talk about the piece *Fidelity* (DeLys 2003) where I sense you "inhabited" an archival recording of Helen Keller – and where, it seems, voices called out to you, touched you, inviting you to work with them?

DELYS: When I first heard the archival recording of an interview with Helen Keller, conducted with the aid of her companion of thirty-four years, Polly Thompson, you might say the voices "touched" me literally. My emotion registered first as subtle physical sensations, as it's often possible to notice when paying close attention to the body while listening.

When the interviewer asks a question, we hear Polly repeat the words softly so that Helen can feel vibrations. Helen reads Polly's lips, with her first finger on the lips, second on the nose, thumb resting on the throat. Helen's utterances are strange to the hearing world's ear, and "uncivilized" in contrast with Polly's perfect British diction, the two voices weaving in counterpoint as Helen strains to reply and Polly repeats her words rolling the "r"s in red *rrro-*ses. As with *If,* the voices in this interview offer the opportunity to appreciate the musical texture of our connectedness to others.

Hearing this the first time, my mind went to the haunting recording of Tchaikovsky's *Vocalise* performed by Clara Rockmore playing the theramin, an early electronic instrument played without touch, accompanied by her sister on piano. In that moment, I recognized that I wanted to make a radio piece that simply set these two recordings – the interview and Clara's soaring voice-like theramin performance – side-by-side to hear what happens when they speak together. *Inhabited* is a perfect description for the way this played out. At the moment of my first hearing, the Helen Keller interview was in conversation with the sisters' performance in ways that I didn't fully understand, although I can now articulate correspondences around touch and voice. I instinctively put a "gash" into the recording so that a forty-five-second portion of the interview is repeated immediately after first hearing. While a number of listeners have spoken to me of a mysterious power that this conversation between two recordings seems to hold, none have mentioned noticing the very obvious repetition. Perhaps under the spell of this ancient disc recording, with its exquisite surface noise, understanding human expression through language recedes as we are taken up, inhabited, mesmerized by the music of voice.

Through her finely tuned musical intuition, DeLys makes sensible the "intimacy of temporality" within silence and the voice (Ihde 2007: 57, 111).[5] Playing sometimes at the noisier end of the music-to-sound arts spectrum is Jon Rose, who is primarily known as an innovative and experimental musician and improviser, but who also has a long association with radio. In 1988, Rose made an extraordinary work for *The Listening Room*, *Paganini's Last Testimony*, which memorably opened with violins screeching Paganini's confession. In that work, the play with, and between, the choruses of people (dead, alive and a bit of both) and violin voices – as well as Rose's play with his own human voice – performed a testimony to the wondrous and multiple potentials of voice as much as to Paganini himself.[6] It was the beginning of my own *enchantment* by Rose's voices, including, years later, his performance with/of Australian fences. As he discussed in "Lines in red sand,"

> In the sense that Paul Klee described the process of drawing as "taking a line for a walk," so it was for me with a string [...]. By 1983 I was using fence wire to string up whole gallery spaces. Two years later, the penny dropped. Why was I making string installations when the continent that I was living on was covered with strings? That became the conceit: Australia was not mapped out with millions of miles of fences; it was hooked up to millions of miles of string instruments.
>
> *(Rose 2012b: 197)*

To me, this wondrous fences project (Rose n.d.1; Taylor 2007) seemed to ask, *what if* fences had a voice, what performance would this evoke, what listening? I posed this question to Rose and his collaborator, Hollis Taylor.

FIGURE 10.1 Jon Rose and Hollis Taylor play a fence in the Strzelecki Desert, Australia 2005. Photo © the artists.

TAYLOR: "What if" – we assumed that the fences all have a different voice – that was the premise for why we had to stop and play so many. If they were the same or similar, we would have stayed in town and saved our energy.

NEUMARK: Can you both say a bit more about performing with these musical voices?

TAYLOR: Inherent in everything we do is the natureculture continuum. We don't mind the gap. Fences reset our perception. To have a voice is to be sung into existence.

ROSE: Sometimes in the outback, the wind is playing the fence (Aeolian), so it is a question of joining the performance, or holding back and listening to the show as an audience member. Whenever upper partials of a string (any length including fence wire) are bowed, the grain of the bowed string (the saw-tooth waveform that inhabits all string music) is removed, and you are left with voice-like harmonics (more like sine waves, in fact) – it is this purity that maybe you are pointing to. Although after decades of playing fences, you get a sense of how one might sound by looking at it, but then there are surprises …

NEUMARK: Can you talk about the collaboration in this project?

TAYLOR: I was the straight man. This was Jon's project, and if I thought it was wacky and avant-garde (and that I was chiefly the chauffeur and the cook), the outback folks made me think twice. Many had already given their fences a tug. To them, fences mean the local music of place, the voice of their paddock, rather than an experimental music session. As for the sound or voice of the fence, I often did not know how they really sounded until later, since most fences are very quiet. Contact microphones gave them their "voice," as captured by the mini-disc recorder. Sometimes we wore headphones, giving me more of a sense of what that instrument was about. Fences, unlike violins, can suddenly turn on you. Weather affects them much more than their smaller cousins. Fences are a type of weather report. I found them frustrating, coming from the violin. On a violin, the notes are where they are, and you can be confident in a performance that you can replicate your rehearsal. Not so for a fence. Fences gave me (forced onto me) the opportunity to improvise in a way I never would have on a violin. Playing a fence is like interviewing a stranger; you have to be ready for just about anything and can't afford to take too strong a stance until you get your bearings.

NEUMARK: Can you expand on the "natureculture continuum," particularly as it plays out in relations to birds?

TAYLOR: I am currently writing a book, *Is Birdsong Music? Outback Encounters with an Australian Songbird.* I discovered the pied butcherbird on our first fence trip [...]. This was an epiphany for me [...]. Originality, creativity, genius – these are 18th-century concepts that are overdue for a rethink, along with human exceptionalism, which is currently being disproven in a number of parameters.

Rose, too, listens to the voices of birds. *Syd and George*, a piece for radio (2007) is

> the story of a 20-year-long interspecies relationship between Syd Curtis, a member of *Homo sapiens* and George, an Albert's Lyrebird or *Menura alberti*, who lives in Lamington National Park, Australia. In parts of the composition, both species tend to morph into each other.
>
> *(Rose 2012a; n.d.2)*

I asked Rose to comment further on the musical voices across species and things and how the figure and performance of "morphing" expresses or plays with that.

ROSE: Years ago, I had a nineteen-string cello; Hollis asked me once, how did I know when to stop (adding strings)? I explained it in terms of abstract expressionism: the painter just looks up and suddenly realizes it's over. I think my perception has changed over the years. Nothing is really over; there is just a pause for breath, maybe – an ubiquitous *work-in-progress*. As with so many of the Aboriginal notions of fluidity between the animate and inanimate, between the living and the dead, between history, myth and the present moment – we just shift states a little. That is not to deny the presence of a performance. Sometimes we play fences *in situ* to a real human audience using amplification: it's a show. The world is inherently musical and, as a musician, it is our job to reveal what is there and maybe convey or share it with other voices from other species and indeed – even other objects that may be in a current state of silence.

To respond to, and perform, the shape-shifting and morphing between things and beings, as Rose does so compellingly, is to listen to and evoke the world's enchantment. As Bruno Latour and Jane Bennett contend, the "morphism" that questions sharp distinctions, such as between nature and culture, and recognizes instead hybridity or "crossings" is "an essential component of an ethical, ecologically aware life" (Bennett 2001: 99; see also 96–98). Partly, too, as Rose says, it is a response to Australian Aboriginal culture, which hears *country* speak.

Turning next to Australian urban spaces takes me to this final conversation with artist collaborators Sonia Leber and David Chesworth.

NEUMARK: I'd like to focus here on the way you work with voice in your engaging and unique installation works for public spaces. Your website (Leber and Chesworth n.d.) raises provocative points about public space and movement (passers-by); about the "call" of the voice, coming not just through words but all sorts of bodily sounds; and about different modalities of voice – beckoning, cajoling, harassing …

LEBER AND CHESWORTH: When we started making sound works in public spaces, we recognized that our works would exist in spaces occupied by people somewhat absorbed in their daily routines, which is quite a different situation to making work for galleries where people actively experience art by choice. The ability for us to create a *situation* was key in many of these works, where people passing through city spaces could feel themselves directly addressed or instantly arrested in some way.

We developed an approach where our fabricated sound environments were declamatory, emphatic and, we hoped, difficult to ignore. We reasoned that if we built up our works around voices calling out to the passers-by, addressing them directly, then the passers-by would listen. We could then shift the audience's experience of the objective space to a subjective experience that would unfold further over time, and an otherwise disinterested public could be transformed into an *audience*.

In one of our first collaborative works, *5000 Calls*, commissioned for the exterior of the Sydney Olympic Stadium, our aim was to create a shifting field of voices built up from the sounds of human effort. We approached people engaged in all kinds of physical effort and mental activity and recorded sounds that were a by-product of those activities. We extracted the sounds they made before language emerged, what we refer to as proto-linguistic sounds – grunts and groans, sighs and exclamations, sounds of pleasure, disappointment, straining and meditating, laughing and crying and many more.

The *5000 Calls* soundscape is built up from thousands of human voice fragments programmed via a computer server to shift and recombine across a large open public area surrounding the main stadium. As visitors move within the space, they experience a number of different "imagined crowds" in changing eddies of affect and sensation, in some ways mirroring the crowds inside the stadium. Some voices are loud commands (commands are an abiding interest of ours as they pre-date language), other voices are more personal and intimate.

At different times, a crowd of breathy sighs and exclamations might develop, and then this might transmute into a field of short commands drawn from many different voices and contexts such as "Keep it going! – Stop! – Get out of here! – Push!" Visitors might be plunged into an active sports team circling all around them, with each voice jostling for attention. These urgent sports calls might shift into a group of infectiously giggling and gurgling kids at play, then the intimate struggles of patients in a rehabilitation hospital.

NEUMARK: You've talked about an "acousmatic presence" of the voices in this piece …

LEBER AND CHESWORTH: Our intention was to mostly exclude the vocalizations of "language," to largely utilize the vast range of what the voice can do beyond the "sense" of speech. This is similar to what Pierre Schaeffer (1966) describes as the acousmatic "sound object," which is experienced as pure "sound in itself."[7] While these non-speech sounds are recognizably vocal sounds – think of an "aaah" sighing sound, for instance – they can also be perceived as "sound objects," stripped of their original meaning and context. These vocal fragments could then be deployed by us in different ways, in unfolding fabrications composed across space and time, with a logic derived from their redeployment by us, rather than the logic of their original source.

There is also a noticeable, shimmering "field of reverberation" that we generated from the voices, that can be described as a kind of "sonic residue" similar to what happens in large cathedrals when a choir stops singing and a lingering trail or reverberation of the voices is heard, beyond the moment of singing. The idea of an uncanny "vocal residue" arose from our fascination with the way traditional cathedrals employed ways of amplifying the voice beyond mortal possibilities, as if the unnatural amplification and lingering aspects of the voice in cathedrals were proof of special powers of the priest and also "proof" of a life beyond death.

NEUMARK: Can you discuss your understanding of voice, site and architecture, including your recent work *This Is Before We Disappear from View*?

LEBER AND CHESWORTH: This was created for the 19th Biennale of Sydney and was situated in a disused coal storage bunker on an ex-shipbuilding island that was once a penal institution. Into this industrial space, enclosed by high walls that obscure vision, we inserted two specific soundscapes. The first element is a choir of constantly rising female voices, in constant upwards *glissandi*, seeping up over the wall, with the loudspeakers remaining unseen. The voices rise and rise in constant upwards *glissandi*, primal and pre-linguistic, unbounded and at times wobbly and almost hysterical.

In contrast, a large metal speaker jammed into a corner emits a singular voice that is hard to identify. Robotic and genderless, and taking on metallic aspects of the speaker enclosure, the voice delivers a series of pronouncements

FIGURE 10.2 Sonia Leber and David Chesworth, *This Is Before We Disappear from View*, 2014, 4–16 channel audio, metal, variable, 25 minutes. Installation view at 19th Biennale of Sydney (2014). Courtesy the artists and Fehily Contemporary, Melbourne. Photo © Sonia Leber.

in measured bursts. The voice persuades us to respond to its guidance and authority. Where the rising female voices are beyond speech but remain corporeal, this voice delivers a spoken monologue that is beyond the body and almost beyond human recognition.

In this work, the voices transform a rather functional space into what Michel Foucault calls a "heterotopia" or a space of otherness.[8] In the blankness of the setting, the voices invite visions and apparitions. The voices also invite questions of proof, doubt, belief and knowledge.

We have developed an abiding fascination that certain architectural forms act on us in ineffable ways, making certain metaphysical "fictions" manifest. While architecture can appear so fixed and unchanging, the human voice can be deployed to shift the reading of a space, to make it more ambiguous, to fabricate an almost infinite array of situations; some connected to the real world, others wholly imagined spaces of "otherness." The human voice can create riddles of identity, situation, agency and philosophical argument. It can also be used to address city passers-by as citizens of a *polis*, raising questions about their agency and relationship to the public domain.

Leber and Chesworth's intriguing works speak of the performative potentials of voice (Neumark 2010) – as voices of crowds call audiences into listening crowds, for example. They speak, too, of the desires of listeners to be both caressed and disturbed by a provocative play with voice as it calls to us in public sites – beckoning, cajoling, harassing.

To close, I return to Jane Bennett whose notion of enchantment resonates wondrously for me with the work of Ravlich, DeLys, Rose and Taylor, and Leber and Chesworth. In their different ways, the voices in these artists' works touch us in all senses, sensually and affectively – imaginatively speaking to Bennett's understanding of the importance of "an energetics of ethics," where affect, aesthetics and sensibility energize and inspire ethical engagements with the world:

> Without modes of enchantment, we might not have the energy and inspiration to enact ecological projects, or to contest ugly and unjust modes of commercialization, or to respond generously to humans and nonhumans that challenge our settled identities. These enchantments are already in and around us.
>
> (Bennett 2001: 174)

This attention to affect, ethics and aesthetics revitalizes the figure of enchantment, and, as I have explored in this chapter, opens up a way to listen to the specificities of voices in Australian sound art as they caress, call out, disturb and intensify. The voices I have chosen to present here are exemplary in the way they *performatively* evoke these qualities of enchantment. In conclusion, I would also suggest that, in turn, these voices in sound art also enrich our revitalized understandings of enchantment itself. As we listen to these sound art voices, we sense that enchantment enables us to "enact" because it is itself a performative enactment. The performativity, which is essential to voice as it evokes, invokes, convokes or provokes, moves from and between bodies and things. Listening to, sensing, this performativity of voice brings to the fore the performativity of affect itself – the very affect, which is so central to enchantment. Affect makes us *feel* investments and attachments, and, more than that – and in ways that are culturally and politically important to understand – affect actually *performs* those very investments and attachments between individuals and things, communities and assemblages.[9] In their performance of the affect that is so central to the experience of enchantment, voices in Australian sound art make vivid the performativity of enchantment – enchantment is not just "there" but it is always becoming, as it is performed.

Acknowledgement

I gratefully acknowledge The Department of Aesthetics and Communication (Section for Aesthetics and Culture), Aarhus University, Denmark, where I have been Guest Professor during the writing of this chapter. I expand on enchanted voices in my forthcoming book (Neumark forthcoming).

Notes

1 For a fuller discussion, see Kouvaras (2013).
2 *Surface Tension* ran from 1985 to 1987 and *The Listening Room* from 1988 to 2003. For a fuller discussion, see Madsen (2008).

3 Ihde's *Listening and Voice* is also important for understanding the power of the poetic in the "auditory imagination" (2007:161–65).
4 See Bennett (2001: 154) and Ihde (2007: 14, 147), about the sonority of language and the voices of things.
5 It is interesting that the inventor of the theramin, Lev Theramin, was a radio scientist and its music, as Steven Connor discusses, "was a product not of removing the body from the circuit but of introducing the body into it. In a sense it was all interference" (2010: 227).
6 "Based on the letters of Paganini himself, the listener discovers a violinist who was as much a faith healer and bewitcher of the masses as conjurer with sound. A full range of violins including the ten string double violin, the baby megaphone violin, the 19 string cello, and amplified bow are used and cut with the ravings of evangelical preachers from America's Bible belt" (Rose n.d.3).
7 See Chion (1999: 18).
8 See Foucault (1984).
9 See Ahmed (2001).

References

Ahmed, S. (2001) "Communities that feel: intensity, difference and attachment," in Koivunen, A. and Paasonen, S. (eds) *Conference Proceedings for Affective Encounters: Rethinking Embodiment in Feminist Media Studies,* Turku, University of Turku, https://susannapaasonen.files.wordpress.com/2014/11/proceedings.pdf.

Bennett, J. (2001) *The Enchantment of Modern Life: Attachments, Crossings and Ethics*, Princeton: Princeton University.

Bourriaud, N. (2002) *Postproduction: Culture as Screenplay: How Art Reprograms the World*, New York: Has and Sternberg.

Chion, M. (1999) *The Voice in Cinema*, trans. C. Gorbman, New York: Columbia University Press.

Connor, S. (2010) *Matter of Air: Science and Art of the Ethereal*, London: Reaktion.

DeLys, S. (2003) *Fidelity*, https://soundcloud.com/sherred.

——(2008) *If*, www.radiolab.org/story/91763-our-podcast-comes-in-all-shapes-and-sizes/.

——(2013) *John Cage and the Question of Genre*, www.thirdcoastfestival.org/library/1258-john-cage-and-the-question-of-genre.

Foucault, M. (1984) "Of other spaces, heterotopias," *Architecture, Mouvement, Continuité*, 5: 46–49.

Ihde, D. (2007) *Listening and Voice: Phenomenologies of Sound*, Albany: State University of New York.

Kouvaras, L.I. (2013) *Loading the Silence: Australian Sound Art in the Post-Digital Age*, Farnham, UK and Burlington, US: Ashgate.

Leber, S. and Chesworth, D. (n.d.) leberandchesworth.com.

Madsen, V. (2008) "Written in air: experiments in radio," in Priest, G. (ed.) *Experimental Music: Audio Explorations in Australia*, Sydney: UNSW Press.

Neumark, N. (2010) "Doing things with voices: performativity and voice," in Neumark, N., Gibson, R., and van Leeuwen, T. (eds) *Voice: Vocal Aesthetics in Digital Arts and Media*, Cambridge, MA: MIT Press, 95–118.

——(forthcoming) *Voicetracks: Voice, Media, and Media Arts in the Post-Humanist Turn*. Cambridge, MA: MIT Press.

Ravlich, R. (2010) *Graveyard Gate*, www.abc.net.au/radionational/programs/360/on-a-raft-all-at-sea—robyn-ravlich-tribute/3039092. Produced 1994, posted online 2010.

——(2012) *Her Father's Daughter*, www.abc.net.au/radionational/programs/intothemusic/nora-guthrie—her-father27s-daughter/4093874.

Rose, J. (2012a) *Syd and George, ABC*, www.abc.net.au/radionational/programs/intothemusic/syd-and-george-by-jon-rose/3933256.

——(2012b) "Lines in red sand," in Zorn, J. (ed.) *Arcana VI: Musicians on Music*, New York: Hips Road/Tzadik.

——(n.d.1) *Great Fences Project*, www.jonroseweb.com/f_projects_great_fences.html.

——(n.d.2) *Syd and George*, www.jonroseweb.com/h_radio_syd_and_george.html.

——(n.d.3) *Paganini's Last Testimony*, www.jonroseweb.com/h_radio_list.html.

Schaeffer, P. (1966) *Traité des Objets Musicaux*, Paris: Seuil.

Taylor, H. (2007) *Post Impressions: A Travel Book for Tragic Intellectuals*, Portland: Twisted Fiddle.

Part IV
Voice in experience and documentation

11

"BODY MUSICALITY"

The visual, virtual, visceral voice

Ben Macpherson

In 1938, German musicologist Alexander Truslit published *Gestaltung und Bewegung in der Musik* ("Shaping and Motion in Music"), a work which explored the relationship between what musicians and performers see, hear and experience in the production of music. Truslit's work was in many ways ahead of its time. It included the concept of the "inner motion" of music (*innere Bewegtheit*) which he suggested was more than simply the intrinsic properties of the sound: "[m]usical motion is internal and encompasses *the whole human being*" (Repp 1992: 267; added emphasis).[1] To demonstrate his thesis, Truslit developed the concept of visual curves to represent such motion (Figure 11.1). Interestingly, Truslit takes care to emphasize that the "curve as such is not important [...] it is only an aid to visualizing the motion" (Repp 1992: 270). The visual representation of musical motion, then, is secondary to the motion itself; a motion which is internal and visceral. This hierarchy of the bodily experience of music claiming primacy over the visual representation provides the starting point for this discussion.

Of particular note is Truslit's position on what the curvilinear visuals represent: they are aids – not to the melody – but "to the motion" (Repp 1992: 270), suggesting that Truslit understood there to be an explicit connection between what was seen *visually* and what was experienced *viscerally*; a relationship that would subsequently affect the orality/aurality of the sound produced. Building on Truslit's concerns, and with reference to contemporary scholarship on his theory by Hans Brandner (2012), this chapter explores the relationship between the visual and the visceral in vocal performance. First, it offers a theoretical position on the way visual representations might evidence a sense of what Brandner has termed "body musicality" (2012); the idea that visual representations of musical intention are explicitly connected to the visceral experience of performance. Then, it constructs a critical historiography of three forms of Western notational practice and a contemporary visual aid to vocal performance, analysing them as aids to "visualizing the [inner,

FIGURE 11.1 Drawing of a visual curve, after Truslit. © Ben Macpherson.

bodily] motion" of music. This historiography extends from the *neumes* of classical antiquity through *orthochronic* stave-notation and graphic scoring, concluding with a 21st-century technological representation of voice. In order to explore an implicit "bodily musical sense" (Brandner 2012) in notational and visual strategies for voice, the problematic relationship between the oral/aural, the visual and the visceral must first be addressed.

The body in visual culture: a position

There can be little doubt that postmodernity is primarily visual, with a reliance on electronic devices that use icons rather than words, computer games, advertising, social media and picture-sharing websites that encourage people to document their lives visually. In the last decade of the 20th century, cultural theorist W.J.T. Mitchell (1994) identified what he called the "pictorial turn" in the increased ocularcentrism of contemporary culture. Detailing this turn, Chris Jenks suggests that "[v]ision is lionised among the senses and treated as wholly autonomous" (1995: 1).[2] Regarding such a common cultural situation, practitioner–scholar Yvon Bonenfant (2014) observes that "[i]t's so hard to dissociate questions of primacy from ocularcentric culture. If you go into the postmodern and poststructural critiques of how we think […], it's very difficult to know."

This reliance on, and privileging of, the visual destabilizes Truslit's concept that visual images are somehow less important than the information they represent. In Truslit's framework, curvilinear visuals were used to denote the inner bodily motion of the music. Yet, early theories of visual culture claim that ocularcentrism "connects us to the truth as it *distances us from the corporeal*" (Keller and Grontkowski 1983: 209; added emphasis). Philosophical difficulties with notions of "truth" notwithstanding, the result of such ocularcentrism – which Adriana Cavarero argues has been endemic in Western culture since antiquity (2005: 42–43) – is that the visceral becomes marginalized in favour of the visual. After all, it is not uncommon for musicians or vocalists to say they "*read* music," or suggest they can "*sight* sing," implicitly preferentializing the visual understanding of music over the visceral, inverting Truslit's concept of "inner motion."[3]

In a further demonstration of the marginalized body, studies of reading and writing habits in antiquity and the medieval period have debated whether it was common to voice the written text aloud, or to read silently.[4] This debate derives in part from Eduard Norden's *Die Antike Kunstprosa*, in which the author recounted the surprise and confusion experienced by Augustine upon finding the bishop

Ambrose reading *silently* (1898: 6). Similarly in 1927, philologist Joseph Balogh published "Voces paginarum" in support of the practice of reading aloud. Referencing Balogh's discussion in his cultural history of lines, anthropologist Tim Ingold writes that "monastic readers would follow the text with their lips as much as with their eyes, pronouncing or murmuring the words. [...] The sounds that came forth were known as *voces paginarum* – the 'voices of the pages'" (2007: 14). Balogh's and Ingold's emphasis on the visual in their consideration of *voces paginarum* seemingly marginalizes the visceral experience of vocalizing what is seen. In short, even in the medieval period, it would seem that ocularcentrism removed "the whole human being" from the equation (Truslit in Repp 1992: 267).

Yet, a comprehensive review of this issue by William A. Johnson (2000) provides a basis to begin considering ways in which the visual and the vocal may have related directly to the visceral in the practices of the medieval period and beyond. Johnson suggests that numerous factors were involved in the practices of reading aloud, including the pagination of scrolls and the idea that written texts were *performative*, intended to be read aloud. Both factors are transferable to a consideration of musical notation for voice, and provide an appropriate framework within which to offer a brief historiography of such notational practices. It is noteworthy that contemporary discussions regarding performativity centre implicitly on concerns of the body in a manner that challenges the primacy of the visual in line with Truslit's thesis.

Indeed, the turn to embodied knowledge – with its roots in the Western philosophies of Immanuel Kant, William James, John Dewey and Maurice Merleau-Ponty – has enabled cultural theorists and neuroscientists to place the *visceral*, rather than the visual, at the centre of lived experience.[5] The work of neurobiologist Antonio Damasio (1994; 2000; 2010) has inverted Cartesian dualisms of mind and body, whilst Richard Shusterman's monograph *Body Consciousness: A Philosophy of Mindfulness and Somaesthetics* drew together philosophical and neurological debates to construct a "critical study [...] of how we experience and use the living body (soma) as a site of sensory appreciation (aesthesis)" (2008: 1). This "sensory appreciation" surely includes experiences elicited from visual and vocal stimuli as part of the performance Gestalt.[6] Crucially, the visual does not claim primacy here, aligning with James's philosophy that: "[t]he world experienced comes at all times with our body as its centre, centre of vision, centre of action, centre of interest" (1976: 86).

In this case, I would argue that any visual stimulus – such as Truslit's curves or musical notation – acts as an aid to visualizing the inner motion of the bodily experience. How, then, might the body act as the "centre of vision" in understanding the visual properties of notational practices for voice? Considering this question through a brief analytical historiography, the following section will focus on the *neumatic* and *cheironomic* notation of the medieval period.[7]

Neumatic and cheironomic notation: visuals of the visceral voice

Neumatic notation depicted the contours and shapes of the intended melody, rather than pitch or rhythmic information, leaving the singer to interpret these shapes

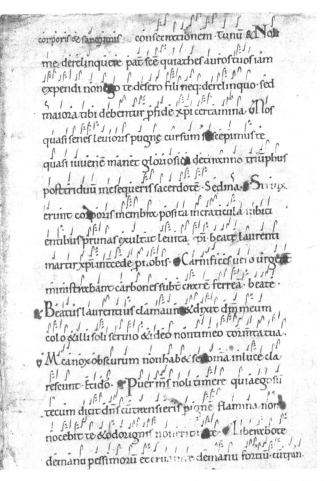

FIGURE 11.2 Fragments of an Antiphoner including parts of offices for Lawrence, Hippolitus, and Peter and Paul. Copyright © The British Library Board, Burney 277, f.70.

from their prior knowledge of the work (Figure 11.2). Of particular importance was the use of *cheironomic neumes*, which were held to represent the gestural movement of the conductor's hand (Parrish 1957: 8). In this sense, the visual representation of melody was implicitly and intimately connected to bodily gesture in a manner similar to Truslit's curves.

Rather than dislocating voice from body, *cheironomic neumes* served to emphasize their *connectedness*. *Neumatic* notation was therefore an "aid to visualizing the motion" (Truslit in Repp 1992: 270). As performance historian Tobin Nellhaus observes, it was not until the 17th century that bodily gesture became "opposed to voice" (2006: 79). In fact, the implicit connection between the visceral and vocal can be seen in the very name of this notation: *neumatic* derives from the Greek *pneuma* ("breath"), and *cheironomic*[8] is a compound word deriving from χείρ, meaning "hand," and νέμω, which means either to dispense/distribute or to manage/regulate.[9] In this sense, *cheironomic neumes* may be (albeit clumsily) translated as something approaching "hand breaths": *embodied* invocations for vocalizing sound, associated with the movement of the conductor's hands as they direct the singers.

Neumatic notation therefore evidenced "body musicality" in two ways: as a sign-system to recall previously embodied knowledge, and a *cheironomic* representation of gestural motion. The visual became what Bonenfant (2014) describes as a "facilitator" of the visceral, embodied voice. Suzannah Biernoff, a historian of visual culture, suggests that "[v]ision, in the medieval world, did not leave the viewer untouched" (2005: 44). Recent neurobiological theories help shed light on this position and articulate the way in which *neumatic* and *cheironomic* notation allowed the body to become a site of *aesthesis*. Damasio has consistently suggested that the experience of sight or sound initiates the neurobiological consciousness of being:

> consciousness [the embodied sense of being] begins as the feeling of what happens when we see or hear or touch [...], it is a feeling that accompanies the making of any kind of image – visual, auditory, tactile, visceral – within our living organisms.
>
> *(2000: 26)*

In a later work, he simply asserts that consciousness is *"felt,"* it is embodied (Damasio 2010: 15; added emphasis). This position suggests that no one sense dominates in the embodied consciousness of lived experience; they all contribute to *aesthesis*, "with [the] body as its centre" (James 1976: 86).

Biernoff further asserts that prior to the 17th century, "there was no mind–body problem" (2005: 42); the visual, vocal and visceral were intimately connected. Written representations of speech and song did not rely on the primacy of the visual as the champions of ocularcentrism might in our postmodern epoch; these visual symbols were understood to represent *embodied* vocalic gesture. In other words, the *voces paginarum* – the "voices of the pages" – were not silent or sonic, but *sensed*. "Bodily musical sense" (Brandner 2012) was therefore implicit in notational (and textual) prac-tices of antiquity and the medieval period. All of this looked set to change, however, with the arrival of the *orthochronic* system of notation.

Orthochronic notation: visual voice over visceral vocality?

By the 17th century, *orthochronic* notation, with pitches placed within and on a series of parallel lines, was established as the predominant visual system in music, and is still used widely in contemporary Western classical and popular music. In contrast to the *neumatic* system, the *orthochronic* score was elevated to its current status as a "fixed" work in the Barthesian sense;[10] the sophisticated indicators of rhythm, tempo, timing, pitch, key, phrasing, pauses, repetition, dynamics and stress found in modern standardized notation helped to ameliorate some of the performative indeterminacies or idiosyncrasies in evidence before such stringent information was provided in the written score (see Goehr 1992: 42). As a result, Ingold suggests that *orthochronic* notation "ceased to be a notation of [bodily] gesture" (2007: 33). The body was removed from the relationship between visual representation and musico-vocal intention in favour of a melody-centric strategy. The utterance subsequently became dissociated from the utterer in a powerful visual demonstration of Cartesian duality.

Additionally, the linearity of the stave format might also be considered problematic in conceptualizing the relationship between vision, voice and body. Musicologist John Sloboda (2005: 5–6) observed that the potential advantages of this system include economy of space, note-clustering, bar-lines and information regarding note-length, key and tempo. Likewise, sequential progressions bound to a linear stave system provide a sense of structure to the cognitive engagement with note-reading.[11] However, such linearity may also constrict the sense of musical shape; performative expressions of embodied musicality do not operate in "straight" lines. Therefore, whilst *neumatic* and *cheironomic* notation implicitly utilized the visual as a facilitator of the visceral voice through indicators of physical gesture, the *orthochronic* system ostensibly focuses on melody – on the voice, rather than the body. Yet, this position can be challenged from an anthropological and psychological perspective, presenting evidence that a focus on visual representations of melodic intent need not distance the corporeal.

Two lines of evidence support a sense of "body musicality" in *orthochronic* notation. In Ingold's anthropological discussion of inscriptions, he defines two "classes of line": threads and traces (2007: 41). Threads are lines which have surfaces and are three-dimensional; they are not inscribed on a surface, but they *have* a surface (for example, a fishing line, the string of a musical instrument or chain-linking). Conversely, the second class of line – the trace – is an inscription etched onto a surface: a signature written on a contract, instructions for a class written on a whiteboard or the grid drawn up in architectural drawings.

This taxonomy has certain consequences when applied to the *orthochronic* system.[12] Sloboda champions *orthochronic* notation as the most complete and coherent, claiming that it "actually embodies […] the structure, or meaning, of the music," and might result in the "correct" interpretation of melodic intent (2005: 5–6). Sloboda's conflation of structure and meaning invites challenge on numerous levels, yet it could be argued that *orthochronic* notation does "embody" melodic intention in a slightly different way; through the dual function of its line-classes.

Jenks argues that "[v]iewing is an activity of transforming the material [we view] into meanings" (1995: 13). Yet, in the act of "viewing" (or "reading") *orthochronic* vocal notation, we are presented with a visually sophisticated set of instructions that remain incomplete.[13] The parallel lines of the staves correspond to Ingold's class of *trace* (2007: 41) – lines inscribed onto the surface of the page. But these are not the lines singers may pay most attention to. In the act of transforming the visual cues into *meanings* – the visual into vocal – it is the notated melody that is the ocular focus. To which of Ingold's line classes do notes, ties, slurs or beams belong? Perhaps they are both a trace and a thread – all at once inscribed onto the surface of the stave, but simultaneously representative of the sounds they indicate. Ingold highlights that *threads* exist in "three dimensional space" (2007: 41), and what is that space if not visceral? In this sense, whilst Sloboda might be incorrect to suggest *orthochronic* notation embodies meaning (2005: 5), it may certainly have more in common with the *neumatic* properties of embodied sound – representing the three-dimensional space of voices "produced by bodies," as Steven Connor has put it (2002: 80).

The sophistication of the visual information present in *orthochronic* notation may focus on melody, but in being written *to be performed*, the making of meaning and the lived experience (*aesthesis*) of the viewing are once again placed with the viewer – the vocalist – in the act of performance. Rather than becoming "detached from the bodily gestures" of the *neumatic* system, perhaps they simply become implicit rather than explicit (Ingold 2007: 33).

Graphic scores: visceral visualization

When considering experimental forms of notation, such as "graphic scoring," one might immediately think of composers such as Luciano Berio (1927–2003) and "Sequenza III for Female Voice."[14] Written for virtuoso Cathy Berberian in 1965, Berio's work employed specific and bespoke "notational solutions" to capture what Linda Hirst and David Wright see as the "sound-image" of the piece: the expressive and extended vocal demands of the work in performance (2000: 198) (Figure 11.3).

Hirst and Wright's use of the term "sound-image" is pertinent here. Without ignoring the specific function of such approaches to notation, this term is a useful way of considering *all* forms of notation; implicit in the idea of the "sound-image" may be the dual classification of notational lines as both *threads* (vocal sound) and *traces* (visual inscription). Berio's "solutions" are expressly indicative of the *performative* demands and range the singer is required to utilize. Performance theorist Erika Fischer-Lichte argues that such sound "brings forth corporeality […] in screams, sighs, moans, sobs and laughter" (2008: 125). In this sense, Berio's score directs all attention onto the body in its performative language and the notation used to express this: "The materiality of the voice reveals the performer's materiality in its entirety" (Fischer-Lichte 2008: 129); the body becomes a site of vocal *aesthesis*.

Berio's notation does not indicate a specific key, there are no bar lines, only occasional intimations of pitch, and the freedom to interpret each ten-second increment of music as the singer wishes.[15] Much like *neumatic* notation, it achieves a sense of "body musicality" in its use of symbols and performance directions. At the

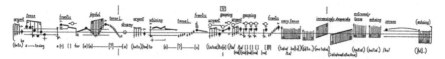

FIGURE 11.3 Four bars from Luciano Berio "Sequenza III für Frauenstimme". © Copyright 1968 by Universal Edition (London) Ltd, London. © Copyright assigned to Universal Edition A.G., Wien/UE 13723. Reproduced by permission.

same time, it demonstrates the logic and sophistication of the *orthochronic* system, suggesting something of an amalgam of historical and modern approaches to writing for voice which honours the implicit appreciation of "bodily musical sense" in the visual representation of vocal performance.

Such graphic notation is not new. In the 15th century, composers experimented with how to "visualize the motion" of the voice (Truslit in Repp 1992: 270). For example, French composer Baude Cordier wrote the chanson "Belle, Bonne, Sage" ("Beautiful, Good, Wise") in the shape of a love heart with *manner notation* in red to indicate specific rhythms, and John Bull's six-part contrapuntal "Sphera Mundi" depicts two circles, one inside the other.[16] Interestingly, both Cordier's and Bull's works are defined as "eye music": "Musical notation with a symbolic meaning that is apparent to the eye but not to the ear" (Dart 1980). Implicit in this term is a sense of the visual connecting the performer to the vocal. Yet, if the world is experienced "at all times with our body as its centre" (James 1976: 86), and Damasio's neurobiology of body consciousness begins "when we see or hear or touch" (2000: 26), then the combination of sight and sound here – the "sound-image" of the notation as both *trace* and *thread* – yet again implies a sense of "body musicality" and *aesthesis*.

The implicit "body musicality" in visual notation for voice, whether *neumatic, orthochronic* or *graphic* not only adds credence to Truslit's thesis from the early part of the 20th century, but demonstrates the importance of embodied engagement with the musical score. Yet, there is a 21st-century form of visual representation that demands consideration: the technological visualization of voice in training programmes or computer applications for student vocalists and performers.

Voice Bubbles: somatic sounds and technical touch[17]

The challenge to a disembodied ocularcentrism in postmodernity has already been explored in notational practices, but what of recent advances in the visual representations of voice via digitized computer software? In February 2014, Bonenfant released the iPad application Voice Bubbles as part of an extended research project designed to encourage children to explore the possibilities of their voice outside of the normative cultural constraints in Western culture. Children can record their voice into the electronic device making any sound they wish, play it back, add effects, and then imitate their own voice in what Bonenfant calls "mirroring games" (2014). Even in this technological representation of voice, there is an evident sense of "body musicality" through the necessity of interaction between the vocalist and the visual representation of voice, in a manner that is different to a vocalist's interaction with notation.[18]

The visuals in this programme bear strong echoes of Truslit's curvilinear diagrams in their representation of the "inner motion" of the body, directly created as a result of vocal production (Figure 11.4). They are not "notational" strategies, but "representational" images.

The voice is visually represented in colourful, crayon-like bubbles, quite literally as "sound-images" (Hirst and Wright 2000: 198). These are conceived by

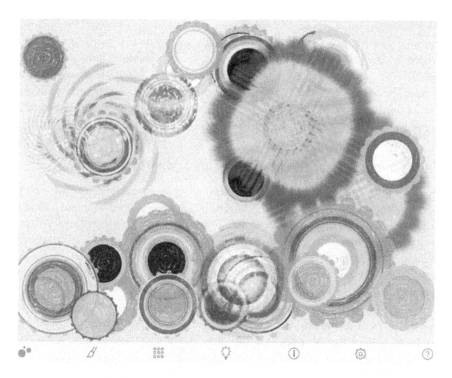

FIGURE 11.4 Voice Bubbles application screenshot. © Yvon Bonenfant 2014.

Bonenfant as "tiny little bodies – like Steven Connor's *vocalic body* – tiny little vocalic bodies" (2014), suggesting an implicit sense of the visceral within the visual representation of voice.[19] The corporeality of the visuals is further evidenced by the fact that they are crayon-like in texture: "rather than [having] a flat look, to help with the sense that it's a body rather than a drawing or a flat thing" (Bonenfant 2014). This sense of texture and depth might be understood with reference to Ingold's two classes of line, functioning as both *thread* and *trace* – a visual aid to the visceral.

Bonenfant explains that this application does not just facilitate a "release experience," but a "sophisticated experience" for the children who play with it (2014), *directly* related to the way in which the visuals depict the body as the sight of vocal *aesthesis*:

> the app tries to detect syllables – and when there is something close to an interruption in the sound like a fricative – it starts a new colour band every time there is a stop in the utterance (hard stop, glottal stop, etc.), and the colour of the colour band is based on the average frequency of the utterances within that gesture [...], it's very difficult to make two bubbles or bands be the same colour. [...] So what we've got is a little visual representation of what the body did.

(Bonenfant 2014)

The "sound-images" of the bubbles therefore contain an inherent "body musicality" representing not only the voice but the *body*. This position is given added credence when Bonenfant acknowledges that once children have created the bubbles, "they'll then switch to the effects mode [...], put an effect on [and] imitate the effect with their own voice. So their body becomes the performer they're imitating, because the visuals of the app help to give their bodies an external symbol" (2014).[20]

The commonality of the visceral, visual and virtual

Bonenfant's observation that the "bubbles" provide an external symbol of the vocalist's body returns this discussion to Truslit's demonstrations of music's visceral quality through visual representation. Whilst written in the third decade of the 20th century, it has clear links to the embodied knowledge of contemporary philosophical and theoretical discourses in performance, and in many ways sits on the continuum from the medieval use of *cheironomic neumes* through to the contemporary application of technology in visually representing the visceral voice.

As Connor argued, the visceral quality of voice is "not simply an emission of the body" but becomes its own corporeality in production (2004: 158). This can be seen in the "hand-breaths" of the *voces paginarum*, wherein the voice was the direct result of a gestural and corporeal expression. Likewise, even in the complex notational practices of the *orthochronic* system, or the visual stimuli found within the "sound-image" of graphic scoring, the incomplete nature of written performance material still requires the voice – the body – to make sense of its information.

As this chapter has demonstrated, the visceral quality of the voice is involved in all visual representations of vocal music and sound: whether in notation for performance, or software for practice. Truslit's work identified the inner motion of music through visual means, which Brandner (2012) developed with reference to "body musicality." In challenging the primacy of ocularcentrism in postmodern cultural analysis through an interdisciplinary framework of cultural studies (Ingold), musicology (Sloboda) and neuroscience (Damasio), this chapter's expansion of what "body musicality" might mean for the way vocalists, performers, composers, students and teachers of voice understand and interact with musical notation – ancient and modern – may enhance approaches to understanding and engaging with "what a body did," or what a body *can do* when it sings (Bonenfant 2014).

Acknowledgements

The development of this chapter has been in no small part due to the assistance of several colleagues and students at the University of Portsmouth, who took part in a field study based around Truslit's musicological diagrams. I wish to thank Yvon Bonenfant for discussing his work and express gratitude to Hans Brandner and Bruno

Repp for their assistance with my early efforts to explore Truslit's little-known musicological experiments.

Notes

1 The citations from Truslit are taken from the edited translation by Repp (1992).
2 This position echoes Berger's claim that "[s]eeing comes before words" (1972: 7). In the Foreword to this volume, Barker makes reference to the McGurk effect, which offers a similar hierarchy of the primacy of the visual in perception.
3 Of course, sight-reading is not a symptom of postmodernity, and has been a practice for much longer than the above comment might suggest.
4 For an extensive review of this debate, see Johnson (2000) and Goody (1987).
5 For the further discussion of embodied philosophy, see Kant (1996), James (1976; 1983), Dewey (2009) and Merleau-Ponty (2002).
6 Bonenfant suggests that "our primacy is largely tactile [...]. I guess we use neither and both [that is, visual and vocal] in terms of primacy" (2014).
7 Due to the length of this chapter, and to ensure its focus, I do not cover all forms of notational practice in Western music.
8 This term is also rendered *chironomic*. I thank Konstantinos Thomaidis for clarifying the spelling of *cheironomic*.
9 Cavarero's exploration of the terminology related to voice as breath and voice as speech is particularly interesting in this respect (2005: 19–32).
10 See "The death of the Author" and "From work to text" in Barthes (1977).
11 For further discussions see Gibson, Folley and Park (2009), Sloboda (2005) and Storr (1997).
12 Ingold's taxonomy of line classes in fact applies to all systems of notation, but is particularly applicable to the *orthochronic* system in this discussion.
13 See Johnson's discussion of the absence of locutionary and illocutionary acts in the texts of antiquity and the medieval period (2000).
14 Musicologist Janet Halfyard has termed this piece "the paradigm of the extended vocal repertoire [... and] the most written about of any piece of contemporary vocal music" (2007: 104).
15 A study of the score might hint at a B minor tonality.
16 The use of colour in graphic notation extends into contemporary approaches to teaching children music in primary school curricula. See Kuo and Chuang (2013), Lee (2013) and Pramling (2009).
17 This section contains extracts from an interview with Bonenfant held on 18th February 2014. The interview discussed many aspects of the "Your Vivacious Voice" project, and whilst this chapter focuses on the Voice Bubbles application, it is hoped further material from the interview will be reproduced in other research platforms. For detailed examinations of his approach to devising and vocal praxis, see Bonenfant (2009; 2011).
18 For a comprehensive report on computer–human interactivity, see Frogtmann et al. (2008).
19 See Connor (2000).
20 This concept of the external symbol – the "bodily musical sense" being visualized – is also seen in the University of Rochester's Vowel Shapes software (2014) designed by "Team Moose" and initiated by Ehsan Hoque (Assistant Professor in Computer Science) and Katherine Ciesinksi (Professor of Voice, Eastman College of Music). The software is designed to enhance the development of vowel shaping for students, who replicate blue circular and elliptical shapes produced by the tutors or tutor on certain vowel sounds. A yellow circle for the student's vowel shape is transposed on top of the tutor's, until the shapes match and the shape turns green. The program therefore represents, in real-time, the vowel shapes of the singer via a visual schematic. Rather than altering the shapes and positions of lips, jaw, tongue or larynx in response to the teacher's vocal sounds, the visual shapes are an aid for the students as they practise.

References

Balogh, J. (1927) "Voces paginarum: beiträge zur geschichte des lauten lesens und schreibens," *Philologus*, 82: 85–109, 202–40.

Barthes, R. (1977) "The death of the author," in *Image, Music, Text,* trans. S. Heath, London: Fontana, 142–48.

Berger, J. (1972) *Ways of Seeing*, London: Penguin.

Biernoff, S. (2005) "Carnal relations: embodied sight in Merleau-Ponty, Roger Bacon and St Francis," *Journal of Visual Culture*, 4(1): 39–52.

Bonenfant, Y. (2009) "Enskinning between extended voice and movement: somatics, touch, contact and the camera," *Journal of Dance and Somatic Practices*, 1(1): 65–87.

——(2011) "Sound, touch, the felt body and emotion: toward a haptic art of voice," *Journal of Media Arts Culture*, www.scan.net.au/scan/journal/display.php?journal_id=126.

——(2014) Interview with Ben Macpherson, University of Winchester, 18 February 2014.

Brandner, H. (2012) *Bewegungslinien der Musik: Alexander Truslit und seine Lehre der Körpermusikalität der Kinästhesie der Musik*, Augsburg: Wissner-Verlag.

Cavarero, A. (2005) *For More Than One Voice: Toward a Philosophy of Vocal Expression*, trans. P.A. Kottman, Stanford: Stanford University Press.

Connor, S. (2000) *Dumbstruck: A Cultural History of Ventriloquism*, New York and Oxford: Oxford University Press.

——(2002) "Violence, ventriloquism and the vocalic body," in Campbell, P. and Kear, A. (eds) *Psychoanalysis and Performance*, New York and London: Routledge, 75–93.

——(2004) "The strains of the voice," in Felderer, B. (ed.) *Phonorama: Eine Kulturgeschichte der Stimme als Medium*, Berlin: Matthew and Seitz, 158–72.

Damasio, A. (1994) *Descartes' Error: Emotion, Reason and the Human Brain*, New York: Grosset/Putnam.

——(2000) *The Feeling of What Happens: Body, Emotion and the Making of Consciousness*, London: Vintage.

——(2010) *Self Comes to Mind: Constructing the Conscious Brain*, London: Vintage.

Dart, T. (1980) "Eye music," *Grove Music Online (Oxford Music Online)*, www.oxfordmusiconline.com/subscriber/article/grove/music/09152.

Dewey, J. (2009) *Art as Experience*, London: Penguin.

Fischer-Lichte, E. (2008) *The Transformative Power of Performance: A New Aesthetics*, London and New York: Routledge.

Frogtmann, M.H., Fritsch, J., and Kortbek, K.J. (2008) "Kinesthetic interaction – revealing the bodily potential in interaction design," http://cs.au.dk/~kortbek/web/Publications/kinesthetic-interaction-fogtmann.pdf.

Gibson, C., Folley, B.S., and Park, S. (2009) "Enhanced divergent thinking and creativity in musicians: a behavioural and near-infrared spectroscopy study," *Brain and Cognition*, 69: 162–69.

Goehr, L. (1992) *The Imaginary Museum of Musical Works: An Essay in the Philosophy of Music*, Oxford: Clarendon Press.

Goody, J. (1987) *The Interface between the Written and the Oral*, New York and Cambridge: Cambridge University Press.

Halfyard, J.K. (2007) "Provoking acts: the theatre of Berio's *Sequenzas*," *Berio's Sequenzas: Essays on Performance, Composition and Analysis*, Basingstoke: Ashgate, 100–17.

Hirst, L. and Wright, D. (2000) "Alternative voices: contemporary vocal techniques," in Potter, J. (ed.) *The Cambridge Companion to Singing*, Cambridge and New York: Cambridge University Press, 192–203.

Ingold, T. (2007) *Lines: A Brief History*, New York and London: Routledge.

James, W. (1976) *Essays in Radical Empiricism*, Cambridge: Harvard University Press.

——(1983) *The Principles of Psychology*, Cambridge: Harvard University Press.

Jenks, C. (1995) *Visual Culture*, New York and London: Routledge.

Johnson, W.A. (2000) "Toward a sociology of reading in classical antiquity," *American Journal of Philology*, 121(4): 593–627.

Kant, I. (1996) *Anthropology from a Pragmatic Point of View*, Carbondale: Southern Illinois University Press.

Keller, E.F. and Grontkowski, C.R. (1983) "The mind's eye," in Harding, S. and Hintikka, M.B. (eds) *Discovering Reality: Feminist Perspectives on Epistemology, Metaphysics, Methodology, and Philosophy of Science*, Dordrecht: Reidel, 207–24.

Kuo, Y-T. and Chuang, M-C. (2013) "A proposal of a color music notation system on a single melody for music," *International Journal of Music Education*, 31(4): 394–412.

Lee, P-N. (2013) "Self-invented notation systems created by young children," *Music Education Research*, 15(4): 392–405.

Merleau-Ponty, M. (2002) *Phenomenology of Perception*, New York and Oxford: Routledge.

Mitchell, W.J.T. (1994) Picture Theory, Chicago: University of Chicago Press.

Nellhaus, T. (2006) "Performance strategies, images schemas, and communication networks," in McConachie, B. and Hart, E. (eds) *Performance and Cognition: Theatre Studies and the Cognitive Turn*, New York and Oxford: Routledge, 76–94.

Norden, E. (1898) *Die Antike Kunstprosa*, Leipzig: Treubner.

Parrish, C. (1957) *The Notation of Medieval Music*, Michigan: Norton.

Pramling, N. (2009) "External representation and the architecture of music: Children inventing and speaking about notations," *British Journal of Music Education*, 26: 273–91.

Repp, B. (1992) "Music as motion: a synopsis of Alexander Truslit's (1938) *Gestaltung und Bewegung in der Musik*," *Haskins Laboratories Status Report on Speech Research*, 265–78.

Shusterman, R. (2008) *Body Consciousness: A Philosophy of Mindfulness and Somaesthetics*, New York: Cambridge University Press.

Sloboda, J. (2005) *Exploring the Musical Mind: Cognition, Emotion, Ability, Function*, New York and Oxford: Oxford University Press.

Storr, A. (1997) *Music and the Mind*, London: Harper Collins.

12

TRANSCRIBING VOCALITY

Voice at the border of music after modernism

Pamela Karantonis

This chapter considers some of the challenges in documenting and writing meaningfully about classical vocal pedagogy as it applies to singing. It is situated within the cultural studies tradition of illuminating and interrogating the power structures embedded in disciplinary practices. Attendant to this is the location of vocal pedagogy as it arises from ideological and cultural investments that underscore perceptions of vocality as a marker of artistic and cultural identity in performance. Key examples span from early-20th-century pedagogical texts and their apprehension of "National Schools of singing," to the postmodern, transnational and even post-national discourse of vocality, communicated through mass media. The power relations that underpin the action of communicating vocal instruction in these examples are examined through the lens of Pierre Bourdieu's reading of pedagogic power.

The historical scope of my case studies begins with a refusal by Viennese officials to authorize Leoš Janáček's published *vocalises* for educational purposes, which I argue is a gesture of cultural, and indeed, colonial standardization of vocal exercises by the Austro-Hungarian Empire. Further examples are considered in print form, such as E. Herbert-Caesari's *The Voice of the Mind* (1951), a pedagogic text that builds upon a successful teaching career established in London in the early 20th century. Subtler tensions were evident in the Cold War period, and by the second half of the 20th century, these cultural biases eventually shifted with the emergent discourse of voice science.

On another level, many of the personalities discussed in this chapter were distinguished voice teachers, successful artists and (occasionally) voice scientists or theoreticians from diverse cultures attesting to different experiences of the classical singing world. The struggle to maintain multiple personae of pedagogue–singer–scientist–philosopher is a fruitful one, as there is a tension between science and an expanding, more circumspect, attitude to the legacy of the operatic tradition as it travels further, geographically and culturally, from the Italian Old School. This attests to a self-reflexive cosmopolitanism in pedagogic writings on vocality, a term associated most fruitfully with Cathy Berberian. The chapter's final shift is from the modernist abstraction of voice training in printed pedagogical texts in the immediate post-World-War-II era, to the postmodern audio documentation of the radio talk-show, and the liberating politics of post-War experimentation with voice in the West. Ultimately, the historical shift from the nationally distinct, culturally defended vocal pedagogies to postmodern vocality is understood as a discourse of vocal empowerment. Significantly, the pedagogical content is read as interdependent with the mode in which it was disseminated.

(Re)contextualizing treatises: from nationalism to scientific universalism

The mainstream cultural history of the Western tradition of classical and operatic singing is that it sprang from an Italian tradition of masterful vocality preceding opera. This cultural bias has a defensible basis empirically; the key works and treatises on the voice should have come to us as a result of the Italian Renaissance. The treatises are too numerous to name here, but included the Neapolitan, Roman and Bolognese Schools, which not only contained the contributions of singers, but of composers and philosophers, writing from the perspective of *listening to* inasmuch as *making* the sound. For example, some 17th- and 18th-century sources by Porpora, Pistocchi and Bernacchi referred only to pitch, trills and the general concept of dramatic expression. Two notable examples are *Opinioni de' Cantori Antichi e Moderni* (1723) by Pier Francesco Tosi and *Pensieri e Riflessioni Pratiche sopra il Canto Figurato* (1774) by Giambattista Mancini (in Cvejić and Cvejić 2008). However, some technical instruction was provided in Mancini's work, which warned against filling up the lungs with too much breath before singing (Cvejić and Cvejić 2008: 100).

There is a definite sense of comparison between the Italian and French Schools in the writing of this period. The Italian School privileged the physicality of the voice, while the French School advocated the linguistic and intellectual. The mind–body dichotomy was addressed in this culturally specific way as early as 1705, with the treatise *Comparaison de la Musique Italienne et de la Musique Françoise* by Jean-Laurent Le Cerf de la Viéville (in Nancy 2013: 69–71). One legacy of this is the belief that the Italian School could provide the technical answers:

> The French tenor Duprez, introduced the tone covering methods in the vocal technique (1830), having returned from Italy. He exploited it so he could avoid the bright and open tone many singers at that time practiced (*la voix ouverte, la voix blanche*). Duprez introduced the technique of the dark, covered voice (*voix sombre, voix couverte*) and thereby succeeded in getting a much lovelier sound.
>
> *(Cvejić and Cvejić 2008: 156)*

This thinking was sustained into the 20th century, with key pedagogic texts from the US supporting the use of Italian vowel sounds as the international model for classical singers (see Vennard (1967) and Miller (1997), among others). This did not mean that every successful opera singer in the 20th century embodied an immanent variation of Italian oral culture. Yet, the cultural power of Italian opera rendered the operatic voice in the 20th century as metonymic for Italy, even extending to the conflation of popular Neapolitan songs performed by tenors with arias from Romantic or *verismo* operas. This conflation of the two categories persists in global, popular cultures to this day.[1] The perpetuation of a certain listening culture was, to some extent, a predicate for the training methods and a singer's anticipation of career success. In Germany in the 1950s and 1960s, the legendary tenor Fritz Wunderlich understood the listening culture in which he was trained and sang all operatic repertoire in German. In fact, it was so rare for him to sing in Italian, that extant recordings of all his major roles in the Italian repertoire tend to be in German and the few YouTube clips of him singing in Italian are the exception rather than the rule (Operbathosa 2010).

While this chapter traverses some rather broad historical examples, it aims to begin within the current ideological legacy of modernism and its treatment of the trained voice as an international phenomenon – abstracted, singular and emblematic of the institutional power that brought it to the ear of the public. This relates directly to the colonial politic that presided at the beginning of the 20th century. It is evident that in this period "excellent" classical singing regarded the Old Italian School as its touchstone, but with the rise of multiple nationalisms in voice training many more nation-states sought to naturalize what were arguably culturally artificial distinctions in modes of singing. Pierre Bourdieu would account for these distinctions as a type of empire-building through pedagogy: "every power which manages to impose meanings and to impose them as legitimate by concealing the power relations which are the basis of its force, adds its own specifically symbolic force to those power relations" (in Bottomore 1990: xv). These symbolic forces underlie the discourses about national traditions and techniques during most of the 20th century.

We begin with a very brief episode in 1899, with Leoš Janáček responding to the Viennese Ministry of Culture and Education about the perceived inadequacy of his book of *vocalises*. Janáček has come to be seen as synonymous with Czech opera. His works such as *Jenůfa* (1904), *Kátya Kabanová* (1921) and *The Cunning Little Vixen* (1924) are still in the list of standard repertory in international opera houses, and yet his effort at a simple school textbook failed through bureaucracy. Janáček's collection of *vocalises*, published in 1899, was titled *Instructions for Singing Lessons*. It was completed while he was a music teacher in Brno at the Czech Men's Teacher-Training Institute. The book was written for the dual subjects of music and singing, and went on to become an informal textbook at Janáček's own organ school in Brno. The foreword by Milena Duchoňová in a recent edition provides an incisive narrative:

> Janáček endeavoured to have the Instruction[s] officially recognized as a textbook of singing for teacher-training institutes and secondary schools, but he never obtained this approval. Two professional judgements on it, drawn

up on the request of the Ministry of Culture and Education in Vienna, did not recommend the Instructions as a textbook.[2] The reviewers rebuked Janáček's Instructions for being incomplete, too brief, and for not having a sufficiently theoretical foundation [...]. Janáček was given these remarks and he accepted some of the criticism.

(Janáček 1980: xiii)

In a draft of a letter addressed to:

[...] the Ministry of Culture and Education in Vienna, Janáček expanded the Instructions by another 35 lessons – of which 22 were new vocalises – corrected the printing errors and added a Postscript. This "newly printed, corrected and supplemented copy" of the Instructions was sent again to the Ministry with the request for approval as a textbook for teacher-training institutes and secondary schools.

(Janáček 1980: xiii)

Duchoňová reports that the work seems to then vanish within the archives: "Not even the Österreichisches Staatsarchiv in Vienna was able to supply any information from the Ministry's archive" about this edition (Janáček 1980: xiii).

In 1899, when the work was published in Brno, the political and ideological leadership of the region resided with Franz Joseph I of Austria, who sought to unify – and in some ways assimilate into a Germanized and Catholicized uniformity – the many diverse cultures in the realm. This brought with it particular challenges in the late 19th century, most evident in the ethnic tension in the Balkans. There is no evidence in the archival material relating to this book of *Instructions* to suggest that there were any political undertones in the Viennese Ministry of Culture and Education's refusal to authorize or endorse Janáček's *vocalises*. However, I would argue that the "failure" here was a combination of what Bourdieu would identify as a legitimated "symbolic" power coming from the administrative centre of Vienna, nationalist politics, and to some degree, Janáček's admission that certain improvements were to be made. Although the composer studied formally in Vienna, the capacity of his music to engage with folkloric idioms at this stage in his career undermined any reputation he might build as a reliable author of standardized *vocalise* patterns. Janáček's foray into what was yet to be labelled as "ethnomusicology" spills over into indulging in the colonial imaginary.[3] Vocal training was therefore subject to the politics of colonialism, not only from Vienna, but also from a long-standing prejudice that venerated the Italian Old School, with the established success of Italian *vocalise* publications such as *Metodo Pratico di Canto Italiano* by Nicola Vaccai (1790–1848), the lively settings of *solfeggio* by Giuseppe Concone (1810–61) and a treatise and practical workbook on the *bel canto* method by the Italianized name-changing German mezzo Mathilde Marchesi (1821–1913).

Added to this illustrious list is the 19th-century Spanish–Italian-born Manuel Garcia, the notable voice teacher, whose father Manuel Garcia the Elder was the teacher of opera stars such as Maria Malibran (1808–36) and Pauline Viardot (1821–1910). The younger Garcia could attract the labels of proto-voice scientist/ethnographer to his work:

> Garcia (1806–1905), the tireless promoter of the laryngeal mirror [...] was a painstaking observer [...]. In his famous *Traité complet d'art du chant 1924* he described the vocal behaviour of the Baskir people and peasants conducting horses in St Petersburg [...] who had the astonishing facility to produce simultaneously two perfectly distinct tunes: one low pedal tone [and] a high pitch melody which he called [...] cantilena.[4]
>
> *(Wendler 2008: 280)*

This description of what might be called "throat singing," is a phenomenon in the regions of Central Asia. Its description in Garcia's treatise on voice points to the pedagogical author as a "collector" of voices and listening experiences, much like a travel writer would collect exotic encounters. In print, it reflects what Edward Said's *Orientialism* did for the analysis of literary travel fiction – in that the observation of the exotic is infused with wonder – but it also reveals a scientific curiosity. In relation to the voice, the late 19th-century aesthetic responses to science, colonialism and exoticism tended to regard a voice that was closer to nature and "the sensual" with fascination and suspicion.[5] In this case, the exotic in terms of classical vocal pedagogy is necessarily perceived as the aberration, tamed by an enlightened classicism. However, Manuel Garcia the Younger was renowned most for his fusion of the Italian Old School of pedagogy with the beginnings of voice science. The more that pedagogy distances itself from this aberration of the "folk" element in voice, the greater its legitimacy.

E. Herbert-Caesari's *The Voice of the Mind* (1951; 1978) is a pedagogic text that makes no apologies for favouring the Italian Old School. Herbert-Caesari (1884–1969) was a voice teacher, establishing himself in 1925 at Trinity College of Music, London. Whilst Janáček's textbook seemed to inconspicuously promote a nationalist agenda and a rediscovery of folk, and Garcia's treatise emphasized the scientifically "correct" inflected by a fascination with the exotic, Herbert-Caesari took the opportunity to warn of the decline of good singing. He cautioned against poorly acquired technique and vocally unsuitable repertoire (usually a euphemism for pop, jazz or folk music). He seemed to target popular influences especially, although his complaint came before rock'n'roll and the rise of the teenager:

> [The] culture of the arts is heading slowly and surely for a chaos of ugliness, a retrogression to the first feeble attempts of primitive man. Witness the slant today in terms of the surrealist daubs, sculptured monstrosities, and architectural atrocities. Is it the deliberate cult of ugliness? Or incapacity?
>
> *(1951: 38)*

Yet, in the 1978 posthumous reprint of the work, there seemed to be a revised defense of the validity of the Italian Old School, not so much for cultural reasons, but scientific ones. Surprisingly, the author argued that: "there is no such thing as a [...] national mechanism" (Herbert-Caesari 1978: 44).

National schools and the cultural arbitrary

This observation was made in the text's 1978 reprint, when voice science was making claims upon the singing community's readership, so when it came to vocal technique, readers were increasingly convinced by the immutable scientific principles that conveniently mapped onto the culturally "superior" Italian *bel canto* tradition. In a sense, the claim of science here is nothing new, as Garcia had pioneered the laryngoscope in the previous century; rather, it is more about the cultural pressure to reconcile a history of singing pedagogy with the scientific "facts." Much of this mapping or overlapping is defensible on the grounds that remedial voice work borrows from principles such as the *voce cuperto* and *coup de glotte* ("stroke of the glottis" or clean cord closure) of the Italian Old School. For example, voice scientists will examine a range of vocal behaviours in the experimental subject that relate to breath, vocal fold function during phonation, range of *vibrato*, pitch stability and larynx position that are prompted by the features of successful classical vocal singing, evidenced by the use of the operatically trained singer as the test subject in one experiment after another. A landmark piece of literature in this respect is William Vennard's extensive study *Singing the Mechanism and the Technic* (1967). It is interesting to consider that much vocal pedagogy, even the principles that have stood the test of time and have been assisted in this respect by the reinforcement of scientific discourse, can fall under what Bourdieu terms the *cultural arbitrary* in a training system:

> Education also requires a continual and productive pedagogic work [...], a process of inculcation which must last long enough to produce a durable training, i.e. a habitus, the product of internalization of the principles of a cultural arbitrary capable of perpetuating itself after the pedagogic action has ceased and thereby of perpetuating in practices the principles of the internalized arbitrary.
>
> *(Bourdieu and Passeron 1990: 27)*

There are two methods of perpetuating these principles of the *cultural arbitrary* in voice studies: through the publication of vocal pedagogical texts, and through practice itself. This extended to the institutional involvement in vocal training, noted by the US pedagogue Richard Miller:

> The modern French Ministry of Culture has long had official inspectors who visit regional conservatories of music to check the condition of vocal pedagogy. Several of these inspectors were highly influential in the post-World War II decades, demanding from regional and municipal conservatory voice teachers absolute conformity to the inspector's concept of the "vocal attack"

> (onset). These techniques are based on strong inward abdominal thrusting at the moment of onset, inducing high levels of airflow at the commencement of phonation [...]. This accounts for the pushed, sharp phonations so characteristic of many French sopranos. [...] It may well be that the English School itself greatly influenced the post-World War II French tendency toward "in and up" techniques of breathing.
>
> *(1977: xxv)*

This culturally determined appraisal of breathing and breath support in French (and subsequently English) singers is not related to language or even the literature associated with the singing. It is specifically to do with the institutional practice of monitoring breathing and the opening of the sound in education, in an example of the *cultural arbitrary* that perpetuates itself both within, and beyond, pedagogy. What is intriguing at the level of cultural politics here is that there should be a contrast in post-World–War-II French institutions with the German and Italian models of voice training. This could be traced both to a centuries-long French tradition of distinguishing its own national approach to vocal training (such as *Le Cerf de la Viéville*) – specifically the desirable traits of a singer's artistry – but perhaps also to the more visceral reaction to any pedagogic or cultural content that may be associated with the Fascist powers – a facet of recent cultural memory. These kinds of oppositions become inscribed upon the bodies of students and deny the spontaneity of an individual vocality. In his text, Miller makes a particular contrast between the French, English, Italian and German schools variously employed by North American singers. The international tensions are literally inscribed on the voice and body when vocalists parody another school: "The Italian will quickly demonstrate the excesses of the low-breath and distended abdominal posture of the German School; the German, in turn will display the higher chest position of the Italian singer." The example flourishes into "the unkind parody of the English dropped jaw [...] easily encountered [...] especially in France and Italy" (1977: xxxix). What is missing is a sense that these models have been convincingly deconstructed by the 1970s and such distinctions have continued into the 21st century in print.

The Serbian pedagogue Dušan Cvejić makes a similar identification with vocal practice and the *cultural arbitrary*: "For some time the German singing school campaigned for the so-called 'soft lump' in the throat (*weicher Knödel*) theory, that is for an active tightening of the throat in order to achieve better tone projection" (Cvejić and Cvejić 2008: 279). Cvejić then offered his opinion of this as a voice scientist, criticizing the practice for encouraging a "tight throat." The example here serves to illustrate that the vocal pedagogue will usually develop a more powerful readership when publishing advice *via negativa*, rather than making proactive statements – we learn of the difficulties of the "tight throat" which prompts our faith in the author of the critique as an advocate of the corollary, the "open" throat. This engenders a philosophy in singers and voice teachers that we often know good singing by what "it is not." The association of the technique with

Germany adds a prejudice to a practice that is arguably universal. This in itself creates a vulnerability to the *cultural arbitrary*; the terms of the critique are not always consistently interrogated.

Consulting singers can reveal persistent essentialist narratives of national differences in the production of the singing voice that move from their training into career decisions. The Spanish tenor Alfredo Kraus observed the challenges of singing French repertoire as a native Spanish speaker:

> [The French style] demands good taste, subtlety, finesse, sensitivity and control [...]. And to Italian and Spanish voices, the French language sometimes seems anti-musical, anti-singing, because it seems to go against the natural musical and vocal line. This always displeases the French, although they, themselves, are the first to admit it.
>
> *(in Matheopoulos 1986: 113)*

Post-national pedagogies

By the late 20th century, it seemed that the discourse of national schools – and indeed the pursuit of international supremacy in singing – was still relatively unchallenged by the postmodern deconstruction of other aspects of learning and knowledge. In popular texts on the "art" of singing, these kinds of tropes persist into the 21st century: "the vocal scene resembles the Tower of Babel, with many voices screaming for attention" (Marek 2007: xxi). The orientalist metanarrative governing classical voice texts had its own postmodern "crisis" with Richard Miller's revised publication on the topic of ever-permeable borders of the national schools, furthered by other pedagogue–singers who dabbled in voice science, such as Cvejić. Miller observed voice lessons in 165 vocal studios in Western countries, finding some internal resistance within each culture to the perceived national school: "some teachers, geographically associated with a national school, often point out its deficiencies with razor-sharp criticism, citing specific national tendencies against which they work" (1997: xxxix).

In that narrative of a confusing deconstruction of any centre of empire in vocal pedagogy, the US was the natural heir of the Italian Old School. Writing in 1997, Miller asserted: "At the risk of chauvinism, it may be postulated that the historic Italian School of singing has its most comfortable home in North America and that the rest of the world is very much aware of that" (xv). Equally, he acknowledged the phenomenon of opera singers coming from many regions of the Pacific and Asia (such as China, Japan and South Korea):

> The upward mobility of the Asian singer on the operatic scene is yet another indication that the historic Italian School of singing is the most nearly universally appealing of all the national schools. Asian singers [...] who adhere to the principles of international vocalism are definitely on the increase.
>
> *(1997: xv)*

The conflation of the Italian Old School and "international vocalism" remains uncontroversial in the discourse.

It is the impact of science that tempers Miller's argument here, as he acknowledged that vocal practices do transcend national systems of training:

> The interchange of information among the related disciplines of vocal pedagogy, otolaryngology, and vocal therapy has greatly expanded. Spectrographic analysis of the sounds of singing is more frequently applied. Fiberoptic and stroboscopic examination of the vocal mechanism during singing is no longer unusual. This new information can be used in all styles of singing. Results confirm that there are commonalities that transcend national or regional vocal pedagogies, while national tendencies continue to exist.
>
> *(1997: xiii)*

This gesture towards a revision by Miller seemed to pave the way for vocal pedagogical approaches that question themselves and their prejudices. Cvejić predicates his voice science upon the need to disclaim cultural supremacy in training, despite the inescapability of the discipline's succession from the Italian Old School: "surely Italy is the place that is pre-eminently responsible for the emergence, development and promotion of beautiful singing, but one should never ignore the contributions made to it by different nations that did a lot to elevate it to where it stands now" (Cvejić and Cvejić 2008: 249).

Cvejić was also a political idealist in promoting thinking about voice beyond nationalized stereotypes of practice. Fellow phoniatrician Jürgen Wendler places Cvejić as a key figure in allowing other voices (both literal and metaphorical) to be heard in the discourse of classical vocal pedagogy:

> Dušan Cvejić was the father of phoniatrics in [the] former Yugoslavia [...]; in 1994, he published together with his wife Biserka, held in high esteem as one of the worldwide leading mezzos at her time, [she sang at The Met in the 1960s] a [...] book on singing, combining scientific as well as artistic aspects [...]. And not to forget Cvejić was the founding president of the Union of European Phoniatricians, a professional as well as scientific organization which – against a sea of plagues – succeeded in keeping colleagues in touch from both sides of the iron curtain whilst Europe was so strongly divided during the cold war.
>
> *(2008: 283)*

There is a sense that by opening the discourse of vocal pedagogy to other disciplines, including voice science and phoniatrics, pedagogues and artists saw national boundaries dissolve. In more recent incarnations, the Union of European Phoniatricians (which still exists) inspired the Pan-European Voice Conference (PEVOC). This is an interdisciplinary event held every few years:

The Pan-European Voice Conference has always been a great scientific, medical and artistic event. It focuses both on fundamental and applied scientific research, and on clinical assessment and treatment. It offers the opportunity for international voice researchers, voice therapists, voice teachers and singers to come together and share their knowledge, ideas and experience.

(Pan-European Voice Conference 2011)

In his keynote at PEVOC in Groningen in 2007, Wendler mentioned the emerging group of voice scientists who like to sing: "they are from Sweden and call themselves 'Stimmbanditen,'" listing their names (2008: 279). It would appear that 21st-century pioneers of voice training are much more open to deconstructing their own labels, as they are open to a climate of globalization that has an air of internationalism similar to the Olympics:

PEVOC is not another society. The responsibility of organising the biannual conferences is passed like a torch in a relay race from one interested voice organization in one country to a like-minded organization in another European country. Thus has been born a tradition, which stimulates European voice research by interdisciplinary exchange and which offers a platform for sharing findings with all who are interested.

(Pan-European Voice Conference 2013)

The shift from a modernist abstraction of voice training as nationally distinct discourses to a postmodern, post-national interdisciplinary web of languages might usefully be addressed as a type of cosmopolitanism. This implies that the citizenship available to the singer, voice scientist and pedagogue comes with an assumption of a relative amount of wealth, education and access to specialist training and technology. However, the commonality of interest in classical voice remains, and the cultural bind of nationhood is brought into question. In his work on cosmopolitan society, Ulrich Beck paints a picture of what might be a travelogue of the jet-setting classical singing star, vocal pedagogue, academic and voice scientist:

All three criteria – indifference to national boundaries, space–time compression and an increasing network-like interconnectedness between national societies – are exemplified primarily by economic globalization. But there are many more examples. As more processes show less regard for state boundaries – people shop internationally, work internationally, love internationally, marry internationally, research internationally, grow up and are educated internationally (that is, multi-lingually), live and think transnationally, that is, combine multiple loyalties and identities in their lives – the paradigm of societies organized within the framework of the nation-state inevitably loses contact with reality. These changing circumstances have prompted a never-ending debate on the condition of the nation-state: Does it still exist or is it already gone?

(2000: 80)

These assumptions about global interconnectedness may be unsurprising in the second decade of the 21st century, as we exploit commercial networks and a relatively unhampered labour exchange of artists to wider audiences. However, it is not so long ago that classical vocal pedagogy and its impact were imbued with the climate of the Cold War. For all the North American certainty of its supremacy in operatic training and talent, in the latter part of the 20th century, productive pedagogy and research was happening behind the Iron Curtain. Could the patrons of The Metropolitan Opera in New York in the 1970s have predicted that by the late 1990s, many of the pre-eminent artists singing the principle roles were not necessarily coming out of the vocal and opera programmes at the Julliard School but Larisa Gergieva's tutelage at the Mariinksy in St Petersburg?

Towards a new audio-transcription?

Equally, it is the efficacy of the radio broadcast, as a means of instructing listeners upon the issues of vocal athleticism, style and technique, that is of interest as a self-reflexive and dynamic mode of conveying concepts related to vocal pedagogy. The final example in this chapter may be asynchronous, in that Cathy Berberian (1925–83) sang, wrote and broadcast about the voice mainly in the 1960s and 1970s. However, her status as a pioneering vocal artist – her polyvocality – places her interests at the intersections of some unlikely opposites: everyday speech and song; the Early Music revival movement and Italian Old School as against extended vocal technique and the audio aesthetics of the microphone; her conquering of the 19th-century salon repertoire along with newly commissioned works; and finally her embrace of musical kitsch and pop while attaining the accolade "the Muse of Darmstadt" (Berberian 2014: 54). This not only places Berberian as a pioneer in what her voice could achieve, but as an artist and scholar who questioned the efficacy of classical vocal pedagogy, and often felt prejudice for her transgressions against the prevailing mainstream musical and dramatic aesthetics of the immediate post-World–War–II era in the West. In 1966, Berberian published the essay "The new vocality in contemporary music" in the Italian journal *Discoteca*:

> What is the New Vocality that appears so threatening to the old guard? It is the voice which has an endless range of vocal styles at its disposal embracing the history of music; as well as aspects of sound itself, marginal perhaps compared to the music, but fundamental to human beings. Unlike the instrument, which can be locked up and put away after use, the voice […] is inseparable from its interpreter. It lends itself to the numerous tasks of our daily lives continuously: it argues with the butcher over the roast beef, whispers sweet words in intimacy, shouts insults to the referee, asks for directions to the Piazza Carità, etc. Furthermore, the voice expresses itself through communicative "noises," such as sobs, sighs, tongue snaps, screams, groans, laughter.
>
> *(in Placanica 2014: 47)*

Berberian advocated an understanding of an embodied voice, continuous with the artist's everyday life. She made the bold claim that the everyday utterance could actually be part of the artistry. This reveals the interdependence of her thinking with her artistic collaborators, such as John Cage and Luciano Berio. It also attests to an embodied-ness that resists the logocentrism of vocal pedagogy in print. When Berberian was invited to present her own radio talk show on the subject of voice, it had the potential to be read as a postmodern essay on vocal technique, philosophy and artistry. However, the mode of transmission added a delightful supplement, in that Berberian used the microphone productively and relished the opportunity to play and comment upon excerpts of other singers, whose efforts were in some way instructive. *Cathy's Solo Talk Show* was approximately seventeen hours of conversation between Berberian and Dutch Radio station KRO producer Frans van Rossum, originally aired in 1979. The material, featuring candid monologues from the singer, interspersed with her "live" playing of recorded vocal excerpts, was a fascinating postmodern listening experience for those who sought to understand the voice better, or perhaps already knew her work at the limits of speech and song, vocalization and composition, theatre and the quotidian, liveness and mediation. While the words convey only half the scenario here, readers can imagine commentary interspersed with the archival recordings:

CATHY BERBERIAN: You know people always ask me what is the difficulty involved and I always say that – Classical music – or let's say non-contemporary music – is easy to learn and difficult to perform and contemporary music of this kind is hard to learn and then easy to perform. Once you know what the mechanism is, once you've got your reflexes conditioned, then it's ok. [… T]he difficulty is not in the vocal cords, it's in the mind as far as contemporary music is concerned … it's the mind that has to react first and then the impulse is sent to the vocal cords and everything is OK. If you are *late* in sending the impulse, then you get bigger holes in the piece [… T]he value of *Sequenza* is that its virtuosity is so impressive that people will not fight its contents. It's almost a trick piece. Without – the bad connotation of a trick there. In the sense that people who ordinarily wouldn't accept an avant-garde piece or […] a *contemporary* piece that's difficult, that's offbeat – will accept *Sequenza* and even get something from it because of its virtuosity. It's a kind of a contemporary version of coloratura, you know. Except that you're really doing a mission when you're doing this piece because it's an important piece.

(Berberian and Rossum 2014)

Berberian's example is significant here, as she was a singer–composer for whom a solid classical vocal technique was vital, yet she used that basis to explore multiple kinds of vocalities that dissolved international borders. Born in the US to Armenian parents, she enjoyed great acclaim in her adopted home of Italy, the Netherlands, Germany and the UK among many places. She sang in multiple languages, including Armenian and Azeri, and was a key force behind reviving some of

Stravinsky's early vocal pieces in Russian. Her notable composition *Stripsody* (1966) mixed the media of singing, speech, vocal parody, cross-gendered voices and the genres of the concert hall, the comic-book and radio programme. With an approach to vocal performance that is now paradigmatic of the postmodern classical voice, Berberian remains instructive as an example of a polyvocal artist. Furthermore, her inscription upon the world of composition was to infuse the musical score with a sense of embodiment. The graphical notations of "Stripsody" were invented by Berberian and then communicated to the graphic artist and left-wing political cartoonist Roberto Zamarin, who brought even more of a lively play of animated images to the final edition in order to prompt vocalists into composing with their voice, given the absence of pitch and rhythmic markers throughout most of the score. This is perhaps the ultimate act of subverting the classical vocal score and its anticipated pedagogic associations.

This chapter has considered the relationship between classical vocal pedagogy and the cultural biases that reside within a nationally determined appraisal of voice training, and the artistry that results from, or grows beyond, that training. Beginning with the example of the oversight of Janáček's contributions to voice education in the Czech Republic, the discussion of colonialism in marginalizing the colonized voice was linked to Bourdieu's *cultural arbitrary* within the pedagogic environment, whereby dominant narratives dictated the practice imparted to students. This underpins many of the assumptions made about "national schools" of singing and the dominance of abstracted pedagogic texts, ironically written by authors who were performers and active pedagogues themselves. Further deconstruction of the relevance of national schools is then possible when findings from voice science suggest a commonality of techniques. There are evident overlaps in the successful classical training traditions among many national and linguistic groups. Finally, the possibility of the radio talk-show as a medium for talking about or guiding the listening practice, and performing the pedagogy, suggests an element of self-reflection that avoids any of the institutional excesses seen in post-World-War-II Europe.

What remains to be seen is whether the YouTube generation of vocal pedagogical contributors can have that same element of cultural power and self-reflection. Given the post-national democratizing potential of the technology and its ability to create a community of participants, voice lessons, masterclasses and lectures can be transmitted to millions of audience members. The acclaimed mezzo-soprano Joyce DiDonato has given masterclasses on vocal technique and interpretation at The Julliard School of Music in New York, which were officially uploaded to You-Tube (Julliard School 2013). The internet also has the capacity to celebrate the autonomous vocality of participants without being "hosted" at the prestigious masterclasses of leading conservatoires. Any kind of voice lesson can be found on YouTube, and it can enjoy mass-media circulation without being conducted by an expert. The content does not have to conform to a standard image of a vocal expert in a studio; some content may comprise a disembodied voice or voice-over with video images. Equally, the democratizing format also tempts those uploading and listening with the pitfalls of seeking the sensationalist item (much like the 19th-century quest for the exotic or virtuosic) and translating the sensational into the bid for popularity (the highest number of "hits"). The question therefore remains as to whether this mode of transmission will develop its own hierarchies and institutionalized spectatorships like the other ideological underpinnings of more conventional, print-based authorship.

Ultimately, in light of the issue of transcription, it can be argued that vocal pedagogues seek some perpetuity and legacy, and often this is through the written transcription of how one should sing. Historically, this has allowed some empire-building, but the writing was always based upon the live phenomenon of the teacher's studio, which remains an enduring factor in the transmission of vocal pedagogy.

Notes

1 I thank Nicholas Till for suggesting this point in relation to my work and reminding me of Barthes's concept of "Italianicity" in *Image Music Text* albeit here for a sonic, rather than visual marker.
2 The label "Instructions" in this extract is adopted by Milena Duchoňová as an abbreviation of Janáček's *Instructions for Singing*.
3 There is the interesting example of singer–teacher Marketa Sagiova (1988) who lived and studied in Budapest and Vienna in the early half of the 20th century, later relocating to Australia. Upon establishing her Australian singing studio, she used Clive Douglas's setting of Indigenous Australian melodies as repertoire in singing lessons for her students.
4 The original title of this work, abbreviated by Wendler here, was *Traité Complet de l'Art du Chant*.
5 An extensive examination of these kinds of associations is offered in Goodall (2002), with provocations upon the vocal and physical components of performances "close" to nature. This includes Oscar Wilde's *Salomé* (1891) as a work revealing the contest between symbolism and biology: "The dance and the voice are the instruments of destinies meted out by natural selection, but who are the dying and who the survivors in the struggle of which they are part?" (Goodall 2002: 210).

References

Barthes, R. (1977) *Image Music Text*, trans. S. Heath, London: Fontana.
Beck, U. (2000) "The cosmopolitan perspective: sociology of the second age of modernity," *The British Journal of Sociology*, 51(1): 79–105.
Berberian, C. (1966) *Stripsody*, New York: C.F. Peters Corporation.
——(2014) "The new vocality in contemporary music," trans. F. Placanica, in Karantonis, K. *et al.* (eds) *Cathy Berberian: Pioneer of Contemporary Vocality*, Farnham: Ashgate, 47–51.
Berberian, C. and Rossum, F. (2014) *Cathy's Solo Talk Show*, http://cathyberberian.com/links/audio/.
Bottomore, T. (1990) "Foreword," in Bourdieu, P. and Passeron, J-C., *Reproduction in Education, Society and Culture*, trans. R. Nice, London: Sage.
Bourdieu, P. and Passeron, J. (1990) *Reproduction in Education, Society and Culture*, trans. R. Nice, London: Sage.
Cvejić, B. and Cvejić, D. (2008) *Art of Singing*, trans. D. Bogdanović, Belgrade: IP Signature.
Goodall, J. (2002) *Performance and Evolution in the Age of Darwin: Out of the Natural Order*, London: Routledge.
Herbert-Caesari, E. (1951) *The Voice of the Mind*, London: Robert Hale.
Herbert-Caesari, E. (1978) *The Voice of the Mind*, New York: Crescendo.

Janáček, L. (1980) *Návod pro Vyučování Zpěvu* (*Instructions for Singing Lessons*): *Zpěv a Klavír* (*Voice and Piano*), ed. M. Duchoňová and L. Faltus, trans. J. Moss-Kohoutová, Kassel: Bärenreiter.

Julliard School (2013) "2013 Joyce DiDonato master class with Avery Amereau & Bretton Brown," www.youtube.com/watch?v=9dNQhI3S5_w.

Marek, D. (2007) *Singing: The First Art*, Lanham: Scarecrow.

Matheopoulos, H. (1986) *Divo: Great Tenors, Baritones and Basses Discuss Their Roles*, London: Harper Collins.

Miller, R. (1977) *National Schools of Singing: English, French, German and Italian Techniques of Singing Revisited*, Lanham: Scarecrow.

Miller, R. (1997) *National Schools of Singing: English, French, German and Italian Techniques of Singing Revisited*, Revised edition, Lanham: Scarecrow.

Nancy, S. (2013) "The singing body in the *Tragédie Lyrique* of seventeenth- and eighteenth-century France: voice, theatre, speech, pleasure," in Symonds, D. and Karantonis, P. (eds) *The Legacy of Opera: Reading Music Theatre as Experience and Performance*, Amsterdam/New York: Rodopi, 65–78.

Operbathosa (2010) *Fritz Wunderlich Handel: Xerxes "Ombra mai fu" (Largo)*, video adapted from vinyl recording, www.youtube.com/watch?v=WivrX29dufw.

Pan-European Voice Conference (2011) "PEVOC 9," www.pevoc.org/pevoc09/index.html.

——(2013) "Mission Statement," www.pevoc.org/mission.php.

Placanica, F. (2014) "'La nuova vocalità nell'opera contemporanea' (1966): Cathy Berberian's legacy" in Karantonis, P. *et al.* (eds), *Cathy Berberian: Pioneer of Contemporary Vocality*, Farnham: Ashgate: 51–66.

Sagiova, M. (1988) *The Art of Singing*, Melbourne: Kynoch.

Vennard, W. (1967) *Singing: The Mechanism and the Technic*, New York: Carl Fischer.

Wendler, J. (2008) "Singing and science," *Folia Phoniatrica et Logopaedica*, 60(6): 279–87.

13

STRANGE OBJECTS/STRANGE PROPERTIES

Female audibility and the acoustic stage prop

Ella Finer

Seeking strategies for political agency and artistic recognition, art historian Dorothy Rowe has drawn attention to the fact that in recent artistic practice there has been "recourse to an extended sensual field as a means of disrupting the dominance of the visual within Western metaphysics" (2004: 148). This chapter explores the constant negotiation of female audibility and visibility within such an "extended sensual field." Of particular interest is how the *sonic property* of voice can be investigated for its "ability to effect surprising forms of subversion," after Gina Bloom's provocation in *Voice in Motion* (2007: 16). How, for example, are the politics of female visibility and audibility implicated together when the voice is staged in specific scenographies/situations? How does the voice become "visible" when the body is absent?

A considerable number of living female artists who are "visible" in terms of recognition and success (however that may be gauged) in the *visual* art world, make explicit use of their own voice. Janet Cardiff's (1957–) audio walks; Georgina Starr's (1968–) personal archive of recorded sound; Laure Prouvost's (1978–) broken English voice-overs; Cara Tolmie's (1984–) vocal narrations of space: all use the artist's voice as an integral component in the form and content of the work.[1] These contemporary artworks demonstrate how voice can be – and *has been* – conceptualized and used as an object with material qualities, as a sound spectacle: a sound *seen*, and a body *not* seen. While Lacan's voice-object in psychoanalysis is well-known and has been augmented by Mladen Dolar (2006), the voice-object considered here is sonic material. It is an object which *makes* the artwork (as paint or plaster might), or *takes* the stage (as a tangible prop might).

Exploring voice as a property of motion and exchange, between bodies on and off the stage, I discuss three instances of the way female voices can manifest as strange material objects, illustrating the ways invisible bodies might vocalize their presence and sound their visibility. Firstly, I consider how the female character has been identified through acoustic vocal properties in Adorno's essay "The curves of the needle" ([1928] 1990), and in the meeting of Gertrude Stein and Ernest Hemingway as illustrated by Anne Carson in "The gender of sound" (1995). Secondly, I address the materiality of the disembodied voice, towards conceptualizing the voice as a theatre/performance material. I close by "listening back" to the spectacle of *The Invisible Woman* (*La Femme Invisible*), one of the preludes to Étienne-Gaspard Robert's (Robertson's) *Phantasmagoria* show of 1798. This illusion, one of many magical acoustic and optical curiosities spectators were invited to experience in anticipation of Robertson's famous magic lantern show, had as its focal point a female voice emanating from a suspended glass orb. I consider this performance as a specific instance in which the female voice is treated as an acoustic stage property in relationship to a ventriloquized object, and more crucially, as an acoustic "prop" in-and-of-itself. In the light of what I have discovered in my own contemporary practice with voice in and out of the body, I show how voice can practise a vital "appearance" as both disembodied and embodied: as a shifting property in the theatre air. Sound is always moving, constantly changing through each vibration. It is this character of sound, as a continually varying entity, that vitally lends itself as a medium to practise with and attend to, allowing a theorization of visibility in audible terms.

Visibility is never a straightforward term. To "have visibility" – which suggests visibility is an attribute to own – is not simply being seen, just as "having a voice" does not refer solely to the ability to talk. Having visibility and having a voice are political positions of agency where, whether the seen or speaking body is present or not, the body (and its voice) is an acknowledged presence in the world. Addressing "the complex and changing relations between visibility and political power," John B. Thompson writes that "prior to the development of print and other media, the visibility of political rulers depended to a large extent on their physical appearance before others in contexts of co-presence" (2005: 33). Continuing on to the advent of print and other media, Thompson arrives at the age of mechanical reproduction when he suggests those in power "increasingly acquired a kind of visibility that was detached from their physical appearance" (2005: 33). Visibility thus became the terminology for practising presence in physical absence.

This negotiation between visibility and invisibility renders unreliable the idea of visibility as synonymous with agency for women artists. As Peggy Phelan asserts in *Unmarked*, "visibility is a trap" and "there is a real power in remaining unmarked" (1993: 6). She unpacks the complexities of visibility politics, arguing that the presumption that "increased visibility equals increased power" surely "bears further scrutiny" (1993: 6). Whilst discussing race and gender in the performances of Moti Roti, Rowe further develops this contention with the visible:

> the investment in the visible as a sign of the real, a sign of presence that has underpinned the philosophy of much of the identity politics practised by sexual and racial minorities over the past few decades, is tactically problematic, because it relies for its effects on the very system of representation that it seeks to undermine.
>
> *(2004: 148)*

Rowe observes that "much aesthetic and cultural discourse is prompted by the desire to dislodge what Martin Jay has described as 'the scopic regimes of modernity'" (2004: 148). How might sound dislodge and challenge what we see, or think we see? My wider concern outside the bounds of this text is to understand how sound operates within the sensual world – and in this specific instance, with what is visible and invisible. Jay's phrase "the scopic regimes" emphasizes the command that the visible holds in modern Western culture and society. To subvert these "scopic regimes," it is vital to examine them; to analyse and understand their negotiation with (supposedly) less authoritative senses. Here, I attend to the voice in relation to "the phallocular visual field" (Rowe 2004: 148), which betrays aspects of power and matters of social inscription, in order to propose theoretical and practical "forms of subversion" and resistant strategies for female artists working with sound and nego-tiating their own visibility. I hope to demonstrate the complexity and subtlety of that which shifts between the visible and invisible, the audible and inaudible. This is especially important as the relationship between the effects of multiple forms of representation (textual, photographic, phonographic) becomes increasingly complex, and the senses of presence they offer give rise to far stranger kinds of visibility that are not so easily delineated into polarized terms of presence and absence. Indeed, the subject of this study – the voice – is a live presence which escapes definition within the binary of presence and absence, oscillating between and within both.

Strange properties

Acoustics can "give voice away." We can identify spaces through their distinct acoustic characteristics and their effects on the voice: imagine the voice in the swimming pool, the supermarket or by the busy roadside. We can be tricked by acoustics: even if we do not believe someone is trapped underground, we might say "you *sound like* you are at the bottom of a well." The audible body is able to shape-shift, to appear in altered locations and transform in character with only subtle changes to its environment. However, the voice that performs live comes to the stage already characterized, already bearing acoustic properties (pitches, volumes, accents, inflections), which have been culturally and socially identified and constructed. Of course, defining the character of the voice happens in the ears of the receiver and discerning the character of the female voice is tied to seeing or imagining (the image of) her body. When that body is absent – or not "ideal" – the voice too can stray from what might be characterized as "female."

The characteristics of voices are often defined as sounding *like* something else, whether taking on the acoustic properties of the space they are in, or igniting an audible version of Elin Diamond's "mimetic apprehension" (1997: 149), in which similar or familiar voice(s) might be heard in another's voice (such as hearing a mother's voice, or that of a well-known historical persona, in a stranger's inflection and tone). The voice even lends itself to stranger metaphorization, such as Gertrude Stein's "laugh like a beefsteak," which Anne Carson identifies as leading to a case of cannibalism when "artfully confused" alongside the factual information that "she loved beef" (1995: 121). Stein's "voice like meat" is of course imposed on her by another listener. Yet, this interpretation of Stein's voice also demonstrates how voice can be characterized through personal factual information; how we "see" or perceive someone starts to shape the way we might hear them.

Carson goes on to describe Hemingway's quick escape from Stein's household "because he could not stand the sound of her voice" (1995: 121); an escape betraying the shock for the receiver when women's voices stray from sounding like one's traditional expectation of the feminine. Adorno's oft-cited dissatisfaction with the "shrill" female voice on recordings is described as the absence of "body as complement" ([1928] 1990: 54). In 1928, he wrote that: "the female voice requires the physical appearance of the body that carries it" without which it sounds "needy and incomplete" (54). Perhaps, four years earlier, Hemingway had also heard the voice without a body in a similar register?

While the disembodied voice Adorno refers to is "needy and incomplete," Stein's speaking voice (as Hemingway heard it) was (quite *un*characteristically) "pleading and begging" (Carson 1995: 121). These descriptions are, of course, always according to the interpreter, so one is bound to reproduce them as interpretations; in Stein's case we will never know what she sounded like in the moment of Hemingway's hearing. While it appears that neither the singer on Adorno's recording, nor Stein, were totally conscious of the live exchange with their auditor, both voices are characterized not only by their lack of body, but also by their lack of apparent composure.

These two examples, albeit extrapolated from two distinct contexts, suggest that the female voice-without-body is impossible to apprehend. While the sound of Stein's voice provokes Hemingway's retreat, a distancing of himself further from voice and body, the singing voice on Adorno's record causes a desire to get closer to the voice, to witness the voice as embodied. For Adorno, the body that the gramophone eliminates is female, whereas Barbara Engh suggests that male bodies, whose voices are "reproduced better," are "identical to the body of the apparatus" (1994: 129). While men sound as complementary to the machinery of the gramophone, Adorno fantasizes about meeting a mythical body that would clarify the sound of the female vocalist. In contrast, Hemingway flees from a present body that he could encounter, even if uncomfortably, as Stein's vocal liveness proves the forceful proximity of her body. Adorno's and Hemingway's reactions to two different vocal "characters" imply not only that certain characteristics in the voice either draw the listener closer or physically repel them, but also that the *character of the live voice* has more agency than the recorded voice in speaking the force of the body's close presence (even when invisible). Of course, the voice in song has a large part to play in the historical seduction of the ear, but as Engh concludes, "in any woman's disembodied voice one sees immediately a reflection of one's own self-desiring glance – *or not*" (1994: 131; added emphasis).

Depending on our subjective connections to a single voice, the sound of the voice can physically *move* us as listeners. While a trained musical ear is able to measure distinct sounds, Jean-Luc Nancy writes that "whether he be a musician or not, for someone who listens, the very instant a sonority, a cadence, a phrase touches him [...] he is propelled into an expectation, urged towards a presentiment" (2007: 66). This expectant listening to music – as "prophecy in the instant" (Nancy 2007: 66) – occurs, too, in listening to the human voice, where we seek to match the voice with our expectations of the body at its source. Our perception or apprehension of characters in the voice also complicates the subjectivity of the speaker. *To sound like* is, of course, to act mimetically; an act full of the complexities of sounding *like*, but not *as*, so that hearing and identifying characters in the voice *distances* the voice from the subjectivity of its speaker. Yet, the characters that appear in the voice practise the shifting patterning of difference into sameness, unmaking mimesis while in the mimetic act, never fully characterizing the voice of another. While skilled actors produce vocal characters that can cause an audience to temporarily transform *sounding like* into *sounding as*, outside dramatic theatre, characters always shift in the voice of another. As seen below with reference to *The Invisible Woman*, pinning a voice to a sound source is as impossible as attributing any single character to the speaking body. In a similar but inverted act, audiences can not only apprehend multiple voices in a single body, but also apprehend a particular solo voice in multiple bodies *and* objects.

Stage properties

In my own practice with sound and staging voices, I have explored how voice in performance may become an acoustic stage property in continuous exchange between character and performing body, and also between this doubled body (of character/performer) and the audience. Bruce Smith writes that "the object the audience hears in a human voice is character" (1999: 245). My interest in working out what this affective object is, has led to my staging of vocal characters and practising with the voice as a type of volatile "stage prop," which as Smith writes, exists "in the air" as well as in the bodies of speaker and auditor. Bloom (2007) finds that voice "has a history of production, ownership and exchange":

> Whereas literary critics have tended to conceive of voice as language, equating it solely with aesthetic and textual concerns, early moderns considered the spoken and heard voice, on and off the stage, to be a substance with economic, theatrical and mechanical dimensions [...]. Like props, voices are often imagined as unmanageable, beyond the control of those who ostensibly operate and "own" them.
>
> *(6)*

Oratory – considered the science of mastering the voice – had to contend with the voice and the impossibility of the speaker's total control. This practice of oratory demonstrated the voice as a sound "substance" in early modern England. P.A. Skantze suggests that the voice could be used for its rhetorical force in public speaking as affect, a persuasion without record: "A form of performance employed to persuade in sound, oratory influences as it disappears into the air, not available for later analysis unless the listener has a perfectly retentive memory" (2003: 98).

Through my own work with the speaking voice as artistic and material stage property, I have considered the complex relationship between manners of speaking and the listener's comprehension. In 2010, I staged *Material Voice in Pitch Black*, in which twenty-eight voices read a scholarly text over four hours; this was an experiment in listening to a form of writing not traditionally written to be read aloud. The density of the writing, its citations and arguments, meant that holding onto the meaning through listening alone became ever harder as the hours passed. When words can be carried away in the voice without record, vocal meaning can be hard to apprehend for long, and sometimes defies comprehension. As Skantze's description of oratory suggests, the live voice without record has to become the property of memory if the listener wants to return to it. Voice can be retained in the bodies of skilled listeners, but however brilliant at remembering the listener is, holding the voice as embodied property over time will inevitably alter it. In contrast to speech making, the voice in theatre demands a different kind of attentive listening, "a doubleness of reception" (Carlson 2003: 51). Rather than holding on to the sounds of speech, theatre audiences continuously let go of what they have heard in order to receive more, in order to move with the pace of the play. Voices materialized in the bodies of the theatre audience are the momentary property of these bodies.[2]

Voice belongs to many bodies in theatre and also to the stage: to the temporality of the performance arc and its duration. While impossible to own this shape-shifting, body-hopping property, the making material of voices encounters problems in technological documentation, as Jane Gaines argues:

> The increased scientific precision as well as the increased availability and prevalence of audio recording and transmitting devices have produced the voice as something susceptible to proprietal claims because it is less and less material illusion and more and more material attribute.
>
> *(1991: 119)*

While sound cannot be bound to the stage in the same way a physical object can (it can neither be tangibly placed nor easily located), the play between what is seen and what is heard – and how they are connected – can offer methods to destabilize any easy "proprietal claim." In my work with sound, I have conceived voice as both *illusion* and *attribute*, rich subject and object, a shifting property (of shifting acoustic properties), which can challenge in its vital "appearance" as simultaneously disembodied and embodied.[3] Because, primarily, "the visible sign systems of ventriloquism […] serve to misdirect the audience to the ostensible source of the sounds or voices" (Davis 1998: 141), the voice must also be considered in terms of what is seen, what is visible on stage in order to negotiate *how* it is being heard, be that a body, an empty stage, a microphone, or in the "illusion" of *The Invisible Woman*, a suspended glass ball.

The Invisible Woman

One of the preludes to Robertson's *Phantasmagoria* show in 1798, *The Invisible Woman* (*La Femme Invisible*) suspended a glass ball (sometimes two) from the ceiling of a contained room, and from a set of tubes a woman's voice emanated, fostering a strange "acoustic presence" (Matlock 1996: 176). Jann Matlock describes the way spectators would transform into auditors on entering the spectacle:

> Spectators were herded into a room containing an elaborate contraption sup-posedly conducting sound from the glass ball (or box) hanging from the ceiling. A chosen spectator was invited to converse with the girl whose bodiless essence was claimed to reside in the suspended container. To the amazement of all onlookers, the unseeable woman could describe spectators, name objects held up below the glass, and even make her breath felt through the tubes.
>
> *(1996: 175)*

The Invisible Woman, whose voice so intimately engaged with the spectators, was hidden in a room above her audience. Able to observe the people below, she could then hold her audience captive listeners, as they wondered at the ability of a disembodied voice to see so clearly. With no body in sight, the glass ball, in effect, became the source of the voice, as if the stage prop produced the voice travelling through the tubes. The suspended glass ball was given voice by a speaker whose capacity to speak came from her capacity to see, to watch her audience's movements and gestures. The fact that people held up their personal objects to the glass ball suggests they assumed the ventriloquized object had the capacity to see, hear *and* speak all at once. Other senses came into play because the glass ball was only one part of a larger set of apparatuses, including the tubing through which "her breath could be felt" (Matlock 1996: 175). The glass ball acted as a singular stage prop, within an elaborate set of instruments, all combining to channel different elements of the woman's voice to the different receiving senses of the spectators.

When the spectacle moved to North America, renamed *The Invisible Lady* and displayed in various forms "most frequently during 1804–5" (Bellion 2011: 234), spectators were encouraged to seek out the source of the voice, to reunite voice with body. Wendy Bellion describes how, in the American exhibitions, *The Invisible Lady* "paradoxically enabled its own disempowerment," for while realizing

> the possibility of a "female gaze": a disruption and an inversion of the hegemonic "male gaze" of power [...] the exhibition helped assuage and even deflate concerns about gender and (in)visibility by encouraging spectators to interact with and ultimately locate the concealed speaker.
>
> *(2011: 234)*

Dolar warns of the "crumbling of the aura" in the location of voice source, as the acousmatic voice "loses its fascination and power" and its "charismatic character"

(2006: 67), but he draws a paradoxical conclusion, in that "the source of the voice can never be seen" (70). To seek out *The Invisible Woman* and make her visible is thus an impossible act of disacousmatization, as "every emission of the voice is by its very essence, ventriloquism" (70).[4] While objects, such as the glass ball, can be placed as stand-in sources, imagined to be the origin of the voice, Dolar suggests that we ourselves mimic these ventriloquized objects, detached from our own voices, as "the voice can never be pinned to a body without a paradox" (2006: 197).

The paradox that the voice can never "match what we see" is continually negotiated and challenged in the theatre, as the staged disembodied voice is lent the visual properties of what is seen. The ventriloquized stage object demands a different attention to listening in correlation with a tangible visual focus, an object of focus with visible dimensions and surfaces, which then translate into the sound of the voice. Ventriloquizing by way of a visible stage prop not only offers another method for lending the voice dimension but also a way in which to emphasize the strange impossibility of ever completely attaching a voice to a single sound source. While impossible to hold as a property for long in any receptive body, Dolar reminds us how difficult it is to ever assign the voice as someone's/something's with complete certainty, as "like a bodily missile," the voice both leaves the body and "points to a bodily interior, an intimate partition of the body which cannot be disclosed" (2006: 71). The audience of *The Invisible Woman* participated in assigning voice to the "origins" of the glass ball and tubing, and in the later iterations of the spectacle in North America (where the woman was revealed), the performance depended on the audience's willingness to accept an illusory voice source. From preserving the mystery of the glass ball, to the subsequent versions of *The Invisible Woman*, the woman's voice in both instances is attributed to what an audience can (or is offered to) physically and visibly locate.

The invisible woman is a spectator of spectators, watching in order to reflect what is visible to her through vocal description. In this illusion, the female voice practises a continual exchange between the bodies of both performer and audience as well as the objects that belong to the illusory stage space (the glass ball and tubing) and the audience's own property (held up to the glass ball for the invisible woman to describe). The voice the audience hears returns visual material in the altered form of audible material with the effect of the echo, reflecting back a version of what has been called out. Perpetually unfixed to any one object, the voice exists as a shifting property in the in-between.

Distancing

Voice carries a body and no body simultaneously: existing as vibrations through space and simultaneously as the aural promise of some*body*. While always giving hope of making its source visible, voice obscures its origins through the patterning of its acoustic material in time and space, through echo and reverberation, dampening and absorption: the sound of the voice in transmission from speaker to listener is always changing. As voice audibly alters, so does the search for the visible body, whose character and identification can subtly transform depending on who is listening, when and in what way. Listening to bodies rather than seeing them – such as Stein, the singer on Adorno's record, and *The Invisible Woman* – sounds their presence as unfixed, only ever partially identifiable. As such, the audibility of the voice will always compel us, as listeners, to construct a contingent visible body. Returning to Rowe's provocation that working in the "extended sensual field" can disrupt "the investment in the visible as a sign of the real," it is important to highlight that neither the contingent visible body modelled from the audible, nor the audible voice alone can be relied upon as "signs of the real," as both are continuously in motion (2004: 148).

I will close with the motion of the echo, returning to think about how the voice exists as a strange object related to, but separate from, the speaking body. The instances explored above (Stein and Hemingway, the singer and Adorno, *The Invisible Woman* and her audience) offer perspectives on female audibility that can help elucidate what happens to the voice between speaker and listener, and how voice can subvert any easy identification or characterization of the body it comes from. In each instance, there are not only unseen bodies, but also marked distances between the unseen bodies and their auditor(s). These spatial and temporal distances hosting the voice offer methods for understanding how voice might exist – even if briefly – outside of the body, as a "thing" in its own right. *The Invisible Woman*'s voice carries through the tubing conduits designed to link her "backstage" with the room in which the spectacle takes place. In transmission, her voice is vibrating energy in the air and pipes between both bodies. Independent of bodies, the voice becomes object (without assigned/presumed character or visible prop) through distance. Jacques Rancière's conception of distance as "the normal condition of any communication" is especially useful here in its definition of mediation as an autonomous component ("thing") in itself (2009: 10):

> There is the distance between artist and the spectator, but there is also the distance inherent in the performance itself, in so far as it subsists, as a spectacle, an autonomous thing, between the idea of the artist and the sensation or comprehension of the spectator.
>
> *(Rancière 2009: 14)*

The spectacle, as the mediation between the artist and spectator, is defined by Rancière as the "third thing that is owned by no one," the thing to which both artist and spectator refer, but which prevents "any uniform transmission, any identity of cause and effect" (2009: 15). What implications does this have for the voice in transmission between performer and spectator/auditor? Bloom argues that it is the "voice's distance from, rather than presence in, the body that constitutes the conditions of agency": that the far, distant voice can be less easily relied on to "perform a speaker's will" undermining "male investments in vocal control" (2007: 17). While Bloom's analysis offers models of relationality from the perspective of Elizabethan drama on page and stage, it resonates interestingly with the idea of Rancière's "third thing owned by no one." Distance complicates any simple or passive attempt at ownership, serving as an intermediary state in which the sounded voice can exist outside of the bodies of both performer and spectator. While the voice originates in the body of the performer and is caught (or maybe glimpsed) by the ears of the spectators/auditors, it exists in the time and space of performance also as "autonomous thing." Brian Massumi's example of an echo as its own event emphasizes a sonic materialization of this distance:

> An echo, for example, cannot occur without a distance between surfaces for the sounds to bounce from. But the resonation is not on the walls. It is in the emptiness between them. It fills the emptiness with its complex patterning. That patterning is not a distance from itself. It is immediately its own event.
>
> *(2002: 14)*

Echo travels through the distance of space – it "bounces" back into resonance in the air and off the "walls" that can neither dispel nor contain it. The space the echo fills, the distance, is a vital space for voice to practise its own autonomy as sonic utterance. This conceptualizing of distance allows voice to remain in play, to host its own reception and condition itself through its own movement. Massumi describes this patterning of the echo, the bouncing of sound "back and forth" as the "relation of the movement to itself: self-relation" (2002: 14). Reckoning with its own transmission, the echo is continually negotiating itself through its collisions with itself, its relation to itself.

Never still, the voice is a property that reverberates in the body and out of it, in the object and out of it, and furthermore, like Massumi's bouncing of the self-relating echo which both bounces off surfaces and patterns itself in the in-between space, representations of voices bounce against objects, while also being objects themselves.

Notes

1 Each artist's work can be found at the following links: Cardiff: www.cardiffmiller.com; Starr: www.georginastarr.com; Prouvost: www.laureprouvost.com; Tolmie: www. vimeo.com/caratolmie.
2 Of course, sound memory is also retained after the performance. After the event, our memories to an extent remix what sounds are remembered into a composition of embodied experience.
3 My recent work has focused on: (1) the performance of recorded and live voices together, composing the textures of present and past sound to negotiate the continuously shifting practice of the listener, and (2) the attachment and detachment of the voice to material documents, such as records, mp3s and tapes. One example is an installation I exhibited in Newcastle's Baltic39 (September–October 2013). The work is an acetate record which was made to be played until it is played out, and the song it holds has deteriorated into noise. For documentation and commentary, see www.youtube.com/watch?v=h2_hSsDQBQE.
4 "Disacousmatization" is a term conceived by film scholar Michel Chion (1999) for the act of restoring voice to voice source. There is, of course, a rich discourse on sound and

the voice in cinema, film and screen studies, where the already disembodied voice is often disembodied again, employed as the vocal complement to the visual narrative, speaking over the image. While I do not discuss the relationship of the female voice in cinema within this chapter, the prolific field includes scholars such as Jane Gaines (1991), Laura Mulvey ([1975] 2003) and Kaja Silverman (1988).

References

Adorno, T. ([1928] 1990) "The curves of the needle," trans. T.Y. Levin, *October*, 55: 48–55.

Bellion, W. (2011) *Citizen Spectator: Art, Illusion and Visual Perception in Early National America*, Chapel Hill: University of North Carolina Press.

Bloom, G. (2007) *Voice in Motion: Shaping Gender, Shaping Sound in Early Modern England*, Philadelphia: University of Pennsylvania Press.

Carlson, M. (2003) *The Haunted Stage: The Theatre as Memory Machine*, Ann Arbor, MI: University of Michigan Press.

Carson, A. (1995) *Glass, Irony and God*, New York: New Directions Publishing.

Chion, M. (1999) *The Voice in Cinema*, trans. C. Gorbman, New York: Columbia University Press.

Davis, C.B. (1998) "Reading the ventriloquist's lips: the performance genre behind the metaphor," *The Drama Review*, 42(4): 133–56.

Diamond, E. (1997) *Unmaking Mimesis: Essays on Feminism and Theatre*, Abingdon: Routledge.

Dolar, M. (2006) *A Voice and Nothing More*, Cambridge, MA: MIT Press.

Engh, B. (1994) "Adorno and the sirens: tele-phono-graphic bodies," in Dunn, L.C. and Jones, N.A. (eds) *Embodied Voices: Representing Female Vocality in Western Culture*, Cambridge: Cambridge University Press, 120–38.

Gaines, J. (1991) *Contested Culture: The Image, the Voice and the Law*, Chapel Hill, NC: University of North Carolina Press.

Massumi, B. (2002) *Parables for the Virtual*, Durham: Duke University Press.

Matlock, J. (1996) "The Invisible Woman and her secrets unveiled," *The Yale Journal of Criticism*, 9(2): 175–221.

Mulvey, L. ([1975] 2003) "Visual pleasure and narrative cinema," in Jones, A. (ed.) *The Feminism and Visual Culture Reader*, Abingdon: Routledge, 44–53.

Nancy, J-L. (2007) *Listening*, trans. C. Mandell, New York: Fordham University Press.

Phelan, P. (1993) *Unmarked: The Politics of Performance*, Abingdon: Routledge.

Rancière, J. (2009) *The Emancipated Spectator*, trans. G. Elliott, London: Verso.

Rowe, D. (2004) "Cultural crossings: performing race and gender in the work of Moti Roti," in Perry, G. (ed.) *Difference and Excess in Contemporary Art: The Visibility of Women's Practice*, Oxford: Blackwell Publishing, 138–55.

Silverman, K. (1988) *The Acoustic Mirror*, Indiana: Indiana University Press.

Skantze, P.A. (2003) *Stillness in Motion in the Seventeenth Century Theatre*, Abingdon: Routledge.

Smith, B.R. (1999) *The Acoustic World of Early Modern England*, Chicago: The University of Chicago Press.

Thompson, J.B. (2005) "The new visibility," *Theory, Culture and Society*, 22(6): 31–51.

14

THE EAVESDROPPER

Listening-in and overhearing the voice in performance

Johanna Linsley

What is so compelling about the voice of a stranger? In lifts, trains, cafés and on the street, I casually strain to hear details of the lives of others. This may not necessarily be an intrusion (I couldn't help but overhear …), but it figures voice as borrowed, and easily – often unknowingly – lent. I have begun seeking out opportunities to eavesdrop, testing out which public places offer the best scope for listening while actively trying to draw the least attention to myself. I have started to have long conversations about what eavesdropping means and how it works. Eavesdropping might tell us something about how we listen more generally, and how we might think about voice in performance. Or maybe I just like listening in.

This chapter teases out some initial threads in an exploration of eavesdropping as a broader methodology for listening to/as performance, specifically related to voices. As such, it operates as a sequence of proposals, hoping that these might be pursued in greater depth in the future. I propose two different configurations for eavesdropping, developing thoughts about the phrases "listening-in" and "overhearing." These phrases help me think about listening as spatial, and socially constructed. To ground this enquiry, I draw on work from the social sciences (Krista Ratcliffe on "ethical eaves-dropping" and Tanja Dreher on "eavesdropping with permission"), art history (Gavin Butt on gossip) and acoustic studies (Salome Voegelin on the phenomenology of sound). I think about how the eavesdropped voice might be used in the creation of new performance by looking at two case studies: a series of performances/events coordinated by Hannah Hurtzig called *The Blackmarket for Useful Knowledge and Nonknowledge*, and A.S.M. Kobayashi's video work *Dan Carter*. These differing projects both use documentation of the voice to stage complex experiences of listening. Ultimately, these analyses help me consider how eavesdropping can help theorists and historians of performance expand how we think about the voice in performance, live and documented.

Documentation of the voice is, in fact, deceptively thorny. As a field, performance studies has developed an extensive vocabulary for talking about visual documentation and archives. The voice has received far less attention, even as the metaphor for the voice (e.g., whose voice is heard?) is present everywhere when discussing archives. Eavesdropping might be a way to think about how we listen to the voices of others (and ourselves), and the responses we create – in the present moment, but also as historians and critics. It is the very instability of eavesdropping, both fragmented and excessive, which gives it such promise. Fragmentary as it is, eavesdropping necessarily locates the listener in a particular space and context. Its excesses, on the other hand, prompt the imagination, which in turn can highlight how much of the world we construct when we listen. Finally, the sense of the illicit, the inappropriate, of outright theft related to eavesdropping, forces us to pause and think about what we are doing when we listen, and who benefits. Each of these facets complicates and enriches studies of the voice in performance.

Eavesdropping as documentation

There has been a recent explosion of interest in documentation within performance studies. Books, conferences, exhibitions and research projects have been produced to approach the topic of performance and its documents with the aim or result of producing new work in response. These include *Perform/Repeat/Record* (Jones and Heathfield 2012), an edited collection which brings together the most prominent scholars in the field such as Rebecca Schneider, André Lepecki and Philip Auslander, as well as the editors themselves. Similarly, the research project Performing Documents (University of Bristol) was initiated in 2012, with the purpose of developing new work in response to performance archives. Numerous exhibitions and articles have been developed around the form of the performance re-enactment. This strategy is often seen as a way to use performance itself to document performance. This wealth of material illustrates the importance of documentation for the study of performance.

The move towards performance documentation is often figured as a reaction to the interest in liveness and disappearance initiated by Peggy Phelan's thinking on the ontology of performance. Phelan's thesis – "[p]erformance's being [...] becomes itself through disappearance" (1993: 146) – spawned a range of responses and rebuttals. However, there have also been scores of re-enactments, re-contextualizations, traces, ruins, potentialities and documents of performances-that-never-were that exceed the simple category of reaction, and stand for a rich strand of thinking in-and-of-themselves. Works like *Performing Remains* (Schneider 2011) show how performance is neither stable (enduring), nor neatly vanishing, remaining in complex and ever-shifting modes. Performance documentation is thus a volatile and significant place for questioning authoritative histories and destabilizing fixed identities and hierarchies of knowledge.

Nevertheless, one significant gap in the study of performance documentation is thinking about the documentation of voice. The *image, time, duration* and the *status of the object* often take precedence. However, one of the most important questions asked about documents, archives and the making of performance history is "whose voice is heard?" This question can be enriched by asking *how* we hear voices.

Why has the documented voice been overlooked for so long? This is in part no doubt because of the general predominance of the visual over the aural in contemporary culture. With specific regard to performance, which has invested so much in disappearance and remains, it may also be that the voice disappears and remains differently from the visual, requiring a different framework for understanding its relation to documentation; as Jean-Luc Nancy points out, "the visual persists until its disappearance; the sonorous appears and fades away into its permanence" (2007: 2). For Nancy, the vibratory quality of the sonorous implies connection and participation between listeners and producers of sound, and these connections are not so easily severed. A ringing in one's ears persists beyond the production of a sound, and a scraped throat acts as a fleshy and undeniable reminder of a shout. At the same time, mishearing is perhaps more linked to misunderstanding than its visual equivalent.

Finally, there is a history of misogynistic associations with the voice, connected to a broader history of connections of the feminine with the body as something ephemeral, unreliable and inessential.[1] Adriana Cavarero writes:

> Feminized from the start, the vocal aspect of speech, and, furthermore, of song appear together as antagonistic elements in a rational, masculine sphere that centres itself, instead, on the semantic. To put it formulaically: woman sings, man thinks.
>
> *(2005: 6)*

As such, voice might be seen to elude documentation in its non-rationality and over-embodied condition, but to unquestioningly accept this could be to reinforce problematic links to femininity. However, it is not enough for feminists to argue that women can and do think rationally and conceptually. We must also insist on the ways rationality itself has an embodied, affective dimension (Ahmed 2004: 170). Documentation of the voice, then, needs to contend with a complex and sometimes antagonistic history, but perhaps also provides an opportunity to think in more nuanced ways about the body and communication.

We need a framework for understanding listening that takes on this complicated configuration of persistence, gaps and unruly bodily politics. We need to be able to think how voice circulates with all its messy and connective properties, and how it is reproduced or represented. This is where eavesdropping might come in.

Theorizing eavesdropping

As a methodology for listening to voice or vocal documents, eavesdropping, listening-in or overhearing, may have much to offer. Yet, like voice, eavesdropping itself has been little theorized. John L. Locke (2010), in his cultural history of eavesdropping, notes that it has been all but ignored in the social sciences and suggests two reasons for this. First, "it feeds on activity that is inherently *intimate*, and is so because the actors are unaware of the receiver, therefore feel free to be 'themselves.'" Second, "it is not *donated* by the sender. It is *stolen* by the receiver" (Locke 2010: 3). These qualities of intimacy and transgression associated with eavesdropping need some further unpacking.

It is important to clarify what might be at stake in eavesdropping as such, and look at how what is problematic about it may also be what is useful. With eavesdropping, the listener may not get the full story, and one may hear things one would have rather not. Likewise, eavesdropping exists on a spectrum, from the casual, disinterested listener tuning in out of boredom or curiosity in a public place, to the more sinister form of eavesdropping that intrudes on privacy, and is also known as surveillance. On the one hand, eavesdropping suggests contingency and openness, the ability to find all voices equally, but also uniquely, interesting, even as the eavesdropper is prone to get things entirely wrong. Some conversations are more interesting to overhear than others, but when it comes to eavesdropping, chance proximity to the speaker counts more than the speaker's social identity (although social conditions of course affect which spaces we find ourselves in, and what we understand when we listen). On the other hand, eavesdropping can also connote oppressive and over-determined authority, the desire to know all and thus control all.

For Nancy, the position of the eavesdropper may be necessary to consider the ontology of listening; what it means "to be immersed entirely in listening, formed by listening or in listening, listening with all [...] being" (2007: 4). This listening-in-entirety is framed by Nancy as a secret:

> What secret is at stake when one truly *listens*, that is, when one tries to capture or surprise the sonority rather than the message? What secret is yielded – hence also made public – when we listen to a voice, an instrument, or a sound just for itself?
>
> *(2007: 5)*

The possibility of approaching the secret of listening, Nancy writes, "consisted first in being in a concealed place where you could surprise a conversation or a confession" (2007: 4). Listening as an entirety is slippery, it seems, and needs to be pounced on unawares.

While this ontological approach is important, I also want to think about what kinds of meanings may be *generated* through eavesdropping. One way to think about this is to consider the distinction between eavesdropping and voyeurism. What is different when we watch in secret, and when we listen in? Eavesdropping seems to require language, while voyeurism often does not. The peeping tom does not necessarily care what you have to say, but when I eavesdrop, I would like you to speak loudly and clearly. This is at least partly because when I eavesdrop, I am creating a history and persona for my subject. This works even for that most unfortunate of eavesdropper, the one who is listening for information about herself. This listener creates herself out of, or in response to, this information. This leads to a crucial point: as important as language is to the eavesdropper, it is not enough. The eavesdropper contributes something to the listened-in on. She makes judgments and uses those judgments to make guesses about the kind of person she is listening to.

So, there is something queasy about this act of eavesdropping that is also an act of creation. Not only does the eavesdropper hide what she is doing, which might be figured as a kind of theft, she also may draw faulty conclusions with sketchy information. Freddie Rokem (2002) considers the eavesdropper in drama as a transgressive character, considering Polonius behind a curtain in *Hamlet*, or Orgon under a table in *Tartuffe*:

> Eavesdropping appears both in tragedies and comedies and it is clearly a transgressive activity. In tragedy the eavesdropper is usually punished in some way for having made this transgression; in comedy the eavesdropper does not always understand the full implications of what he or she learns by this transgression.
>
> *(2002: 171)*

This transgression is no doubt in large part what is compelling about eavesdropping. Taking language that is not one's own disturbs the stability of private language as such. If it is not to be dismissed as simply unethical, we must find something valuable in the transgressive dimension of eavesdropping, or at least the de-stabilizations it might produce.

Ratcliffe proposes to recuperate eavesdropping as a form of ethical listening, stripping associations of the "busybody" and framing it instead as "a rhetorical tactic of purposefully positioning oneself on the edge of one's own knowing so as to overhear and learn from others and […] oneself" (2006: 105). Ratcliffe uses eavesdropping in the context of critical race and whiteness studies, as a method for listening that discourages privileged activists from using this privilege (even with good intentions) to dominate conversation and discourse. Dreher usefully expands on this politics of listening with her defense of "eavesdropping with permission" (2009). She draws on her own experience as a white, middle-class academic, in situations such as a series of workshops she co-organized on "the politics of gendered protectionism faced by Indigenous and Muslim women in Australia" (2009: 1). Importantly, it is the anxiety and fraught emotions associated with eavesdropping which give it a modest value for Dreher. Being a good listener might normally be linked to the creation of "safe" spaces for dialogue, but this can also have the unintended consequence of privileged people still in some sense "owning" these spaces. For Dreher, eavesdropping is valuable because it shifts the focus:

> [R]ather than "creating" space, for privileged listeners the goals of redistributing safety and risk, or shifting entrenched patterns of comfort and discomfort within spaces of conversation and interaction might serve as more modest but better aims. Turning to focus on unsettling comfort and security that rests on white occupation of the space of Indigenous sovereignty might enable a white

middle class feminist to work for safer spaces while alert to the pitfalls of "creating" or claiming space.

(2009:16)

Dreher condemns stealing or violating trust which eavesdropping might seem to promote (hence "eavesdropping with permission"). Nevertheless, it is precisely the attention to difficult or uncomfortable feelings that eavesdropping produces which gives it value in social justice work.

In the context of art history, the fraught associations of eavesdropping can also usefully reconfigure how we think about and value knowledge. I am taking a cue from Butt's (2005) work on gossip, particularly his study of the informal networks of information that circulated around homosexuality in the post-World-War-II art world in New York City. Discussing forms of "hearsay," he notes that they are "by most standards of academic or authoritative discourse, 'nonnormative' or 'deviant' forms of evidence"; this evidence is deviant because it "remains unverified by some authorized body or mode of validation" (Butt 2005: 6). This deviance becomes, for Butt, an object of study in its own right. We learn a lot about formations of homosexual identity in post-war New York by considering the mechanics of gossip. It is also a historiographic shift, a shift in how we might *do* art history. Butt continues:

> I am interested in how gossip, even though "unreliable," can nevertheless be seen to *bear witness*, to act as *trace* of some historical real – of some event, act or identity. […] Thus I am concerned with gossip's testimonial power to make evident that which could not be seen, which was not clear, and which was not disclosable – to consider the evidence of gossip's conventionally *non*evidential meaning.
>
> *(2005: 7; original emphasis)*

Gossip, then, becomes a way of thinking about absence, and the impact of particular absences or vaguenesses as such. To consider homosexuality in the US in the 1950s should necessarily be to grapple with what was not officially evidenced as much as what was.

If gossip can be used to think about absence, eavesdropping might be an alternative way to think about excess: excess of language and excess of identity. At the same time, absence in the form of the fragment is also illuminated by thinking about eavesdropping. In the following two sections, I consider how configurations of fragmentation and excess, understood as eavesdropping, offer ways to think about documentation of voice in performance.

Listening-in

There is a big room full of people. The room is a theatre, though it is not set up like one. In the middle, taking up most of the space, are rows of card tables, about fifty in all, each set with two chairs placed opposite one another. On the outer edges, there are bleachers set up to view the action in the centre. A gong rings loudly and the seats in the middle of the room and on the edges begin to fill up with people. Voices also start to fill the room along with the bodies, creating waves of sound and action.

Hannah Hurtzig's *Blackmarket for Useful Knowledge and Nonknowledge* is an ongoing project that uses voice as a component part of the work, but in nuanced and complex ways that make it useful for thinking through the phrase "listening-in" as one configuration of eavesdropping.[2] It is an event based ostensibly on the exchange of information, though never in a straightforward or uncritical sense. In each of the sixteen iterations of the project thus far, "clients" (as audience members are dubbed) are able to buy half-an-hour of time from a variety of experts. The profile of these experts depends on the theme of the event. The themes tend to be wide-reaching, even baroque, and range from "Encyclopedia of Dance Gestures and Applied Movement in Humans, Animals and Matter" (Berlin, 2006), to "The Repaired, Enhanced and Dead Body" (Riga, 2014).

When I visited the *Blackmarket* in 2008 in Vienna, the theme was "Who Will Have Been to Blame." Of the nearly one hundred experts at this event, there were economists, lawyers, climatologists, arts professionals, a chief rabbi, an astrologist and many more. This eclectic mix is part of the point. In this *Blackmarket*, knowledge is unregulated, and there are no guarantees about what you are going to get. The interactions with experts are one-on-one and spoken, rather than in written text, and to this end, a certain unreliability is built into the experience of knowledge transfer at the *Blackmarket*, which is at least in part related to the prominence of voice.

There are multiple facets in this event of oral exchange, but for now I want to return to the big room full of people and full of voices. What struck me at the Vienna *Blackmarket* was how located this listening was, and how the event was constructed to call attention to this fact of listening. When I was lucky enough to purchase half-an-hour with an expert – not a guarantee, as there is an elaborate queuing and bargaining system to dispense the slots – I was given a number corresponding to one of the tables in the main space. I took my place opposite my expert, and immediately was aware of a very literal listening-*in*. The forced and sometimes awkward privacy of the one-to-one exchange was constantly violated by the voices from the other tables. It was often impossible to resist listening-in on the conversations surrounding us, which reinforced the feeling of being *in* space, not only visually, but aurally.

Voegelin (2010) discusses how listening is always located and proximate to the sound being listened to. This is part of what distinguishes listening from seeing.

> Seeing always happens in a meta-position, away from the seen, however close. […] The visual "gap" nourishes the idea that we can truly understand things, give them names, and define ourselves in relation to those names as stable subjects, as identities.

(Voegelin 2010: xii)

As mentioned above, this disconnected assuredness of the visual contrasts with the uncertainty of the aural. Voegelin connects this uncertainty with listening's necessary located-ness:

> By contrast, hearing is full of doubt: phenomenological doubt of the listener about the heard and himself hearing it. Hearing does not offer a meta-position; there is no place where I am not simultaneously with the heard. [...] Consequently, a philosophy of sound art must have at its core the principle of sharing time and space with the object or event under consideration.
>
> *(2010: xii)*

All listening is a sort of "listening-in," though with eavesdropping, the one who makes the sound may not know she is "with" the listener.

Back at the *Blackmarket*, the sense of listening-with,-among and ultimately-*in*, means listening is especially fragmented. While listening to my expert discuss the role of women in Lars von Trier films, my attention is constantly tempted by the other voices surrounding me. Interestingly, this is somewhat shifted when I take up the offer of authorized eavesdropping available at the *Blackmarket*. During the rounds where I have not been able to purchase an expert, I can borrow headphones and a short-wave radio receiver. In every round, a handful of lectures are broadcast so people sitting in the bleachers can "listen-in." This is eavesdropping with a twist. The expert and client pair *know* they are being broadcast but they do not know who can hear them. Similarly, I, as the listener, cannot be sure who is speaking. There are approximately one hundred people in the main space and picking out a single pair is difficult. This curiously disembodied eavesdropping is no less an act of listening-*in*, however. Listening to these conversations is far more consuming than the face-to-face encounters, as other noises are blocked out, and the social obligations of visual recognition (eye contact, head nodding, smiling) are not present.

These broadcasts are recorded, and become the primary documentation of the event, far exceeding the visual records (some photographs and video). The audio recordings are meticulously indexed and are publically available on the *Blackmarket* website. In this way, the documentation offers its own form of listening-in, where the spatial located-ness of the live event is replaced with a virtual surrounding of information. Within this sea of information, there is no meta-position that takes in knowledge as an entirety, even as there is both a temporal and spatial gap between what is heard and who is speaking. Each recording I listen to exists in relationship to the others, via cross-indexing, and although I feel this proximity, I do not perceive any kind of complete or internally coherent system. Voegelin discusses knowledge that comes from listening as something that "does not pursue the question of meaning, as a collective, total comprehension, but that of interpretation in the sense of a phantasmagoric, individual and contingent practice" (2010: 5). The listening-in I experience at the *Blackmarket*, and after, is sometimes overtly framed as eavesdropping and sometimes not, but it produces just this type of slippery and contingent knowledge.

Overhearing

The question of knowledge is central to the second configuration of eavesdropping I want to explore, framed as "overhearing." Voegelin notes that "listening discovers and generates the heard" (2010: 4). In listening, we bring something to the heard, which is both a desire to know, but also a range of associations, biases, experiences and misperceptions that exist prior to the heard. I am thinking about "overhearing," then, as a kind of listening that exceeds the heard. By calling attention to this excess, however, we can also understand something of the conditions that construct what it is we listen to.

Here is an extreme example of overhearing. At some point before 2005, a man named Dan Carter donated his answering machine to a charity shop in Toronto, but forgot to remove the tapes. Artist A.S.M. Kobayashi found these tapes and listened to them, creating a fifteen-minute video piece, *Dan Carter*, in response.[3] The video stages the messages left for Carter from a range of participants in Carter's life – both close family and impersonal strangers – using voice recordings themselves, and pairing them with elaborate, though low-budget, props, costumes and sets. Kobayashi, a young Japanese–Canadian woman, plays all the parts. We see her take on a range of bodies, diverse in age, race, gender and size, though we never hear her voice.

While some of the messages gesture to micro-intimacies that underlie these lives, many are stark in the difficult private moments they reveal. There is a sequence of calls from Carter's ex-wife and daughter, asking where he is and whether he plans to pick up his young son for the weekend. The sequence ends with a short call from the son, who speaks quickly and stumbles on his words before hanging up. The final section of *Dan Carter* is a long, winding message from Carter's fiancée, which begins with sexually suggestive whispers and ends with her grocery-shopping list for a weekend away with both of their children that she is planning. This unnamed woman's desires and insecurities are laid bare in this call, and listening to it feels like the most blatant eavesdropping imaginable.

Much of Kobayashi's work centres on the (re-)creation of elaborate scenarios based on found documents. In addition to Dan Carter's answering machine tapes, Kobayashi has also worked with YouTube videos, the detritus found in an abandoned hotel and a note from an adolescent boy offering oral sex to a male classmate. Although a young artist, she has already developed a body of work based on second-hand knowledge, or what has been dubbed a "thrift gaze" (Nightingale Cinema 2013). Of all of the found documents Kobayashi uses, these voice machine tapes are among the most affecting. The rich semiotics of the voices indicates class, nationality and age, which inform Kobayashi's visual portrayals. They also disclose less tangible affective registers like desire and disappointment. These voice messages are unsettling in how private they are, and how illicit Kobayashi's eavesdropping feels. They produce a complex geometry of relationships between listeners and speaker which I will attempt to trace below.

In *Dan Carter*, the viewer (and in this case, listener) occupies the position of eavesdropper. We are overhearing one end of a telephone call. We do not hear the response. However, the person leaving the message also does not receive a response, but speaks into a machine knowing she will be heard later. In this way, we are also in the position of Dan Carter. We are simultaneously in the place of an eavesdropper and an intimate partner. Finally, we are aware that we are not the only listeners; the audience is hyperaware of the artist's listening. Kobayashi asserts her presence as a listener excessively, casting herself not only as part of the narrative she listens in on, but as *every* part.

This is a very literal "overhearing," the imposition of the listener (and her associations, biases, desires) "over" what is listened-to. Kobayashi creates a persona for each of the listened-in on, including a material history, a style, a physicality – all grounded in the documented voice. These personae are fragmented. We are aware that we are only getting brief glimpses, and this is underlined by the editing style of the video, which jumps, and stops and starts. At the same time, the personae in *Dan Carter* are also excessive. Kobayashi plays over a dozen characters, some of whom we are never introduced to in the actual recording. She imagines friends, colleagues, casual acquaintances, partly prompted by the voices, and partly pure invention. Meanwhile, from a visual perspective, the piece is practically bursting at the seams with *stuff*. The props, wigs, make-up and set dressing all speak to an over-the-top aesthetic that nevertheless refuses to tip into caricature. Instead, the creation of these personae speaks to the mutability of identity (*vis à vis* race, gender, class or nationality). Yet, the visible labour that goes into these representations shows that while identity may be mutable, it nevertheless requires effort. Identity is constructed, and these constructions take work. Kobayashi's overhearing tells us something about what is at stake in the creation of stories about other people, and us. These stakes should be taken into account whenever we listen in.

Of course, Kobayashi's (or rather Dan Carter's) answering machine messages are not documents of intentional performance. It is fair to assume that neither Carter nor the people in his life intended them to be used as an art project, nor know that they have been. I believe that Kobayashi has developed a strategy of listening *as* performance, what I have been calling overhearing, that might be useful in thinking about all sorts of vocal documents. However, I want to think further about the particular consequences of listening to a voice that does not know it is being heard.

Eavesdropping and reciprocity

This final section looks more broadly at eavesdropping as a methodology for doing performance studies. This might be in relation to things like oral histories as well as the documentation of voices in performance, as I want to emphasize that this thinking comes from a consideration of listening to voices as such. However, there might also be value in considering eavesdropping in the context of performance history and critical responses to performances even more broadly. This might frame performance studies as a kind of forensic practice, returning to the scene, piecing together what happened through hearsay and bits of overheard conversations. This would be a discipline that acknowledges its own relationship to desire and its potential for unreliability, while still trying to get some things right. Nevertheless, there is something uneasy about eavesdropping that I have alluded to throughout; and has to do with eavesdropping and reciprocity.

Cavarero (2005) opens her monograph with a story about eavesdropping. It is a reading of an Italo Calvino story, a parable on listening in a collection devoted to each of the five senses. The story is of a king who is trapped by his own logic of surveillance. He has constructed a palace that allows him to listen to everything that goes on around him, knowing that his overthrow is always possible. The people of the court know they are being listened to, and so the very timbre of their voices takes on a tone of artificiality and death. One day, the king hears a woman sing outside the palace, and is reminded of the possibility of a different kind of listening. For Cavarero, this is a moment of recognizing how voice can be "a sort of invisible, but immediately perceptible, nucleus of uniqueness" (2005: 2), far different from the stilted and inexpressive voices of the court. Importantly, the woman's voice comes from outside the web of surveillance that structures the royal court, for "this voice emerges from the world of the living that is outside the deadly logic of power" (Cavarero 2005: 2).

This moment of eavesdropping teaches the king something about the uniqueness, not only of the voice, but of the individual who produces the voice. This uniqueness is inherently physical. The fleshy, corporeal uniqueness of the (human) body can also be perceived visually, but transferring attention from the visual to the aural also transfers attention from the surface of the body (especially the face) to the interior of the body, "the fleshy cavity that alludes to the deep body, the most bodily part of the body" (Cavarero 2005: 4). Sonority is impalpable, yet "comes out of a wet mouth and arises from the red of the flesh"; importantly, this transfers the understanding of human "essence" away from ideas of ineffable, secret cores to the idea of "a deep vitality of the unique being who takes pleasure in revealing herself through the emission of the voice" (Cavarero 2005: 4).

To whom does this unique being reveal herself? Part of the vitality of the song comes from the fact that the woman does not know she is being listened to, and so does not guard herself. The king eavesdrops, in other words. However, at the end of the story, the king joins the song, revealing his own unique, vital, fleshy self. In this way, listening "is no longer a question of intercepting a sound and decoding or interpreting it, but rather of responding to a unique voice that signifies nothing but itself" (Cavarero 2005: 7). As well, while the voice reveals nothing but itself, it must be heard for this revelation to occur. This is where reciprocity comes in, not in a joint effort to communicate, but "the reciprocal intention to listen" (Cavarero 2005: 5). This, for Cavarero, is where ethics joins listening, in the constituent communality of the individual.

What does this say about eavesdropping, then, which is surely non-reciprocal in essence? Is it left in the royal court, hearing everything and listening to nothing? One response might be to return to eavesdropping as a framework both for studying performance and for creating performance itself. In this way, while we do not respond to those we listen-in on and overhear, we do reciprocate. This works both for performance that literally uses eavesdropping as material, and for a broader understanding of performance studies that listens to performance and then creates historical and critical works, which can never be identical to the live, but exist in their own right.

However, I also want to reserve a space precisely for the uncomfortable dimensions of eavesdropping. Its fragmentation, its excess, its sometimes lack of reciprocity should not be ignored. To conclude, I want to consider the different configurations of eavesdropping I have looked at, in light of the tensions they can create.

Eavesdropping as methodology

This chapter considered eavesdropping as "listening-in," suggesting that this type of listening locates us, and draws attention to the spatial context of the voices we encounter, putting us in relation to them. The located-ness of listening-in also means that we risk mishearing or misrecognizing certain voices that are produced outside the field we occupy. Similarly, I have thought about eavesdropping as "overhearing," which allows us to think about identity as constructed and unfixed, but also about the labour that goes into these constructions. However, it is crucial to remember that listeners risk silencing voices with imposed biases and interpretations. Finally, I have proposed that eavesdropping might be a way to listen to the uniqueness of the voices we hear, and to consider how this individual uniqueness is necessarily a function of community. I have also, though, highlighted the problem of surveillance without reciprocity, which controls and flattens.

These notes of caution are not meant to undermine the value of eavesdropping as a methodology. On the contrary, it is precisely the way eavesdropping creates occasions for self-criticality that may be its ultimate strength. Listening to voice in performance, whether live, recorded or standing metaphorically for historical or critical studies of performance, is complex and riddled with problems. This chapter, then, proposes eavesdropping not as a way of resolving complexity or overcoming problems, but as a way to highlight and critically approach them.

Acknowledgements

Thanks to Rebecca Louise Collins for her insight into eavesdropping and her reference to Voegelin's work.

Notes

1 See also Clément (1989), Dunn and Jones (1997) and Schlichter (2011).
2 For documentation of previous *Blackmarkets*, see Hurtzig (2005–14).
3 For documentation of *Dan Carter*, see Kobayashi (2006).

References

Ahmed, S. (2004) *The Cultural Politics of Emotion*, New York: Routledge.
Butt, G. (2005) *Between You and Me: Queer Disclosures in the New York Art World, 1948–1963*, Durham: Duke University Press.

Cavarero, A. (2005) *For More than One Voice: Toward a Philosophy of Vocal Expression*, trans. P.A. Kottman, Stanford: Stanford University Press.

Clément, C. (1989) *Opera, or the Undoing of Women*, Minneapolis: University of Minnesota Press.

Dreher, T. (2009) "Eavesdropping with permission: the politics of listening for safer speaking spaces," *Borderlands E-Journal*, 8(1): 1–21, www.borderlands.net.au/vol8no1_2009/dreher_eavesdropping.htm.

Dunn, L. and Jones, N. (eds) (1997) *Embodied Voices: Representing Female Vocality in Western Culture*, Cambridge: Cambridge University Press.

Hurtzig, H. (2005–14) *MobileAcademy*, www.mobileacademy-berlin.com/.

Jones, A., and Heathfield, A. (2012) *Perform/Repeat/Record: Live Art in History*, Bristol: Intellect.

Kobayashi, A.S.M. (2006) *Dan Carter*, www.asmk.ca/HOME/index.php?/video/dan-carter/.

Locke, J.L. (2010) *Eavesdropping: An Intimate History*, Oxford: Oxford University Press.

Nancy, J-L. (2007) *Listening*, trans. C. Mandell, New York: Fordham University Press.

Nightingale Cinema (2013) *Thrift Gaze*, http://nightingalecinema.org/thrift-gaze/.

Phelan, P. (1993) *Unmarked: The Politics of Performance*, London: Routledge.

Ratcliffe, K. (2006) *Rhetorical Listening: Identification, Gender, Whiteness*, Carbondale: Southern Illinois University Press.

Rokem, F. (2002) "Witnessing Woyzeck: theatricality and the empowerment of the spectator," *SubStance*, 31(2–3): 167–83.

Schlichter, A. (2011) "Do bodies matter? Vocality, materiality, gender performativity," *Bodies & Society*, 17(1): 31–52.

Schneider, R. (2011) *Performing Remains: Art and War in Times of Theatrical Reenactment*, Abingdon: Routledge.

Voegelin, S. (2010) *Listening to Sound and Silence: Toward a Philosophy of Sound Art*, London: Continuum.

Part V
A polyphonic conclusion

15

WHAT IS VOICE STUDIES?

Ben Macpherson, George Burrows, Diana Van Lancker Sidtis,
Yvon Bonenfant, Lyn Darnley, Amanda Smallbone,
Nina Sun Eidsheim, 'Femi Adedeji, Jarosław Fret and
Konstantinos Thomaidis

Ben Macpherson

For me, the idea of voice studies represents the intersection of two concerns: one material, the other metaphorical or methodological. Whilst voice is often inextricably linked to performative or illocutionary acts, the idea of studying voice offers us the opportunity to extend our thinking beyond practical or pedagogic concerns and into the realm of the theoretical and philosophical. Inroads into this have been made from Plato onwards, and we might think more recently of Dolar, Cavarero or Chion. There is some way to go, however. Opera studies, (ethno)musicology, musical theatre scholarship and pedagogy, have all discussed voice from disparate perspectives, but a coherent platform for the interdisciplinary exploration of voice at large is needed. The reason, for me, is that if (to paraphrase T.S. Eliot) next year's words have "other voices," then scholarship in performance studies, cognitive studies, reception theory and cultural studies at large, needs a framework in which to interrogate these changing voices, modes, lenses and frameworks.

Whilst my immediate interest in many ways lies in the academic study of what voice is, and what it can do or be, I remain aware that outside of the metaphoric realm, the study of voice – and any theoretical work that develops as a result of it – must at base always return to the praxis and practice of working *with* voice. I readily think of Beckett's *Breath* (1969) as an example of voice in performance, with its screaming, rhythmic breaths, disembodied onstage in that short performance. Yet, this study of voice is only possible – and useful – when it links to what we hear, what we feel, what we understand voice, in this context, to be – a sound sculpture, a postdramatic text.

I came to voice through performance studies, and my experience as a composer/ lyricist writing for musical theatre, a discipline which is focused most on pedagogy and the signification of registers, ranges and voice qualities at the service of character and narrative. Practices and pedagogies that focus on twang, belt, speech quality – I am thinking about Estill, for example – signify a particular approach to "doing" voice, and one that provides a great breadth of possibility. Yet, my turn to what voice *is* conceptually, convinces me that even in this popular art-form, the voice in performance needs to be re-envisioned, expanded and explored. So voice studies on a personal level, involves seeking to explore the concept of voice as a medium in-and-of itself. In particular, I am fascinated by extended voice and the dramatic use of *vocalese*, historically and in contemporary practice. I have a continuing interest in the vocal qualities of non-singing performers in musical theatre; the peculiar voice quality that isn't quite speech, and yet is not really *Sprechstimme*; the dramaturgical and performative reasons for Henry Higgins or Desiree Armfeldt not really *singing*. Rex Harrison. Richard Harris. Judi Dench. The musicality *of* the voice, *in* the voice.

This is not about melody or pitch, or the "correct" way of performing a character. Perhaps it is about timbre and texture, things that fascinate me most – possibly because I experience them more than study them. Practitioner–scholar Yvon Bonenfant believes that voice can equal touch: that there is a tactility – a visceral quality – to voice. I believe this to be true, and I believe that even in the realm of musical theatre the ability to touch audiences with voice, and to be touched, is the entire *raison d'être* of sung performance. Yet, this is just one aspect of voice. Louis Colaianni has suggested that sound is multi-sensory: "It can be both heard and felt. It can even be seen with the mind's eye. It can almost be tasted and smelled" (1994: iv). This is even more accurate when it comes to voice: the bodily expression of sound made by an individual – or a collective – for a reason, or for no reason. Multi-sensory, embodied and intensely present; the process, performance and experience of voice deserves and demands to be studied in-depth.

George Burrows

I have always sung in choirs and my understanding of what we might call voice studies derives from choral singing during my school days in suburban Bedfordshire in the 1980s. My father, a respected Handel scholar, ran a local church choir and I was recruited to the trebles along with my two brothers. Among my white, middle-class school friends, my singing as a treble was considered decidedly "uncool" and even morally suspect; it hinted at some deviant sexuality, perhaps especially in the church setting.

One year, the choir performed my father's edition of Handel's *Foundling Hospital Anthem* (Burrows 1983) and among my fellow soloists was a countertenor, from an Oxbridge college choir. I had never heard such a voice before: the tone seemed so unadulterated, pure and clarion. Afterwards, I told everyone I met about the profound impression this voice had made on me and was surprised by the strongly judgmental reactions I received. If there was something morally suspect about singing as a treble, there was something *especially* questionable about admiring a countertenor's falsetto.

As I got older I realized voices profoundly articulate subjectivity and mediate gender and sexuality – from "that place down below" (Middleton 2006: 93) – in a highly complex way, which is too often oversimplified. Throughout school and university I continued to sing and to listen to singers, at times struggling to come to terms with differences between my experience of singing and its reception, especially in the face of my increasingly evident self-understanding and heterosexuality. These personal struggles seemed to reflect the tensions apparent between vocal expressions and the subjectivity and social meanings they articulate.

Illuminating such tensions seems to me a foundational basis of voice studies. As a postgraduate music scholar, I thrilled at a body of literature that we might consider fundamental to this conception; the studies of unconventional voices in various disciplines and genres (Barthes 1977), and the more philosophical accounts of the relations between voice and subjectivity (Koestenbaum 1993; Silverman 1988). However, what perhaps speaks loudest to me now of these tensions is psychoanalytic discourse around voice and the broad remit for voice studies this might facilitate.

In Lacanian psychoanalysis, the voice is one of the crucial part-objects equated with the "object cause of desire" (*objet petit a*) (Lacan 1977: 315). It is only partly an object because within Lacan's taxonomy it also represents (or covers over) the unsymbolizable remnant of the unknowable Real that does not wholly fit within the Symbolic order of knowledge. Because it represents the incompleteness or inherent tension within Symbolic "reality," it is both beguiling and terrifying, and we find within this a sort of morbid fascination or thrill (*jouissance*).

From this perspective, voices always represent a sort of unfathomable excess in subjective relations; the incompleteness of symbolic castration as a process of subjective formation and social relativity. Voices fundamentally signify something intangible, but are always-already alluring and meaningful. Voices, thus defined, always-already escape symbolic structure (e.g., their apparent relationship to the vocalizing body) and suggest in their illusiveness that some more abundantly enjoyable transgression is occurring "behind the scenes" of subjectivity. All voices are thus sort-of falsettos, because as much as we may wish to equate a voice with the body or person of the Other, we cannot ever completely *know* them through it but are nevertheless drawn to it as some intangibly beguiling marker of subjectivity.

To define the voice in such a way need not limit voice studies to vocal utterances of one sort (e.g., singing) or another (e.g., speech). We may also consider the rhythmic "voice" of drumming (Mowitt 2002) or the female "voice" in cinema (Silverman 1988), opening the discourse of voice studies to a much broader set of intersections and interdisciplinary discourses. This seems to me to be a very exciting prospect as it points towards the value of the sorts of tensions and struggles concerning the vocal which I experienced as a young male singer. It should take us beyond the too-simple and supposedly "moral" messages that are too easily ascribed to voices that will in any case always-already escape such superficial definitions.

Diana Van Lancker Sidtis

Voices are all around us. In species that ambulate, fly and swim, vocalization has evolved to distinguish friend from foe, express the self and discern the intentions of the other. The survival value is high (Sidtis and Kreiman 2011). Animals recognize voices of their extended kin from fleeting acoustic impressions, many accomplishing this prodigious task from birth. Attitudes, moods, personality and emotions, along with gender, age, size and demographic detail, are detectable in the vocal signal. In humans, functions of vocal nuances include linguistic signalling for word meanings, grammatical structure, theme and structuring of discourse. This rich cornucopia is transmitted by a similarly large array of auditory–acoustic characteristics (e.g., fundamental frequency, vocal tract resonances, mode of vocal fold vibration, temporal parameters, articulatory setting and positionings, prosodic contour, syllable structure, as well as numerous idiolectal features) leading to a many-to-many relationship between informational bundles and auditory–acoustic parameters. Partly because of the long-standing hegemony of vision, scientists and scholars have only recently begun to investigate the information transmitted in voice.

It is an empirical tradition to decompose the object of study into constituent parts, and to examine the structure and function of those constituents. This approach, while yielding some preliminary insights, violates the nature of the voice. All voices constitute complex auditory patterns. For personally familiar voices, it has proven unfruitful to construct a hierarchical or additive list of features that might specify all the voice patterns in one's arsenal. Features such as breathiness or crisp articulation provide primary cues to one voice's identity, but have no status in another's. The characteristics triggering individual voice recognition are unique to that voice.

Judgments regarding personal, psychological, emotional and attitudinal characteristics, derived from voice, also defy reductionistic operations. Some generalizations can be made regarding elementary parameters: sad utterances are typically soft in amplitude, low in pitch and slow of rate; sarcasm might include pharyngealization and a sprinkling of nasality. Such generalizations pale given the many nuances of vocal expression in the speaker–listener process.

In perceiving a voice, attention can be proportioned to acoustic–auditory features or to the overall Gestalt. A determining factor in how perception proceeds – whether by featural analysis or Gestalt recognition – is the listener's familiarity with the voice. Cognitive processes differ for familiar and unfamiliar voices (Van Lancker and Kreiman 1987). Familiar voices engage a large expanse of cerebral systems, due to the aura of associations clustered around their mental representation (Kreiman and Sidtis 2011) and the engagement of arousal, memory and attentional systems, whereby unique cues trigger recognition. In contrast, discriminating between unfamiliar voices engages a greater role of featural processing. Featural elements figure importantly in the discrimination of unfamiliar voices while pattern recognition predominates for familiar voices.

I was privileged to experience an academic background that, over the long term, proved favourable to voice studies. Following graduate studies in linguistics at Brown University, membership in the UCLA Phonetics Laboratory afforded training in speech science, acoustic theory and neurolinguistics, leading later to formal graduate work in communications sciences and disorders. Recently, the complexity of vocal processes in biology has been met by an equally impressive intensification of cross-disciplinary study. The ubiquity of voice in our world has aroused engagement from disparate disciplines in the sciences and the liberal arts. Psychological, neurological, medical, physiological, sociological and linguistic assays are contributing massive gains in understanding of vocalization and its many functions. Encouragingly, many of these groups are sharing their perspectives, expertise and knowledge towards the greater goal of successful elaboration of the role of voice in biology and in human affairs.

Yvon Bonenfant

Frank Baker was the main vocal pedagogue at Bennington College, Vermont, where I studied for part of my undergraduate degree. When I knew him, he was over 70 years old. He could not "sing"; he vocalized in a charming and peculiar way because his speech control was damaged from suffering strokes. He sat in a wheelchair in his home, where one went for twenty-minute private lessons twice a week.

His teaching methods were unorthodox. He dangled a finger in the air, saying "Sing!" – trailing his finger through space. He made intense eye contact. His main concern during lessons was trying to get me to open my mouth more, and undo my tightly vowelled pseudo-bite. One day, he dangled his finger right inside my mouth. I quote him: "Since you were born, they shut you up [...] you're beautiful. Open your mouth. Sing!"

Frank was not my best technical teacher. I acquired my vocal skills and endurance, and learned healthy technique from more scientifically based principles over a longer period and with input from many others. However, Frank's pedagogy had a transformative effect. How do we account for this? How do we explain or understand what Frank's talents were, and why and how students responded to him?

Frank's relationship with vocal pedagogy is not all that interesting from a pedagogical perspective. It could not have been studied scientifically, except in a qualitative manner. Nor was it particularly methodical. It was based on experience and instinct, which are ephemeral and ineffable attributes of the cultural, social and individual construction of human identity. Lessons with Frank were about the relationship with him, and about his work on the somatic qualities of vocalization and its relationship with ego, which rebounded and resonated into the cavities of relationship with oneself and one's own vocal body. I suppose these lessons mostly consisted of what we might call vocal transference and counter-transference.

The ways we use voice have neuropsychological, physiological, psychological, technical, anthropological and linguistic components. Like other forms of physical gesture, the voice is, in part, a product of both our genetic makeup and of socialization and culture. Unlike other physical gestures, it is deeply dependent on the ways language use "trains" our vocal tracts to "dance out" speech. We enact cultural "choreographies" with our tongues and faces. We use words, yet we also make vocal sounds which have little to do with linguistic choreography. These range from the un-encultured babbles of early infancy through to the profound sobbing, ululating or angry roaring of adults.

The ways we perceive our own voices, and are perceived by others, are so tightly intertwined with identity and cultural value systems, we are rarely conscious of the vocal assumptions that inhabit us. Yet, these assumptions have a massive impact on our everyday lives. Our voices are policed by us and by culture. We set limits about what they are able to do and in what contexts. We even police timbre. Let's consider the "difficult-to-gender" voice in most Western cultures. It disturbs. Why? It does not play by the gestural "rules."

As a practitioner–scholar, I have been particularly concerned with the ways voicing might be perceived and felt to function on the tactile or haptic registers, and why that might matter. My practice has included collaboration with, and inspiration from, a psycholinguist, a speech therapist and a range of literatures from across somatics, neuroscience, physiology, and performance and cultural studies. I have also been concerned with how and why voice and identity interrelate. This kind of exploration can only happen within a truly interdisciplinary framework, which we might call voice studies, which explores the voice as a kind of nexus, where numerous aspects of ourselves, our cultures, our bodies, our creative impulses, our aural perception, language and desires collide. This nexus embodies politics, and this nexus resonates, physically. It acts on matter. It acts on us.

Lyn Darnley

There was a time when voice studies was clearly defined. There were distinct areas of study such as speech and language therapy, elocution and singing. The first dealt with the physiological study of the voice, its physical and developmental disorders. The second focused on the artistic use of the voice for performance, including accent and dialect, often working to establish a "preferred" Received Pronunciation. Verse and text were at the centre, and posture, gesture and stage craft were significant. Classical singing training used structured formal breath and resonance exercises to explore the musical boundaries of the voice. These disciplines have evolved and widened their focus considerably in the last century. Additionally, the study of linguistics took a more academic view of language form and context, while etymology was concerned with language roots and the changes in word meaning.

Today, such categorization is harder. There is a greater understanding that voice is central to our very being, and to communication through every medium, in a social, artistic and personal context. The voice is now seen as a Gestalt with many factors, including physical and emotional states, familial patterns, confidence, status and – significantly – choice. We cannot separate voice and speech. The links between language and personality have opened new areas of research into forensic psychiatry, trauma management and respect for regional dialects.

The ways in which voice and language can empower and control have been developed by those interested in public and media communication, resulting in cross-fertilization between disciplines and a deeper understanding of the complexities of the subject. Interdisciplinary organizations have sprung up, facilitating knowledge transfer and debate. Further development has occurred through the focus on the theory of practice in universities; drama school degree programmes now require training actors to commit their practice to paper. At voice conferences today, it is common to encounter movement experts, Alexander and Feldenkrais teachers, phoneticians, philosophers, etymologists, musicians, rhetoricians, actors, academics, social anthropologists, historians, ENT surgeons, hearing specialists and psychologists, NLP practitioners, trauma specialists, amongst many others.

The role of British theatre is considerable in the development of this field, with some of the earliest training recorded in journals or biographies coming from the apprentice system of the Elizabethans and the work of actor–managers, with evidence of both systems in the stock companies of the 19th century. Inspired by training in Europe and the elocutionists of the 18th century, the first drama schools in London were attached to music institutions. Influences from such practitioners as Italian Gustave Garcia, American Hermann Vezin, Austrian Rudolf Steiner, German Alfred Wolfsohn, French Michel Saint-Denis and Polish Jerzy Grotowski, brought new energies and cultural perspectives. Changes in styles of acting and theatre architecture demanded new approaches to voice. The influence from the UK is enormous, with the legacy of such teachers as Elsie Fogerty, Gwynneth Thurburn, Clifford Turner, Rose Bruford, Iris Warren and Cicely Berry, who have all had a formative impact on contemporary approaches.

The sudden explosion of interest in voice is evidenced by the opportunities to specialize in the subject. The Royal Central School of Speech and Drama started the first course in the UK in the 1980s. This course is now an MA, and Birmingham School of Acting, Guildford School of Music and Drama and Guildhall School all offer similar courses. Other courses run in Australia, and certification in methodologies such as Lessac, Linklater, Estill and Fitzmaurice can be achieved in the US or the UK. Trinity Guildhall and LAMDA offer international training, with centres throughout the world and a particular presence in India, Africa, Australia and Asia.

"Giving Voice" Conferences (Royal Welsh College and then Aberystwyth University), Care of the Professional Voice (UK), Voice Research Society, British Voice Association, Voice Care Network, British Association for Performing Arts Medicine (BAPAM) as well as international groups, Pan-European Voice Conference (PEVOC), American Theater in Higher Education (ATHE) and Voice and Speech Trainers Association (VASTA): these are some of the many bodies that have encouraged the multi-disciplinary mix that constitutes the study of voice to flourish.

From a personal perspective I believe voice studies should include considerable practical work. The vocal challenges that actors and other professional communicators face should be experienced personally, not merely theorized. There is no better way to study the voice and understand the practice of others, than to explore and experiment with one's own practice. I favour a multi-disciplinary training, rather than focusing on a single technique. This allows for a strong foundation in anatomy and physiology that can be individually and imaginatively adapted to the learning styles and personal needs of actors and students.

My answer, then, is that voice studies can be focused on any one of the many specialized vocal disciplines or take a more general multi-disciplinary approach to the voice and its many applications.

Amanda Smallbone

I feel uneasy when asked to respond to any question that implies the need for a definition, no less so than when it relates to a new area of enquiry. Such questions can lead us into the trap of unwittingly reifying an emerging field before it has had a chance to blossom. We run the risk of limiting its potential before exploring the uniqueness and fluidity of its shapes and forms, undermining the very purpose of opening up these possibilities in the first place.

Instead, voice studies can and should serve as a potent call to the imagination for those of us working across the broader area of voice. Rather than ask what it *is*, I wish to suggest an adjustment that focuses on what voice studies could *become*. Where might we identify and creatively excavate new inter- and trans-disciplinary relationships out of which fresh and distinctive discourses can emerge across the continuum of voice praxis? How might we take advantage of the intersections of disciplines that interface *with* voice? This requires us to be brave. Daring to risk muddying carefully guarded disciplinary boundaries in the hitherto compartmentalized world of voice is not something to be taken lightly. For many, much will be at stake, but this is where the excitement lies. It affords us the opportunity to release the voice – even temporarily – from historical disciplinary shackles, revealing a rich vein of new enquiry, and encouraging an open sharing.

I should perhaps add a qualifying note. In advocating a realignment of our framing of voice within the wider academy, I am not dismissing the importance of established, tried-and-tested canonic pedagogies, techniques, repertoires, critical framings or methodologies – these must always form the foundations of voice-based practice. My assertion is that this emerging field surely allows us to reassess our relationship with them – to take them out of the cupboard and dust them off, as it were – in order to see them with fresh eyes and consider new ways of applying them.

These ideas are currently being explored at the University of Winchester where, as programme leader of an undergraduate degree in voice studies, I have been fortunate enough to oversee the development of an innovative curriculum that draws on the multiple potentials of praxis across singing and speaking, study and training. The curriculum includes voice anatomy and physiology, performance skills and group vocal practices, workshop leadership and theoretical contexts. As such, it facilitates the development of vocal competency and confidence, alongside a solid engagement with a range of theoretical concepts through academic writing and thinking. A strong interface between practical and theoretical work is emphasized, promoting an engagement with, and understanding of, current practices as research methodologies.

This represents a rare departure from established models of vocal study and training at undergraduate level, which traditionally frame the voice within carefully delineated disciplinary boundaries. For example, singing and speaking are often bifurcated; studied discretely or separately on music or drama-related programmes. Most importantly, this new model invites students and staff alike to explore and develop their own vocal practice, interrogate what voice might mean for them across a broad spread of contexts, and make their own connections between them. This, then, is the *thinking and doing* of voice, explored in Chapter 1 of this collection, and which, for me, represents the very basis of the voice studies turn.

On a personal note, I would add that working within and around this new paradigm has had a profound effect on my work as a singing teacher, lecturer and performer. Coming from the background of a conservatoire training in Western classical singing, it has enabled me to appreciate the solid grounding this training gave me (which I had so often taken for granted and even found restricting) whilst at the same time encouraging me to take risks in identifying and applying new and fertile interdisciplinary ideas and connections across all aspects of my work. In a sense it has released *my* voice from the constraints of what it *should* do to what it *could* do.

Nina Sun Eidsheim

As voice is central to a number of vastly different areas of enquiry, I do not pretend to be able to formulate a unified or widely held notion of what the study of voice may be. However, I do think quite a lot about which differing and contrasting notions of voice may benefit from closer contact with each other, and this concern underpins my research, editorial work, teaching and organizational efforts.

As a musicologist, placing voice at the centre of my research programme has been neither a given nor a predefined path. When, in 2001, I transitioned from purely performative to academic work, I was met with baffled looks when I replied (to the perennial question) that my work was on "voice." The standard response was often simply "What do you mean?" followed by questions such as "Do you mean vocal repertoire? Lyrics? Vocal pedagogy?" "No, I work on questions around the material voice," I would reply, explaining that I consider issues including the relationships and possible boundaries between the subjective, collective, public, private, material and ideological voice.

The situation is different as we write in 2014. Since I first heard people, myself included, using the term "voice studies" in 2009, the possibility of voice as an area of enquiry is not only more broadly recognized, but institutional validation has appeared in the form of support for conferences, panels, research groups and publishing. While I do not pretend to provide an exhaustive list, I want to acknowledge some of the individuals and groups who have been instrumental to my own research, to the building of a scholarly community, and to expanding our collective perspective. In conversation with colleagues across the US, I have found that it can be challenging to stay informed about all voice-studies-related efforts, so I also offer these notes as a resource in this regard.

In the fall of 2009, VoxTAP, the Voice Studies Working Group at UC Berkeley, was founded by Caitlin Marshall and Robbie Beahrs while they were graduate students in, respectively, Performance Studies and Ethnomusicology. I had the privilege of serving as their faculty advisor, a role James Q. Davies (Music, UC Berkeley) also took on informally. In the same year, Douglas Cook (Biomechanical Engineering, NYU Abu Dhabi) and Martin Daughtry (Ethnomusicology, NYU) formed the NYU Voice Consortium, and Brian Gill (Vocal Performance, Voice Science, NYU) later joined them. The Society for Ethnomusicology special interest group on voice was founded in 2012, co-chaired by Katherine Meizel and Eve McPherson. The initiation of two large voice-centred projects in 2013 saw the Neubauer Collegium for Culture and Society's *The Voice Project* directed by Martha Feldman (Music) and David Levin (Germanic Studies, Cinema and Media Studies, Theater and Performance Studies) at the University of Chicago, and the Centre for Interdisciplinary Voice Studies, from which this volume has emerged. Finally, the UCLA Voice Consortium has existed in various forms for around 20 years, focusing more on the scientific and medical facets of voice studies. Key people include Alwan Abeer (Electrical Engineering), Jody Kreiman and Bruce Garrett (Head and Neck Surgery) and Patricia Keating (Linguistics).

With Annette Schlichter (Comparative Literature, UC Irvine), I organized a number of interdisciplinary voice studies initiatives, from an invitation-only weekend symposium (2010), to a quarter-long UC Humanities Residential Research group entitled *Vocal Matters: Technologies of Self and the Materiality of Voice* in 2011, both of which took place at the UC Humanities Center. Currently, I co-convene the UC Multicampus Research Group "Keys to Voice Studies: Terminology, Methodology, and Questions Across Disciplines" with Schlichter, and work with the UCLA Center for Digital Humanities to create a voice studies website offering insights into key terminology, concepts and methodologies, and provide listings of researchers, syllabi and bibliographies.

As James Q. Davies said in a recent conversation, after decades of intense critique of the concept and the meticulous work of questioning the canon, it may have been inevitable that voice has now become a topic in its own right. I will add that while intense debate around voice has been recorded since Aristotle, with the academic (re)turn to the sensorium, materiality and sound, we may be able to take on the topic equipped with new resources. Indeed, perhaps the interdisciplinary study of voice can help bring into relief the intersections of medicine, science, history and critical study.

'Femi Adedeji

For me, voice studies is the art and science of voice pedagogy, performance, technology and research/criticism in a given context. It is a systematic examination of the multifarious aspects of the theory and application of the human voice. Voice studies encompasses the physiology/mechanism, capabilities, training, maintenance, criticism of the voice and its application to specific tasks such as speech, chanting, singing, acting, preaching and healing as defined by a people's culture.

Thompson proposed that socio-cultural ideals and values need to be considered over theoretical premises: "singing is for the listener and hence it is 'good' or 'bad' according to how it sounds, not according to how it conforms to a theory or method of production" (1975: 1733). In Africa, the conceptualization, aesthetics and usage of voice have many peculiarities. Firstly, music (particularly singing) is essentially text-bound. Each ethnic group has its culturally acceptable norms as conditioned by language/dialect. Therefore, voice studies includes phonetics within the ambit of the ethnic language alongside what I am here calling universal principles.

Vocal aesthetics in Africa go beyond the sonic. Hence, what is considered beautiful in Western classical singing is not necessarily the same in Africa. For instance, vocal "colour" plays a significant role in determining several styles and genres, especially in the chanting styles of the Yoruba of Africa. The same melody and text may be sung with different timbres or colours, resulting in chanting voices like *Iyere Ifa* (used for the worship of the Yoruba god of divination), *Ijala* (used for the worship of the Yoruba god of iron and technology), *Esa* (used for ancestral worship) or *Orisa Pipe* (used for invoking the gods). Additionally, the African concept of voice has both physical and metaphysical dimensions. Africans believe that voice is also "spiritual," more so that the producing parts of the body are physical, while the product, "human sound," is not. The Yoruba therefore describe the voice as a raw egg that if dropped to the ground and broken into pieces, can no longer be gathered together. It means that once released, voice cannot be withdrawn. Furthermore, the voice as a metaphysical property is used to bless or curse, and such pronouncements are binding, as in various incantations. Moreover, there are enchantments to make someone's voice desired or detested. The Yoruba also believed that someone could be trapped, harmed or even killed through the voice. Hence, people are warned to be mindful of their vocality. This belief accounts for why indigenous itinerant singers and actors pay homage to witches and the "powerful rulers" of the universe before the commencement of their performances on stage.

Consequently, no straightjacket method may be imposed on voice students. However, the chosen method must be acceptable, effective and consistent within the given cultural context, with the use of voice based on indigenous parameters, such as age and gender. Vidal's (2008) pragmatic approach of starting from "the known" to "the unknown" is an appealing method for children learning how to sing. In which case, the student is introduced to "beautiful" singing within their cultural context before learning the principles. To Africans, hermeneutics is the goal of voice studies. What a song is saying (meaning) is paramount; this implies that the ideal voice is heard clearly and understood in terms of textual content.

Voice studies should not be limited to voice teachers, but rather be a multi-disciplinary endeavour, involving theologians, metaphysicians, medical experts, linguists, dieticians, sociologists and gender scholars. This approach provides a balanced understanding of the relationship between the spiritual aspect and the biology of the voice, from an African perspective. Further, voice studies should be contextualized in order to be effective in its usage and relevant to society. For example, Yoruba diction, indigenous voice aesthetics and various stylistic techniques as identified in chanting voices mentioned earlier are employed in training chanters and singers. Finally, the submissions here are fundamental to understanding non-conventional approaches to voice training and useful in the promotion of empathetic intercultural voice studies for scholars outside the African cultural milieu.

Jarosław Fret

In my work, I like to draw a line connecting the two horizons between which the practice of voice oscillates. Voice Constitution is created in the space between these horizons, as defined by two opposing sentences: "I *have* a voice" and "I *am* a voice." In the work of an actor, we often forget that having a voice is not only a tool – a means of expression – but that through "being" a voice in-and-of ourselves we live, and we enlarge our presence and extend the field of our actions.

Thinking about "a stage of voice" I understand it as a "field of human experience." Theatre practice becomes a medium to translate our experiences from one domain to another, from the field of *lived* experience (liturgy, funerals, birth) to *condensed* experience in re-composed (stage) work. In this process of translating human experience from one stage to another, we operate in three registers: transmission, transition and transgression, bringing vocal material from its anthropological source into the form of contemporary art.

With this process of translation, the oscillation between a power of social oppression – which is hidden in our vocal communication – and a sacred model of our identity – which is indeed the voice *within* us – becomes another important issue. Being "ourselves" vocally, both within society itself and as a result of societal forces, is inherent in thinking about a voice forced to express these problems (the issue of actors' voice material as a question of "vocabulary").

I will now outline a theory of the pneumatics of an actor from the perspective I describe as Voice Constitution. This perspective understands every vocal action with its complicated physical components as a result of the human effort to communicate a fragment of one's life in all its complexity. Pneumatics is an incorporated consciousness of the body struggling with its mortality against the entropy of communications, finding in this struggle a sense of *doing* (doing life and doing art). Pneumatics in us is a sign of gods and the song of gods in our bodies, being disconnected and searching for new breath connection in/through air.

Konstantinos Thomaidis

Every definition of voice is a working definition. A medical practitioner defines voice through its physiological characteristics so that its functions are assessed and facilitated in the case of pathologies or disorders. A casting director in opera looks for a voice that achieves a set of aesthetic standards – and in some cases, exceeds or challenges them. Writers talk about voice, meaning their idiosyncratic take on language or the way their characters arrange words in the verbal universe they inhabit (and inevitably create), or musicians might allude to their instrument's voice. Elsewhere, politicians reflect on the *vox populi*, and rhetoricians strive for effective communication, while dialect coaches have an acute ear for vocal inflection. Even terms such as "the singing voice" would have a completely different meaning for a folk singer, a composer or a musical theatre actor. Voice in this sense is not only a series of physical and acoustic phenomena, but crucially, the assumptions that shape its making and perception. This pluralism is to be celebrated and a definitional consensus might be irrelevant.

If so, how would one go about defining voice studies? The study of voice is, like voice, a practice; its contextual pragmatics matter. Any study of voice is therefore contingent, emergent and vested with (social, political, cultural) value. Who voices, who listens and how they voice and listen is significant. Of equal concern are why they voice, in which context and circumstance. Likewise, if their voice is examined, what is the reason and methodology for this examination? When Polish theatre company Gardzienice traversed their communist state's borderlands to save minority singing cultures from extinction, they deployed a hands-on vocal archaeology. When Korean *p'ansori* was pronounced an Intangible Cultural Heritage by UNESCO, discography became a means to circulate the repertoire, advertise it internationally, preserve it, or – according to the "old masters" – ossify it. Reaching the apogee of *bel canto* technique was not unrelated to the (hugely debated) invention of the laryngoscope by Manuel Garcia. Forensic recognition reorganizes our perception of voice in ways that are, perhaps, at odds with the aesthetic appreciation of jazz vocalism. Methodology is the practice of the practice and determines its supposed object of study, voice – as much as voice determines the methodology of its examination.

It is for the purposes of this book, then, that I wish to outline two perspectives on voice studies that I find particularly intriguing. The first stems from my experience, the second seeds what I envision as a new direction. Having trained as an actor and classical musician in Greece, I had an almost fixed definition of what voice is and does in each respective strand of work. Differences appeared to be only stylistic, and therefore superficial, not affecting what voice essentially was. Embarking on a doctoral project on comparative voice studies in 2007, I soon came to realize that, when borders are crossed, questions around voice become much more complex. Who, how and what voices express become less pertinent than who has agency in voicing, who has agency in listening, who benefits from voicing, and in what ways. More importantly, any essentialist understanding of voice seemed redundant. It wasn't that voice was performed in various stylistic ways. Voice was revealed as performative, transforming and generating the identity of its voicer. I am very aware that I speak in different tones and inflections as a Greek actor–musician and as a Greek-born-intercultural-voicer-based-in-the-UK. The muscularity of my phonemes, my vocal range, even the way I breathe or filter my harmonics, are all fundamentally different. Yet, this is not just me voicing in different ways. These different voices put me in decisively different subject positions. Each voice makes me the voicer who produces it. Voice studies is just starting to grapple with these issues.

As a coda to my thinking and this volume, I wish to share a personal inkling that has to do with methodology. In the last few years, the return to the voice has been establishing interdisciplinary bridges. My own research and practice have benefited from dialogues between performance studies, actor training, opera studies, pheno-menology and ethnomusicology. Voice studies is surfacing as an inter-discipline; borrowing, rebranding and radically alternating approaches. Yet, could what appears to be our object of study – voice – also be used as a methodological tool? What could be the vocal analysis of a landscape? Urban architecture? A religious practice? What would the vocal analysis of democracy in crisis be like? I do not mean studying the role of voice in democracies in crisis; this is still seeing voice as a topic. I mean analysing the landscape or democracy *through* voice. How could such an analysis be conducted? And what would it reveal?

References

Barthes, R. (1977) *Image Music Text*, trans. S. Heath, London: Fontana Press.

Beckett, S. ([1969] 2006) "Breath," in *The Complete Dramatic Works of Samuel Beckett*, London: Faber and Faber.

Burrows, D. (ed.) (1983) *Handel: Foundling Hospital Anthem*, London: Peters Edition.

Colaianni, L. (1994) *The Joy of Phonetics and Accents*, Kansas City: The Joy Press.

Koestenbaum, W. (1993) *The Queen's Throat: Opera, Homosexuality and the Mystery of Desire*, London: GMP Publishers.

Kreiman, J. and Sidtis, D. (2011) *Foundations of Voice Studies: Interdisciplinary Approaches to Voice Production and Perception*, Boston: Wiley-Blackwell.

Lacan, J. (1977) *Écrits: A Selection*, trans. A. Sheridan, London: Tavistock.

Middleton, R. (2006) *Voicing the Popular: On the Subjects of Popular Music*, New York: Routledge.

Mowitt, J. (2002) *Percussion: Drumming, Beating, Striking*, Durham: Duke University Press.

Sidtis, D. and Kreiman, J. (2011) "In the beginning was the familiar voice: personally familiar voices in the evolutionary and contemporary biology of communication," *Journal of Integrative Psychological and Behavioral Science*, 46(2): 146–59.

Silverman, K. (1988) *The Acoustic Mirror: The Female Voice in Psychoanalysis and Cinema*, Bloomington: Indiana University Press.

Thompson, O. (1975) *The International Cyclopedia of Music and Musicians*, New York: Dodd Mead.

Van Lancker, D. and Kreiman, J. (1987) "Unfamiliar voice discrimination and familiar voice recognition are independent and unordered abilities," *Neuropsychologia*, 25: 829–34.

Vidal, T. (2008) "Music education in Nigeria: entering the 21st century with a pragmatic philosophy," *Journal of the Association of Nigerian Musicologists*. Special Edition: 1–20.

INDEX